Questions of Influence in Modern French Literature

Edited by

Thomas Baldwin

James Fowler

and

Ana de Medeiros

Preface, selection and editorial matter © Thomas Baldwin,
James Fowler and Ana de Medeiros 2013
Remaining chapters © Contributors 2013

All rights reserved. No reproduction, copy or transmission of this publication may be made without written permission.

No portion of this publication may be reproduced, copied or transmitted save with written permission or in accordance with the provisions of the Copyright, Designs and Patents Act 1988, or under the terms of any licence permitting limited copying issued by the Copyright Licensing Agency, Saffron House, 6–10 Kirby Street, London EC1N 8TS.

Any person who does any unauthorized act in relation to this publication may be liable to criminal prosecution and civil claims for damages.

The authors have asserted their rights to be identified as the authors of this work in accordance with the Copyright, Designs and Patents Act 1988.

First published 2013 by
PALGRAVE MACMILLAN

Palgrave Macmillan in the UK is an imprint of Macmillan Publishers Limited, registered in England, company number 785998, of Houndmills, Basingstoke, Hampshire RG21 6XS.

Palgrave Macmillan in the US is a division of St Martin's Press LLC,
175 Fifth Avenue, New York, NY 10010.

Palgrave Macmillan is the global academic imprint of the above companies and has companies and representatives throughout the world.

Palgrave® and Macmillan® are registered trademarks in the United States, the United Kingdom, Europe and other countries.

ISBN: 978–1–137–30913–6

This book is printed on paper suitable for recycling and made from fully managed and sustained forest sources. Logging, pulping and manufacturing processes are expected to conform to the environmental regulations of the country of origin.

A catalogue record for this book is available from the British Library.

A catalog record for this book is available from the Library of Congress.

Questions of Influence in Modern French Literature

Palgrave Studies in Modern European Literature

Published in association with the Centre for Modern European Literature, University of Kent, UK

Series Editors: **Thomas Baldwin, Ben Hutchinson, Anna Katharina Schaffner and Shane Weller**

Editorial Advisory Board: Brian Boyd, Michael Caeser, Claus Clüver, Patrick ffrench, Alison Finch, Robert Gordon, Karen Leeder, Marjorie Perloff, Jean-Michel Rabaté, Andrew Michael Roberts, Ritchie Robertson, Hubert van den Berg

Many of the most significant modern European writers and literary movements have traversed national, linguistic and disciplinary borders. *Palgrave Studies in Modern European Literature* is dedicated to publishing works that take account of these various kinds of border crossing. Areas covered by the series include European Romanticism, the avant-garde, modernism and postmodernism, literary theory, the international reception of modern European writers, and the impact of other discourses (philosophical, political, psychoanalytic and scientific) upon modern European literature.

Titles include:

Thomas Baldwin, James Fowler and Ana de Medeiros (*editors*)
QUESTIONS OF INFLUENCE IN MODERN FRENCH LITERATURE

Anna Katharina Schaffner and Shane Weller (*editors*)
MODERNIST EROTICISMS
European Literature After Sexology

David Williams
WRITING POSTCOMMUNISM
Towards a Literature of the East European Ruins

Forthcoming titles:

Larry Duffy
FLAUBERT, ZOLA AND THE INCORPORATION OF DISCIPLINARY KNOWLEDGE
Righting the Epistemological Body

Ros Murray
ANTONIN ARTAUD
The Scum of the Soul

Palgrave Studies in Modern European Literature
Series Standing Order ISBN 978–1–137–02455–8 (hardback)
(*outside North America only*)

You can receive future titles in this series as they are published by placing a standing order. Please contact your bookseller or, in case of difficulty, write to us at the address below with your name and address, the title of the series and the ISBN quoted above.

Customer Services Department, Macmillan Distribution Ltd, Houndmills, Basingstoke, Hampshire RG21 6XS, England

---

For Alison Finch, an important influence

Contents

Series Editors' Preface	ix
Preface	xiii
Acknowledgements	xxiii
Notes on Contributors	xxiv

Introduction:
Influence: Form, Subjects, Time   1
Daniel Brewer

1   Voltaire, Dante and the Dynamics of Influence   18
  Russell Goulbourne

2   Post-Revolutionary Uses of Pascal   32
  Philip Knee

3   The Survival of Sade in French Literature of the 1950s   46
  Perrine Coudurier

4   Jules Laforgue, Hartmann and Schopenhauer: From Influence to Rewriting   58
  Madeleine Guy

5   Text, Image and Music: Paul Valéry's Melodrama *Sémiramis* and the Influence of the Ballets Russes   71
  Natasha Grigorian

6   Influence as Appropriation of the Creative Gesture: Henri Matisse's *Poèmes de Charles d'Orléans*   84
  Kathryn Brown

7   Samuel Beckett's Funerary Sculpture   99
  Claire Lozier

8   'Périmer d'avance': Blanchot, Derrida and Influence   111
  John McKeane

9   Figuring Influence: Some Influential Metaphors in Derrida, Valéry and Freud   126
  Paul Earlie

10	Roland Barthes's Ghosts: Photobiographical Influence and Legacies *Fabien Arribert-Narce*	140
11	'Le Cycle de Nestor': Patrick Pécherot's Rewriting of Léo Malet *Angela Kimyongür*	154
12	Jacques Roubaud's Rejection of *Japoniste* Influence: *Tokyo infra-ordinaire* *Lucy O'Meara*	166
13	Ghosts of Influence? Spectrality in the Novels of Marie Darrieussecq *Carine Fréville*	180
14	'Now I See Me, Now You Don't': Working with/against Paternal Influence in Marie Nimier's *Photo-Photo* *Ana de Medeiros*	194

Bibliography 208

Index 219

Series Editors' Preface

Many of the most significant European writers and literary movements in the modern period have traversed national, linguistic and disciplinary borders. The principal aim of the Palgrave Studies in Modern European Literature series is to create a forum for work that takes account of these border crossings, and that engages with individual writers, genres, topoi and literary movements in a manner that does justice to their location within European artistic, political and philosophical contexts. Of course, the title of this series immediately raises a number of questions, at once historical, geo-political and literary-philosophical: What are the parameters of the modern? What is to be understood as European, both politically and culturally? And what distinguishes literature within these historical and geo-political limits from other forms of discourse?

These three questions are interrelated. Not only does the very idea of the modern vary depending on the European national tradition within which its definition is attempted, but the concept of literature in the modern sense is also intimately connected to the emergence and consolidation of the European nation-states, to increasing secularization, urbanization, industrialization and bureaucratization, to the Enlightenment project and its promise of emancipation from nature through reason and science, to capitalism and imperialism, to the liberal-democratic model of government, to the separation of the private and public spheres, to the new form taken by the university, and to changing conceptions of both space and time as a result of technological innovations in the fields of travel and communication.

Taking first the question of when the modern may be said to commence within a European context, if one looks to a certain Germanic tradition shaped by Friedrich Nietzsche in *The Birth of Tragedy* (1872), then it might be said to commence with the first 'theoretical man', namely Socrates. According to this view, the modern would include everything that comes after the pre-Socratics and the first two great Attic tragedians, Aeschylus and Sophocles, with Euripides being the first modern writer. A rather more limited sense of the modern, also derived from the Germanic world, sees the *Neuzeit* as originating in the late fifteenth and early sixteenth centuries. Jakob Burckhardt, Nietzsche's colleague at the University of Basel, identified the states of Renaissance Italy as prototypes for both modern European politics and modern European cultural production. However, Italian literary modernity might also be seen as having commenced 200 years earlier, with the programmatic adoption of the vernacular by its foremost representatives, Dante and Petrarch.

In France, the modern might either be seen as beginning at the turn of the seventeenth to the eighteenth century, with the so-called 'Querelle des anciens et des modernes' in the 1690s, or later still, with the French Revolution of 1789, while the Romantic generation of the 1830s might equally be identified as an origin, given that Chateaubriand is often credited with having coined the term *modernité* in 1833. Across the Channel, meanwhile, the origins of literary modernity might seem different again. With the Renaissance being seen as 'Early Modern', everything thereafter might seem to fall within the category of the modern, although in fact the term 'modern' within a literary context is generally reserved for the literature that comes after mid-nineteenth-century European realism. This latter sense of the modern is also present in the early work of Roland Barthes, who in *Writing Degree Zero* (1953) asserts that modern literature commences in the 1850s, when the literary becomes explicitly self-reflexive, not only addressing its own status as literature but also concerning itself with the nature of language and the possibilities of representation.

In adopting a view of the modern as it pertains to literature that is more or less in line with Barthes's periodization, while also acknowledging that this periodization is liable to exceptions and limitations, the present series does not wish to conflate the modern with, nor to limit it to, modernism and postmodernism. Rather, the aim is to encourage work that highlights differences in the conception of the modern – differences that emerge out of distinct linguistic, national and cultural spheres within Europe – and to prompt further reflection on why it should be that the concept of the modern has become such a critical issue in 'modern' European culture, be it aligned with Enlightenment progress, with the critique of Enlightenment thinking, with decadence, with radical renewal, or with a sense of belatedness.

Turning to the question of the European, the very idea of modern literature arises in conjunction with the establishment of the European nation-states. When European literatures are studied at university, they are generally taught within national and linguistic parameters: English, French, German, Italian, Scandinavian, Slavic and Eastern European, and Spanish literature. Even if such disciplinary distinctions have their pedagogical justifications, they render more difficult an appreciation of the ways in which modern European literature is shaped in no small part by intellectual and artistic traffic across national and linguistic borders: to grasp the nature of the European avant-gardes or of high modernism, for instance, one has to consider the relationship between distinct national or linguistic traditions. While not limiting itself to one methodological approach, the present series is designed precisely to encourage the study of individual writers and literary movements within their European context. Furthermore, it seeks to promote research that engages with the very definition of the European in its relation to literature, including changing conceptions of centre and periphery, of Eastern and Western Europe, and how these might bear on questions of literary translation, dissemination and reception.

As for the third key term in the series title – literature – the formation of this concept is intimately related both to the European and to the modern. While Sir Philip Sidney in the late sixteenth century, Martin Opitz in the seventeenth, and Shelley in the early nineteenth produce their apologies for, or defences of, 'poetry', it is within the general category of 'literature' that the genres of poetry, drama and prose fiction have come to be contained in the modern period. Since the Humboldtian reconfiguration of the university in the nineteenth century, the fate of literature has been closely bound up with that particular institution, as well as with emerging ideas of the canon and tradition. However one defines it, modernity has both propagated and problematized the historical legacy of the Western literary tradition. While, as Jacques Derrida argues, it may be that in all European languages the history and theorization of the literary necessarily emerge out of a common Latinate legacy – the very word 'literature' deriving from the Latin *littera* (letter) – it is nonetheless the case that within a modern European context the literary has taken on an extraordinarily diverse range of forms. Traditional modes of representation have been subverted through parody and pastiche, or abandoned altogether; genres have been mixed; the limits of language have been tested; indeed, the concept of literature itself has been placed in question.

With all of the above in mind, the present series wishes to promote work that engages with any aspect of modern European literature (be it a literary movement, an individual writer, a genre, a particular topos) within its European context; that addresses questions of translation, dissemination and reception (both within Europe and beyond); that considers the relations between modern European literature and the other arts; that analyses the impact of other discourses (philosophical, political, scientific) on that literature; and, above all, that takes each of those three terms – modern, European and literature – not as givens, but as invitations, even provocations, to further reflection.

Thomas Baldwin
Ben Hutchinson
Anna Katharina Schaffner
Shane Weller

Preface

If we are to explore the concept of influence as it has been understood and experienced by French writers and artists from the eighteenth century onwards, we will need to find moments of clarity and to uncover discursive spaces within a conceptual landscape whose terrain is notoriously difficult to map. French-language writers from the eighteenth century to the twenty-first, including Constant, Derrida, Diderot, Flaubert, Foucault, Gide, Helvétius, Roubaud, Rousseau, Sartre, Tocqueville, Valéry and Voltaire, have been concerned not only with the question of influence in apparently concrete, literary or artistic senses, but often also in rendering the concept problematic in itself. While some of these writers have conceived of influence in terms that reflect a more or less ordinary usage, others have been less sure of their ground and are thus, perhaps, more radical. Be they more or less radical in that sense, the essays in this volume examine the relations of influence among the arts of France. In the process, they describe points of contact between literature and the other arts, and question the assumptions underlying key theories of influence (not all of them French).

Undoubtedly, the most celebrated theory of influence in the last 40 years is Harold Bloom's. In his preface to the 1997 edition of *The Anxiety of Influence: A Theory of Poetry*, Bloom accounts for the absence of a reflection on Shakespeare from the 1973 edition of his work. He suggests that he 'excluded' Shakespeare, 'one of the most influential of all authors during the last four centuries', because he 'was not ready to meditate on Shakespeare and originality'.[1] Subsequently, he grumbles that 'the entire movement of our current School of Resentment is towards eradicating Shakespeare's uniqueness' and that 'Neo-Marxists, New Historicists, French-influenced theorists all demonstrate their cultural materialism by giving us a reduced Shakespeare, a pure product of the "social energies" of the English Renaissance'.[2] According to Bloom, 'the French have never valued originality'.[3] What, though, is originality? It is, as Bloom himself acknowledges, a concept at least as vague and in need of explication as influence. As the essays in this volume demonstrate, for a number of French writers and artists over the last three centuries, assigning value to such things as originality requires close scrutiny of the complex and often fugitive notion of influence.

Bloom also argues that 'strong poets make [poetic] history by misreading one another, so as to clear imaginative space for themselves'.[4] His corpus consists largely of English and American poets, especially Milton and the Romantics. The hypothesis that writers practise creative misreadings of those who precede them, and that these are a symptom of the 'anxiety of influence', is a powerful one that is not restricted to poetry.[5] However, it seems curiously timeless, being unbound by history, context and genre. It would be facile to remark that Bloom's work has generated its own anxiety of influence among other (strong) theorists, but it has certainly been subject to radical questioning and reappraisal. One example is Paul H. Fry's essay 'How to Live with the Infinite Regress of Strong Misreading'.[6] Fry relativizes and historicizes Bloom by placing him in a twentieth-century tradition of thinking 'about' influence, with reference to T. S. Eliot, Bakhtin, Jauss and Gadamer. He summarizes his findings as follows:

> Bloom distinguishes too sharply, for the good of his own position, between his own psychological wars among poets and the philological tracing of verbal influence he dislikes and [...] actually reintroduces historical change in a salutary way just insofar as he himself participates in verbal source hunting.[7]

Put in more immediately accessible terms, we might suggest that Bloom's work on influence creates a superficial distortion designed to mask a highly significant tension between the idea of a general, transposable meaning for 'influence' as somehow self-evident (X is chronologically prior to Y, which it helps to explain), and the view that 'influence', like any term used to discuss literary and visual artefacts, must be understood in its historical context. While a number of the contributors to this volume engage with Bloom's views, they do not accept them uncritically. Indeed, a number of them can be said to take on the very task – questioning the self-evidence of influence – that Fry describes.

This task has been underway for some time, of course, and was prominent in a variety of fields before the publication of Bloom's text. Indeed, nowhere, perhaps, has life been made more difficult for the concept of influence – and the notion of authentic 'origin' by which it is often accompanied – than in the work of Jacques Derrida, and of 'deconstruction' more generally. While, as Alison Finch has observed, Derrida himself is capable of taking the term 'influence' for granted,[8] his approach to influence in *L'Écriture et la différence* (*Writing and*

Difference) is decidedly more hostile: 'Nous parlons ici de convergences et non d'influence; d'abord parce que c'est là une notion dont le sens philosophique ne nous est pas clair' ('Here, I am talking about convergences, not influence: first of all, because that is a notion whose philosophical meaning is not clear to me').[9] 'La Structure, le signe et le jeu dans le discours des sciences humaines' ('Structure, Sign and Play in the Discourse of the Human Sciences') was published in 1967, some six years before the appearance of Bloom's work (Derrida's text was first delivered, in fact, as a conference paper at Johns Hopkins University in 1966). In this text, Derrida focuses on what he perceives as the weaknesses of Lévi-Strauss's structural anthropology.[10] In so doing, he highlights the pitfalls of a belief in a certain kind of influence. 'Structure', on this view, has been understood as a system organized around a centre, a fixed origin, and it is precisely such organization and 'fixing' of 'structure' that serve to limit its 'play'.[11] Derrida provides a long list of names that have been given to the conception of a founding centre: origin, end, *arkhe*, *telos*, *eidos*, *ousia*, consciousness, God, man, among others, all of which are essential to the history of Western metaphysics and its understanding of 'self-present' being. For Derrida, in its nostalgia for a single, definitive origin existing before or behind all substitutes, the modern period (the limits of which remain difficult to determine)[12] evinces a growing awareness of 'centre' or 'origin' as an unattainable object of desire. It is because of the very nature of language that perpetual substitution – or *différance* – must take place: language masks absence with presence, and its differential mobility depends on its lack of centre. In light of Derrida's observations, and as a number of the contributors to this volume demonstrate, to understand influence as a straightforward active/passive relation between a writer X (an irreducible 'origin') and another writer Y (a recipient) is to show symptoms of a deep-rooted attachment to a 'metaphysics of presence'.[13]

In a similar vein, the work of Roland Barthes illuminates the movement or 'play' of language between works of art (and critical writing on them). Barthes's views on 'intertextuality', as expressed in 'Texte (théorie du)' ('Text [Theory of]') and elsewhere, are essential for an understanding of the relations that obtain between artworks. These views are explored in more detail in Daniel Brewer's Introduction and inform the analysis in a number of the subsequent contributions. They also reflect Barthes's take on the concept of influence itself. In a somewhat tetchy interview with Renaud Matignon published in *France-Observateur* in 1964, Barthes insists that 'je ne crois pas aux influences' ('I do not believe in influences').[14] For Barthes, it is 'languages' (understood as 'des formes que l'on peut remplir différemment' ['forms that can we can fill up differently']) rather than 'ideas' that are transmitted between texts: 'c'est pourquoi la notion de *circulation* me paraît plus juste que celle d'*influence*; les livres sont plutôt des "monnaies" que des "forces"' ('this is why the notion of *circulation* seems to me to be more suitable than *influence*; books are "currencies" rather than "forces"').[15] For Barthes, the task of the critic is not to discover hidden truths about authors or their works, still less to pinpoint their influences; nor is it to produce a replica of the literary text. It is, rather, to bring about a 'contact of languages'[16] through 'integration'[17] and 'rewriting'.[18] Indeed, 'la "preuve" critique, si elle existe' ('critical "proof", if it exists') seeks not to discover 'l'œuvre interrogée, mais au contraire à la *couvrir* le plus complètement possible par son propre langage' ('the work in question, but rather to *cover* it as fully as possible with its own language').[19] We are thus invited to view the relation of 'influence', if we dare to call it that, not as 'X acting upon Y', but as a 'contact' between X and Y in which the circulation and rewriting of linguistic 'forms' are played out.

This view allows, of course, for the possibility that 'Y acted upon X'. In *Patterns of Intention: On the Historical Explanation of Pictures* (in a section entitled 'Excursus against Influence'), Michael Baxandall expounds on this very possibility. He questions the usefulness of what he describes as a 'Humean' image of causality (one billiard ball, X, hitting another, Y) as an account of the workings of artistic influence, arguing that the following is a more suitable metaphor for the ways in which works of art make contact with one another:

> An image that might work better for the case would be not two billiard balls but the field covered by the billiard table. On this table would be very many balls [...] and the table is an Italian one without pockets. Above all, the cue-ball, that which hits another, is *not* X, but Y. What happens in the field, each time Y refers to an X, is a rearrangement. [...] Arts are positional games and each time an artist is influenced he rewrites his art's history a little.[20]

For Baxandall, to say that Cézanne influenced Picasso, for example, as a matter settled only in terms of direct and 'one-way' causation, is not only to risk blurring the 'differences in type of reference' that Picasso makes to Cézanne, and to be blind to 'the actively purposeful element [...] of Picasso's behaviour to Cézanne', but it is also to ignore the fact that Picasso 'changed forever the way we can see Cézanne [...], whom we must see partly diffracted through Picasso's idiosyncratic reading: we will never see Cézanne undistorted by what, in Cézanne, painting after Cézanne has made productive in our tradition'.[21]

While a number of the essays collected here examine influence in relation to the visual arts, and consider a range of prismatic effects of the kind that Baxandall describes, they also consider the 'diffractions' of images by texts as they occur in ekphrastic descriptions (verbal representations of visual representations). The situation is complicated by the fact that such descriptions may turn out to be 'notionally' ekphrastic, if for instance they purport to 'represent', in words, a non-existent painting. If, as Murray Krieger suggests, 'ekphrasis is, in effect, an epigram without the accompanying object, indeed without any object except the one it would verbally create',[22] then in what sense can the visual image be said to influence its own description in words?

This collection was planned as French focused without being limited to French literature. While it demonstrates the short-sightedness of Bloom's complaint about 'the French', its purview also opens onto interdisciplinary and comparative approaches. Of course, we do not claim an absolute specificity for French approaches to influence; nor that they constitute an 'origin' or 'centre' for which others are mere substitutions; nor that the views of French artists, authors and theorists regarding influence are somehow more valuable than those of their European or American counterparts, for example. We believe, nevertheless, that some of the most fruitful and distinctive engagements with the concept of influence in the course of the last 300 years have been produced by French writers and artists, and that the essays contained in this volume are a vivid reflection of that.[23]

The essays have been arranged in an order that attends to chronology and theme alike, which forms a number of overlapping time spans. The first two essays engage with texts spanning the late medieval to the early nineteenth century, a period during which the earlier meaning of influence[24] was increasingly displaced by alternative meanings. In 'Voltaire, Dante and the Dynamics of Influence', Russell Goulbourne revisits the relationship between one of the great *philosophes* of the Enlightenment and an Italian late medieval writer with whom he has rarely been connected. This allows us to see the relationship between Voltaire and Dante in a new light (indeed, to see it rather than not). In 'Post-Revolutionary Uses of Pascal', Philip Knee examines echoes of Pascal in conservative thinkers of the early nineteenth century, in particular Chateaubriand, Maistre and Lamennais. From this discussion there emerges a nuanced account of Pascalian influence. It is as though Chateaubriand and the other writers studied here 'invent' their precursor

Pascal, or make him (over) in their own image. The third piece, by Perrine Coudurier, takes the reader back as far as Sade, and forward to the mid-twentieth century. Her subject is an intriguing post-war surge of interest in the 'divine Marquis' in French intellectual circles. The 1950s saw writers such as Georges Bataille, Simone de Beauvoir, Maurice Blanchot, Pierre Klossowski, Jean Paulhan, Raymond Queneau and Pauline Réage stage various 'returns' to Sade. A complex pattern of fascination and repulsion emerges, as these mid-century writers sift through Sade for explanations of social, cultural and/or historical phenomena (including the Holocaust).

The following two essays span works from 1885 to the early 1930s. Madeleine Guy examines the ways in which Jules Laforgue was influenced by Schopenhauer and the latter's disciple Eduard von Hartmann. This influence went deeper than a selective borrowing or citation: in particular, Hartmann's *Philosophie des Unbewussten* (*Philosophy of the Unconscious*) inflected the vision/version of Schopenhauer that Laforgue 'inherited'. Subsequently, Laforgue re-reads literature under the influence of these thinkers, and vice versa. This 'circulation' of influence can be traced in Laforgue's early work, *Le Sanglot de la terre* (*The Sob of the Earth*), written in verse; and, in prose, the *Moralités légendaires* (*Moral Tales*), especially 'Hamlet ou les suites de la piété filiale' ('Hamlet or the Consequences of Filial Piety'), 'Salomé' and 'Lohengrin, fils de Parsifal' ('Lohengrin, Son of Parzival'). Natasha Grigorian reflects on the verbal, visual and aural affinities between Paul Valéry's musical drama *Sémiramis* and Sergei Diaghilev's ballet *Schéhérazade*. Focusing on the verbal and visual aspects of the musical drama, this essay examines parallels between *Sémiramis* as a 'spectacle total' and the libretto and costume design of the ballet *Schéhérazade*, as produced by the Ballets Russes in 1910. Kathryn Brown extends the span of the two preceding pieces 'forward' to Matisse, and 'backward' to the work of a fifteenth-century poet, Charles d'Orléans, rewritten by Matisse in the form of a *livre d'artiste*. Produced between 1941 and 1944, this artist's book differs from Matisse's other ventures in this area by virtue of the fact that Matisse not only illustrates, but furthermore copies, in his own hand, the selected verses of the poet. Brown also examines Rilke's 'quotation' of Charles Baudelaire in *Die Aufzeichnungen des Malte Laurids Brigge* (*The Notebooks of Malte Laurids Brigge*) and Jorge Luis Borges's fictional 'review' of Pierre Menard's (re)composition of Cervantes's *Don Quixote*. Each case posits influence as a performative act in which one artist identifies with another through the re-enactment of creative gesture; this gives rise to a tension between 'mere' copying and 'pure', original creation.

There follow chapters on Beckett, Derrida and Barthes that throw up a complex web of connections among writers, thinkers and artists of various epochs and cultures. Claire Lozier's essay 'Samuel Beckett's Funerary Sculpture' considers the importance of late-medieval funerary sculpture for an understanding of the lives, or rather half-deaths, of a number of Samuel Beckett's supine characters. The first of two pieces on Derrida, by John McKeane, is entitled '"Périmer d'avance": Blanchot, Derrida and Influence'. Derrida expressed the view in an early article that Blanchot's reading of madness is essentialist. Blanchot went on to rewrite certain texts of the 1950s from 1969–73; these revisit the topic of madness, and present it as non-essential. From Blanchot's writing, Derrida's commentary and Blanchot's rewriting, it emerges that Blanchot undergoes/exercises the influence 'of' deconstruction. The other piece on Derrida, by Paul Earlie, is entitled 'Figuring Influence: Some Influential Metaphors in Derrida, Valéry and Freud'. Earlie situates Derrida's *Mal d'archive: une impression freudienne* (*Archive Fever: A Freudian Impression*) within the context of his writings on psychoanalysis and deconstruction in general. At issue, above all, is Derrida's relation to that mighty precursor Freud. Earlie shows how in *Mal d'archive* Derrida distinguishes between concept and notion in order to suggest that influence should be rethought in terms of 'impression', an idea that is not bound by the presence/absence dichotomy that Derrida rejects. Fabien Arribert-Narce explores key texts by one of the major thinkers of influence: Roland Barthes. More specifically, he re-examines Barthes's writings on the photographic image and their importance for a wide range of novelists, artists and theorists, with particular emphasis on the 'photobiographical' elements of their work.

The closing four pieces focus on primary texts written since the beginning of the twenty-first century. Angela Kimyongür's piece shows a modern-day writer engaging or re-engaging, aesthetically and ideologically, with a popular crime writer of the 1940s. Patrick Pécherot's revival of the character of private detective Nestor Burma, originally conceived by Léo Malet in 1943 in *120 rue de la Gare* (*120 Station Street*) and featuring in his *Les Nouveaux Mystères de Paris* (*New Mysteries of Paris*) series, is not quite pastiche and certainly not parody. The extent of Malet's influence on Pécherot's trilogy is evident not merely in the regeneration of Burma, but also in a range of narrative features as well as in the predominant role played in the three novels by Paris and the language of the city. Lucy O'Meara considers aspects of the most recent in a series of waves of 'japonisme' beginning in the mid-nineteenth century. The postmodern Japanese city has become a rich locus in French literature, and contemporary responses to Japan tend, perforce, to constitute either an extension or a repudiation of the aestheticentric tradition of 'japonisme' in previous French writing. Particularly interesting in this regard is the work of Jacques Roubaud, a long-time scholar of Japanese literature.

In the penultimate chapter, Carine Fréville explores the role of absence, loss and mourning in the writing of Marie Darrieussecq. The latter presents the phantom ('le spectre') as supplementing the impossibility of finding an adequate verbal expression of trauma (usually the death of a child). This connects her writing to that of Nicolas Abraham, Maria Török and Didier Dumas; Derrida's *Spectres de Marx* (*Spectres of Marx*) provides a further important reference for comparison. In Darrieussecq, the fantastic thus allows an otherwise impossible response to the trauma of losing an object of love. Darrieussecq's vision is further enriched by an 'intermedial intertext' that includes Patrick Modiano, Hervé Guibert, James Joyce, Louise Bourgeois, Bernard Faucon and Francesca Woodman. The closing piece, by Ana de Medeiros, is on Marie Nimier. A thread that runs through a large number of Nimier's texts (and not only the autobiographical ones) is the 'puzzling-out' of Roger Nimier's image and its influence on his daughter. In *Photo-Photo* there is a passage in which Karl Lagerfeld, whom the narrator seems to have adopted as a father substitute, offers the narrator a mirror. He proceeds to show her her own 'image' in the person of a double named Frederika, whom he encourages her to meet. This interaction can be read as a survival of the Imaginary within the Symbolic; it suggests a return to an Imaginary dream of self-in-other, yet is inaugurated by the symbolic Father to whom one owes the vital 'mirror'. *Photo-Photo* can thus be seen to continue Nimier's quest to establish the influence of what *is not* over what *is*; the haunting of an absent 'presence' by a 'present' absence, usually paternal.

As soon as we consider the range of its uses, we see that the term 'influence' cannot be exhaustively defined – that it does not go to a single conceptual essence. This does not mean, however, that it must defeat all scholarly investigation. Wittgenstein (influentially) rethought concepts and their relation to words in terms of family resemblances. The present collection has discovered such resemblances among concepts activated by the word 'influence', and provides some of the materials and methods that are necessary for both greater precision and flexibility in our use of the word.

Notes

1. Harold Bloom, *The Anxiety of Influence: A Theory of Poetry*, 2nd edn (New York and Oxford: Oxford University Press, 1997), p. xiii.
2. Ibid., p. xv.
3. Ibid.
4. Ibid., p. 5. Bloom further explicates his theory of influence in *A Map of Misreading*, 2nd edn (New York and Oxford: Oxford University Press, 2003).
5. In any case, Bloom uses 'poem' loosely, as when he talks of Freud's work as a 'poem' (*The Anxiety of Influence*, p. 9).
6. *Modern Language Quarterly*, 69.4 (December 2008), 437–59.
7. Ibid., p. 438.
8. See Alison Finch, 'The French Concept of Influence', in *'When familiar meanings dissolve…': Essays in French Studies in Memory of Malcolm Bowie*, ed. by Naomi Segal and Gill Rye (Oxford and Bern: Peter Lang, 2011), pp. 235–48 (p. 247). Finch's example is Jacques Derrida's reference to 'l'influence reconnue de Condillac' ('the well-known influence of Condillac') in *De la grammatologie* (Paris: Minuit, 1967), p. 393. All translations are our own.
9. Jacques Derrida, 'Violence et métaphysique', in *L'Écriture et la différence* (Paris: Seuil, 1967), p. 164 (cited by Finch in 'The French Concept of Influence', p. 247).
10. See Derrida, *L'Écriture et la différence*, pp. 409–28.
11. See ibid., pp. 409–10.
12. Derrida names Freud, Heidegger and Nietzsche as among the most radical 'decentralizing' thinkers (see ibid., p. 412).
13. Ibid.
14. The interview was, in fact, published under this very title. See Roland Barthes, *Œuvres complètes*, ed. by Éric Marty, 5 vols (Paris: Seuil, 2002), II, pp. 615–19.
15. Ibid., II, p. 616. Emphasis in original.
16. Ibid., II, p. 617.
17. Ibid., II, p. 505 ('Qu'est-ce que la critique?').
18. See 'Table ronde sur Proust', in Gilles Deleuze, *Deux régimes de fous: textes et entretiens 1975–1995*, ed. by David Lapoujade (Paris: Minuit, 2003), pp. 29–55 (p. 30).
19. Barthes, 'Qu'est-ce que la critique?', II, p. 505. Emphasis in original.
20. Michael Baxandall, *Patterns of Intention: On the Historical Explanation of Pictures* (New Haven, CT and London: Yale University Press, 1985), p. 60. Emphasis in original. It may of course be argued that Hume's investigation into causality is more sceptical, and also more sophisticated, than Baxandall asserts.
21. Ibid., pp. 61–2.

22. Murray Krieger, *Ekphrasis: The Illusion of the Natural Sign* (Baltimore, MD and London: Johns Hopkins University Press, 1992), p. 16.
23. See here Alison Finch's arguments in 'The French Concept of Influence', which are a powerful presence in many of the discussions in this volume.
24. For instance 'Qualité, puissance, vertu qu'on prétend qui découle des astres sur les corps sublunaires' ('Quality, force, virtue that is said to be exercised by the stars on the sublunary bodies'; see *Dictionnaire de l'Académie française*, 4th edn [1762]).

Acknowledgements

The editors would like to thank the team at Palgrave, especially Sacha Lake, Paula Kennedy, Sally Osborn and Linda Auld, for their patient and generous support.

Notes on Contributors

Fabien Arribert-Narce is a JSPS (Japan Society for the Promotion of Science) Postdoctoral Fellow at the Tokyo University of Foreign Studies, Japan. He completed his PhD (*co-tutelle*) in French (2011) at the University of Kent, UK and the Université Paris III–Sorbonne Nouvelle, France. He is the author of a forthcoming monograph, *Photobiographies: pour une écriture de notation de la vie (Roland Barthes, Denis Roche, Annie Ernaux)* (2013), and has published several journal articles and book chapters on European photobiography.

Thomas Baldwin is Reader in French and Co-Director of the Centre for Modern European Literature at the University of Kent, UK. His publications include *The Material Object in the Work of Marcel Proust* (2005), *The Flesh in the Text* (co-edited with James Fowler and Shane Weller, 2007), *The Picture as Spectre in Diderot, Proust and Deleuze* (2011) and *Text and Image in Modern European Culture* (co-edited with Natasha Grigorian and Margaret Rigaud-Drayton, 2012).

Daniel Brewer is Professor of French at the University of Minnesota, USA. He is the author of *The Discourse of Enlightenment in Eighteenth-Century France: Diderot and the Art of Philosophizing* (1993) and *The Enlightenment Past: Reconstructing Eighteenth-Century French Thought* (2008). He has co-edited, with Julie Candler Hayes, *Using the Encyclopédie: Ways of Knowing, Ways of Reading* (2002) and, with Patricia Lorcin, *Spaces of War in France: Experience, Memory, Image* (2009); and edited *The Cambridge Companion to the French Enlightenment* (2013). He is presently working on a book on the experience of time and regimes of historicity in eighteenth-century French culture.

Kathryn Brown is Assistant Professor of Art History at Tilburg University, Netherlands. She is author of *Women Readers in French Painting 1870–1890* (2012) and has published widely on nineteenth- and twentieth-century French painting and literature, aesthetics and contemporary art. Recent articles have appeared in *The Journal of Aesthetics and Art Criticism*, *American Art* and the *Forum for Modern Language Studies*. She is editor of, and contributor to, *The Art Book Tradition in Twentieth-Century Europe* (2013) and *Interactive Contemporary Art: Participation in Practice* (forthcoming with I. B. Tauris).

Perrine Coudurier is *Attaché temporaire d'enseignement et de recherche* at the Université de Lorraine, France. She is currently completing a doctoral dissertation on the French novel and the concept of terror in the 1950s, at the Université Paris IV–Sorbonne, France, where she also teaches courses on twentieth-century French literature, information science and communication. Her research assesses questions of memory, the art of writing post-World War II and literary French history from 1945 to the present.

Paul Earlie is a Laming Junior Fellow at the Queen's College, Oxford, UK. His DPhil thesis examined the influence of psychoanalysis on the development of deconstruction in Derrida's writings, from his early phenomenological work to his later reflections on 9/11. His current research project focuses on the legacy of the Greek sophists in post-war French thought.

James Fowler is Senior Lecturer in French at the University of Kent, UK. He has written extensively on the eighteenth-century French novel and French philosophy, and has recently developed research interests in a number of British writers, including Samuel Richardson. His publications include *Voicing Desire: Family and Sexuality in Diderot's Narrative* (2000) and *The Libertine's Nemesis: The Prude in 'Clarissa' and the 'roman libertin'* (2011). He edited *New Essays on Diderot* (2011) and co-edited *The Flesh in the Text* (2007) with Thomas Baldwin and Shane Weller.

Carine Fréville completed her PhD on the representations of trauma in the works of Marie Darrieussecq, Malika Mokeddem and Lorette Nobécourt at the Centre d'Études Féminines et d'Études de Genre at the Université Paris VIII, France. She has published articles on spectrality and mourning in the works of Darrieussecq; on the rewriting of traumatic events and on identity and gender issues in the works of Mokeddem; and on abortions and maternal violence in the works of Nobécourt.

Russell Goulbourne is Professor of Early Modern French Literature at the University of Leeds, UK. His publications include *Voltaire Comic Dramatist* (2006) and a translation of Rousseau's *Reveries of the Solitary Walker* (2011). He is currently writing a book on the culture of posterity in eighteenth-century France.

Natasha Grigorian is a Research Associate in Comparative Literature at the University of Konstanz, Germany, and University of Vienna, Austria. In her research, she focuses on late nineteenth- and early twentieth-century European literature and visual art. She is the author of a recent monograph, *European Symbolism: In Search of Myth (1860–1910)* (2009). Together with Thomas Baldwin and Margaret Rigaud-Drayton, she is co-editor of a collective volume, *Text and Image in Modern European Culture* (2012). Her current research project focuses on the legacy of symbolism and counterfactual thought experiments in literature.

Madeleine Guy is a former student of the École Normale Supérieure in Paris. She is currently a PhD student in French literature at the Université de Poitiers, France. Her thesis, titled 'La Bibliothèque imaginaire de Jules Laforgue', is a study of the rewritings of several authors in Jules Laforgue's collection of novellas, *Moralités légendaires*.

Angela Kimyongür is Senior Lecturer in French in the School of Languages, Linguistics and Cultures at the University of Hull, UK. Until recently, her research focused on the fiction of Louis Aragon; she has authored two monographs and numerous articles on his work. She is currently working on French crime fiction. Recent publications include 'Patrick Pécherot, Eugenics and the Occupation of France' in *Violence and War in Culture and the Medias* (2012); '"The Beast never dies": Maurice Gouiran and the Uses of War Memory', *Journal of War and Culture Studies* (2011); and 'Dominique Manotti and the *roman noir*', *Contemporary Women's Writing* (2012).

Philip Knee is Professor of Philosophy at Université Laval, Quebec, Canada. His publications include *Qui perd gagne. Essai sur Sartre* (1993); *Penser l'appartenance. Enjeux des Lumières en France* (1995); *La Parole incertaine. Montaigne en dialogue* (2003); and two edited collections of essays: *Rousseau juge de Jean-Jacques. Études sur les Dialogues*, with G. Allard (2003) and *Rousseau et le romantisme* (2011).

Claire Lozier is Lecturer in French at the University of Leeds, UK. She is the author of *De l'abject et du sublime: Georges Bataille, Jean Genet, Samuel Beckett* (2012) and of several articles and book chapters on the work of these authors. Her current research project examines the presence of the Baroque in the work of Georges Bataille.

John McKeane is Lecturer in French at the Universities of Cardiff and Oxford, UK. He works on modern French writing and thought. His doctoral thesis addressed Maurice Blanchot's fragments and dialogues, and he has recently been working on a younger generation of thinkers including Philippe Lacoue-Labarthe and Jean-Luc Nancy. In addition to various articles, his publications include a co-edited collective volume entitled *Blanchot Romantique* (2010) and a translation of Nancy's *Adoration (the Deconstruction of Christianity, II)* (2012).

Ana de Medeiros is Reader in French and Life Writing at the University of Kent, UK, and the Academic Director of the University of Kent at Paris. She works mainly on postcolonialism, feminism and life writing, and has published on a number of authors including Assia Djebar, Marie Nimier, Marguerite Yourcenar and the Lusophone writer Lídia Jorge. With Carine Fréville she recently co-edited a special issue on women and wounded bodies for the *International Journal of Francophone Studies* (2012). Her current research project focuses on the absent father in contemporary French autobiographical writing.

Introduction:
Influence: Form, Subjects, Time
Daniel Brewer

Writing never takes place in a vacuum, nor does reading. Both acts are always mediated by the writing or the reading of other texts, be they scripted, visual or otherwise symbolic. This much seems clear. If we wish to understand the nature of this mediation, just how much help can the notion of influence provide us? The term 'influence' is strikingly absent from the current critical vocabulary of literary scholarship and teaching. It is as if we have had to develop numerous other terms to articulate this mediation, whether it is explicit and manifest, needing only to be restated, or cloaked and covert, requiring extensive interpretive pressure to be teased out. Some of the terms used to describe this mediation of other texts are synonymous with influence, but most reflect a guarded reassessment of the notion, if not a critical one.

The question arises: Of what value to literary studies might the concept of influence be today? Not much, some might argue. From the vantage point of French Studies, a discipline long defined by a relentless and bracing self-questioning of foundational concepts, influence might well appear to be a dated concept, if not a pre-critical one. To put it most provocatively, the term 'influence' could be said to hearken back to a distant disciplinary past, a golden age of literary study, when the work of great scholarly figures implied a seemingly total recall of masterworks of unquestioned value, of literary canons whose individual texts might change but not the notion of the canon itself, and of national traditions that freighted numerous ideologies, from 'author' to 'literature' to 'nation'. Under the influence of 'influence', thus understood, these models of academic teaching and scholarly writing set the goal of recalling influences, of establishing filiations, and of selecting the good ones from the others. The seekers of influence took the history of literature as their object, but in a way that implied the history of other subjects as well, including authors and readers, but also the communities, societies and cultures in which these authors and readers were located. Looking back to the earlier times of our discipline, and to the discourse on literature it produced, we may ask whether the study of influence opened onto that larger social and cultural history, or whether the study of influence was part of an aestheticizing recontainment strategy, designed to engage with literature but only by bracketing it off from such a history, if not from history *tout court*. Did the study of textual influences belong to a strategy designed ultimately to be a bulwark against any thoroughgoing and critical understanding of the social, the cultural and the political?

In the following pages, I propose to unpack some of the elements of this all too telegraphic introduction to the question of influence. My vantage point will be a disciplinary one, involving the discipline of French and Francophone Studies. Ultimately, that vantage point would need to be viewed itself in relation to numerous other literary, critical and theoretical traditions, traditions representing disciplinary practices that must be contextualized and historicized. Setting out in such a disciplinarily self-reflexive fashion might well lead us quite some way towards the goal of generating a critical history of French Studies, viewed in terms of the way scholars and teachers negotiate the issue of influence. I will leave it to others, however, to fill this gap and to write this history.[1] What I do propose, though, is to turn the question of influence back on our scholarly and critical practice. I would like to explore how the shifting sense of influence is symptomatic of disciplinary debates, revalorizations and reconfigurations. Tracing some of these shifts can thus allow us to reflect on the influence of influence on our understanding of French and Francophone Studies. In this reflection on the practice of literary studies, we should be wary of adopting a pragmatic discourse of practical value, to which I alluded in my opening question – 'Of what value is influence?' Given that we all work in academic cultures and institutional settings in which the discourse of economic instrumentality is all too steadily gaining ground, I wish to pry an understanding of influence away from an instrumentalizing discourse of value and use. Rather, the question with which I wish to grapple ultimately is double, involving first whether influence might be understood in ethical terms, signalling an ethics of literary practice, and second whether this ethical understanding of influence has come to define – or more critically should come to define – the practice of French Studies (and literary studies) more generally.

Among the keywords of French Studies, those terms designating the paradigmatic ways of reading and of attaching meaning to texts, 'influence' is not readily to be found. 'Influence studies' doesn't trip off the tongue the way 'postcolonial studies', 'feminist studies', 'gender studies', 'cultural studies' or even 'discourse analysis' and 'genetic criticism' do. Yet there are clusters of terms and critical perspectives that intersect with 'influence', designating three sets of relations: the relation between texts; the relation between texts and subjects; and the relation between texts, subjects and time. Involving key aspects of our disciplinary practice, 'influence' as it intersects with these other relations may help us understand something about the business of 'doing French' after all.

One term that articulates the relation between texts, or the formal influence of one text on another, is 'citation'. 'Nous ne faisons que nous entregloser' ('All we do is gloss one another'), suggested Michel de Montaigne, elaborating in the *Essais* a way of writing that assays and displays writing as the endless rewriting of the already written. The 'we' of the Montaignian *entreglose* designates not simply the multiplicity of 'us authors', but the plurality of the writing subject itself, a subject split apart and multiplied by the words, styles, voices and texts that traverse it, the texts the Montaignian subject dialogues and debates with, the texts it desires and incorporates within, the texts it cannot allow to die and be forgotten. Citation is second-hand writing, or writing at one remove, as Antoine Compagnon suggestively terms it in *La Seconde main ou le travail de la citation* (*The Second Hand or the Work of Citation*). Citation is a telling feature of early modern texts for whose authors writing is not yet a form of property, and borrowing the writing of others not yet a form of plagiarism or thievery, whether discursive or economic. But this polyvocal, citational writing cannot simply be policed stylistically by calling it imitation or pastiche. Rather, the presence of citation in Montaigne's text is the mark of writing's inevitably being under the discursive influence of others, traversed by other styles, other voices, other texts, even other media. Writing is rewriting, its inevitable figure being that of the palimpsest, as examined by Gérard Genette in *Palimpsestes: la littérature au second degré* (*Palimpsests: Literature in the Second Degree*). To phrase this 'second degree' feature of literature, one could say that literature always writes itself, that it writes none other – or no other – than itself, figuring its influence on itself through the constitutive *mise-en-abyme* of literature.

We might begin here to historicize this understanding of an otherwise universal trait of literature, locating this work on literary theory in the context of textual theory formulated in the late 1960s and 1970s. The intellectual history of the period should not be unfamiliar, thanks to such intellectual historians as François Dosse, author of the two-volume *Histoire du structuralisme* (*History of Structuralism*).[2] As a simple reminder of the paradigm-shifting events of the time, I would mention Julia Kristeva's work on intertextuality, and Roland Barthes's *Encyclopaedia universalis* article on 'Texte (théorie du)' ('Text [Theory of]'). For Kristeva, the literarity of the literary text resides in its confrontation with other texts and the ensuing transformation of these other texts. A 'mosaïque de citations' ('mosaic of citations'), as she put it, the literary text is a constitutively productive form, always engaged with other texts or semiotic codes and designed to generate a new encoding of the world.[3] Similarly, Barthes will claim that every text is an intertext: 'd'autres textes sont présents en lui à des niveaux variables, sous des formes plus ou moins reconnaissables: les textes de la culture antérieure et ceux de la culture environnante; tout texte est un tissu nouveau de citations révolues' ('other texts are present within it on various levels, in more or less recognizable forms: the texts of prior culture and those of surrounding culture: all texts are bygone quotations newly rewoven').[4] With cultural studies not even a speck on the horizon of literary history, and with *les études culturelles* even less visible, Barthes's move of attaching texts to past and present culture is telling. What Barthes calls the presence within one text of multiple other texts of culture means that the work of the text cannot be dissociated from the contexts of culture, nor can the cultural context be well understood without grappling with the productive work of its texts. The work of Mikhail Bakhtin, translated in the 1980s, defined that relation between text and culture as a polyphonic space, characterized by the confluence of a variety of linguistic, stylistic and cultural elements. But more significantly, for Bakhtin the space of the novel was one of conflict, in which certain voices sought to silence others, the powerful discourse of the monological seeking to reduce the novel's fundamentally subversive dialogism. Through Bakhtin, the examination of dialogical influence offered a way to mount a critique of power. In such a project, the work of Michel Foucault, of course, is not far off.

But rather than cover some familiar Foucauldian ground, I would point out that attention to influence guarantees no easy access to a critical understanding of power. On the contrary, the study of influence may lead instead to recontaining such an understanding, amounting to a retreat from Barthes's original insight concerning the linkage between text and culture. To the extent that the study of influence turns away from the cultural anchoring of textuality, it risks retreating within a restrictive concern with form. The investigation of influence becomes no more than the search for sources that engender the text, itself understood as the locus of an endless yet ultimately imprisoning interplay of forms. Conversely, the study of influence runs a second risk, namely, turning away from the textual anchoring of culture. In a historicist understanding of influence, the cultural is at risk of being reduced to an empirical object that unproblematically constitutes the real, itself taken to be an object easily accessible and directly describable, with little consideration given to the manner in which symbolic forms mediate the relation between texts, subjects and the world.

At this point, my story about influence has encountered two forms of critical closure, which we can call the twin reefs of textual formalism and historicist empiricism. Attention to form may employ refined classificatory schemes and interpretive techniques to tell us much about relations between texts, and attention to cultural objects and institutions may rely on fine-grained descriptions of the empirical to make it seem as if we can grasp what joins us to the world and to each other. But the price paid for this particular form of understanding is a high one; namely, that of a productive engagement with the question of subjectivity, with what constitutes the subject as such. With the question of the subject now raised, we reach a second set of relations of influence.

If we accept, for a moment, the disciplinary divide that separates the so-called hard sciences from the human ones, subjectivity seems to be what must be removed in order to know the world. From the perspective of science, subjectivity appears to be that kind of perception, experience or affectivity that must be bracketed off in order to generate objective knowledge, those ever-elusive Cartesian clear and distinct ideas. In the humanities, however, it is precisely through subjectivity as perception, experience or affectivity that self and world come to be known. Subjectivity does found knowledge in the humanities after all, and it offers a basis for action in the world. Yet it remains a less than certain ground. One of the hallmarks of critical thought in the area of literary studies (and elsewhere) has been to explore that ungroundedness, notably by calling into question the primacy and priority of the subject over language, over writing and over thought.

One of the consequences of this theoretical work concerning subjectivity is that one can no longer engage with the question of 'the' subject, except perhaps by grappling with subjectivity in all its messy multiplicity. It is as if subjectivity involved nothing less than negotiating that heterogeneous, polymorphous plurality of being; that is, the condition of being both in one and in another, as if being one involved always being subjected to the difference of another, the differences of others, difference in and from oneself. To give a sense of this transformative intellectual work concerning subjectivity, let me mention three different areas of critical reflection. These areas at one time may have seemed extrinsic to literary studies, but at present they exert from within this field an ongoing influence on a wide range of pedagogical and interpretive practices.

The first of these areas is philosophy. By philosophy, I do not mean a universal mode of inquiry or a specifically institutional discipline, but instead contemporary, post-war, European philosophy, understood as a form of questioning that, among other things, marks the limits and the limit conditions of thinking the universal, together with the limits of the latter's institutionalization. One might even characterize this European philosophy more precisely as French philosophy. Following Vincent Descombes,[5] what defined this way of philosophizing – perhaps, one might venture, what was most French about it – was its probing questioning of the relation between self and other. Descombes begins his intellectual reception history in 1933, the year in which Alexandre Kojève began teaching his course at the École Pratique des Hautes Études, a course that was to continue until 1939. Kojève's course marked a return to Hegel in France, and it played an enormously influential role in shaping what Descombes calls 'the generation of the three H's' – Hegel, Husserl and Heidegger. Descombes's book appeared in 1979, and so his intellectual history – which runs from Kojève, Merleau-Ponty and Sartre, through semiology, Foucault and Althusser, Derrida and Deleuze, and on to Klossowski and Lyotard – would need to be brought up to date. What is the influence of French philosophy on literary studies from 1980 to 2013? Among the proper names that suggest the lineaments of that history, we might propose Philippe Lacoue-Labarthe, Jean-Luc Nancy, Luce Irigaray, Emmanuel Levinas, and of course many others. As far as the question of influence is concerned, the point I wish to make is double: first, that there exists a mode of inquiry in France that we can characterize as contemporary French philosophy; and second, that literary studies is a domain not only shaped by contemporary French philosophy, but in which that philosophizing work has taken place as well.

A second area of theorization concerning subjectivity, and one that has had considerable influence on literary studies, is Freudian and post-Freudian psychoanalysis. The obvious reference here is to the work of Jacques Lacan, but also to the generation of practitioners and theorists who were influenced by Lacan's writing, including Didier Anzieu, among others. Freud's texts having entered the public domain in January 2010, the question has been raised whether a return to Freud, or a turn to a new Freud, will generate a way of understanding the subject that is in sync with the present situation. Writing recently in a special issue of *Le Monde* devoted to Freud, Élisabeth Roudinesco asked whether a new Freud can be imagined, one whose concepts can be applied to critical issues of the twenty-first century. One might return to this 'conquérant des lumières sombres' ('conqueror of dark lights'), Roudinesco suggested, so that 'la question de la psyché, du désir et de l'inconscient redeviennent, au même titre que celle du Bonheur et de la révolution, une idée neuve dans le monde' ('the question of the psyche, of desire and of the unconscious becomes once again, along with the question of happiness and the revolution, a new idea in the world').[6]

A third area of influence on literary studies is Marxian and post-Marxian political theory, which undertakes to grasp the subject not in its psychic dimension, but in its social dimension, however provisional such a distinction must ultimately be. Following on from Louis Althusser, theoretical work and analytical practice in this area have focused on revealing and effectively critiquing the discursive, symbolic construction of social reality, a construction that is ideological insofar as it purports – or is taken – to pass for the real. This brand of practical critique has aimed to articulate how the dominant forms of culture are reproduced; it has also investigated how other modes of cultural practice, agency and production might serve to resist and subvert the reproduction of dominant forms of culture. Just as recent psychoanalytic theory has delineated the contemporary psychic subject, seeking to articulate the symptoms of the discontent that characterizes life in contemporary civilization, so too political theory has attempted to formulate a new political subject, to reinvent, if possible, new forms of plural identity that could define the global, post-national political subject. Given the contemporary fact of globalization, a system that encourages – and more often imposes – movements, encounters, exchanges, flows and flights that exceed older paradigms, redefining them or sometimes simply attempting to bypass them, the question confronting political theory at present is that of rephrasing these paradigms of subjectivity, of reconfiguring the fraught concepts of nationality, citizenship, sovereignty, democracy and political belonging. For instance, in his book *Nous, citoyens d'Europe? (We, the Citizens of Europe?)*, Étienne Balibar proposes the idea of transnational citizenship, a concept that moves discussion beyond ideas of socio-political identity based on the paradigm of nation, and at the same time rejects the solution of ethnic communitarianism and multiculturalism.[7]

In sum, important theory work concerning the question of subjectivity is located in the fields of philosophy, psychoanalytic theory and political theory. But it has taken place within the field of literary studies as well.

Sometimes it has been smuggled in across disciplinary checkpoints, and at other times it has been the logical extension of a porous interdisciplinarity. As a result of this influence, the subject that literary studies confronts seems increasingly to be one that exists *après-coup*, set down in the wake of bygone being. This subject is a constructed one, its identity plural to be sure, played out and performed in the shifting, labile terms of place, gender, race, history, language, nationality, sexuality, religion, ethnicity and so forth. The plurality of this subject is such, moreover, that it never founds being once and for all, never regrounds the subject in lost plenitude or presence. The identity of this subject is one that never can be full, and it corresponds to no project that can ever be fulfilled. This constructed subject is no more than the untimely aftereffect of fragmented identity, but no less than the dynamic performance of a desire to be at one with oneself and with others.

The interpretive and analytic methodologies of contemporary literary studies are traversed by this theoretical work concerning subjectivity. As a consequence, we have devised particularly refined ways to articulate how identity formation works, a process driven by subjects' desire for being and for being together in a community, however imagined it might be. This desire for being and for being together is one that can also generate strategies of resistance to monological, centralizing and repressive modes of being. The influence of this theoretical work on subjectivity is visible in all areas of French literary studies, from the medieval period to that of *l'extrême contemporain* ('the contemporary extreme'). However, it is in the area of Francophone Studies that the influence of this theoretical work has been particularly productive, a consequence on which I would like to dwell for a moment.

As a disciplinary object, Francophone Studies has emerged on the scene fairly recently, taking on different configurations and aims in various academic and institutional settings. In other words, 'doing' Francophone Studies in France, in the United Kingdom or in the United States involves working with differing canonical texts and writers, as well as engaging with differing interpretive approaches and aims. Without proposing to write the intellectual and institutional history of Francophone Studies, one might nonetheless suggest that one version of such a history would examine the changing notion of the Francophone subject in a specific set of texts, as well as the various interpretations of these texts in several nationally specific institutional settings, in order to reveal the local aims to which they are put. Imagine, for example, the different readings the following texts received at various times during the last 70 years, and in various national and institutional contexts:

Aimé Césaire's *Cahier d'un retour au pays natal* (*Notebook of a Return to the Native Land*), Franz Fanon's *Peau noire, masques blancs* (*Black Skin, White Masks*) and Patrick Chamoiseau, Raphaël Confiant and Jean Bernabé's *Éloge de la créolité* (*In Praise of Creoleness*). Through the reception history of these texts, one could imagine writing the emergence of the field of Francophone Studies in a variety of national contexts. Many other texts would need to be added to this list, such as the recent manifesto 'Pour une "littérature monde" en français' ('Towards a "World Literature" in French'), first published in *Le Monde* in 2007. This manifesto argued for a new way of reading the writer who writes in French, by prying apart language and writing from the stranglehold imposed on it by the concept of nation. The debate this manifesto generated has by and large been salutary for French and Francophone Studies, even though it is not certain that the problematic notion of the national can effectively be bypassed by doing away with the label of 'Francophone' in the name of a new cosmopolitan utopianism.

Up to now, I have discussed the question of influence by relating it to the two conceptual issues of form and the subject. I would now like to discuss influence by turning to a third conceptual issue, that of time, which I will approach from the angle of history and memory. But before turning to time, let me make two extended asides.

The first of these concerns disciplinary transfer, the movement of ideas between different ways of knowing. The assumption that runs throughout the present discussion of influence is that it can be helpful to think of our work in literary studies as mediated by a specific discipline. By discipline, I mean not so much a field of learning and research as a way of knowing, which can be understood in terms of a practice that is discursive, epistemological and institutional in nature. One of the effects of this practice is to establish not only what we can say about a particular object, but also what we cannot say, what is outside accepted practice, beyond disciplinary bounds. I stress the question of disciplinarity because it has been suggested that the current state of the humanities has been influenced by a paradigmatic shift in disciplinary practice, resulting not in oft-invoked interdisciplinarity, but rather in what has been called 'post-disciplinarity'. Louis Menand, author of *The Marketplace of Ideas*, lists four main characteristics of post-disciplinarity: 1) methodological eclecticism – when we behave in post-disciplinary fashion, we claim we can legitimately borrow interpretive questions and analytic techniques from other disciplines; 2) boundary crossing – disciplines have porous boundaries, and so a professor trained in literary studies may claim she can legitimately write or teach on music, film, fashion or architecture;

3) post-professionalism – given demographic and structural transformations within the democratic university, as well as changes, both real and perceived, in the professional and economic value of humanities degrees, our academic and pedagogical work is not limited to credentializing and professionalizing students; 4) the role of the public intellectual – we claim we can legitimately write for or speak to non-academic audiences, aspiring to acquire a voice other than a pedagogical one and to speak in fora other than that of the classroom.[8]

The disciplinary change to which these four characteristics attest is not even across all fields in the humanities. Some fields have become more post-disciplinary than others, and post-disciplinarity is expressed in different ways in different national academic cultures. By way of example, Menand observes that in the United States, the work of Jacques Derrida is taught more frequently in English departments than in philosophy departments. In France, though, no one would take Derrida's work to be that of an *angliciste* instead of a *philosophe*. In other words, the post-disciplinary condition makes it possible to do things – teach, speak, write – that could not be done in a more strongly disciplinarily defined context. However, the price to be paid for this post-disciplinary *laissez faire, laissez passer* is what Menand calls paradigm loss: the rejection of traditional paradigms of knowledge, or just indifference towards them. The question must be posed, then: what would constitute literary studies in a thoroughly post-disciplinary world? What other paradigms enable us to know that world? Or, to put the question in a less avant-garde, optimistic tone, how much paradigm loss is too much?

The question of disciplinary transfer is related to a second form of influential exchange; namely, cultural transfer. First proposed by Michel Espagne and Michael Werner in the 1980s, the concept of cultural transfer was designed to analyse how Western cultures 'importent et s'assimilent des comportements, des textes, des formes, des valeurs, des modes de penser étrangers' ('import and assimilate foreign behaviours, texts, forms, values and modes of thought').[9] Building on reception theory as formulated by Hans Robert Jauss and Wolfgang Iser in the 1960s and 1970s, the theory of cultural transfer affirms that the meaning of texts is not intrinsic to them and instead is shaped by readers' cultural backgrounds and personal experiences. However, cultural transfer differs from reception theory in significant ways. Reception theory, with its notion of a horizon of expectations, offers the promise of a rigorous hermeneutics well attuned to the complexities of the meaning-making process. Yet reception theory risks idealizing that process and reducing its complexity via disembodied, dematerialized (and thus dehistoricized) concepts such as 'idea' or 'influence'. Aiming to rematerialize and rehistoricize the understanding of culture, the theory of cultural transfer proposes to account for such objects as books, journals, newspapers and films in their materiality, connecting them materially to institutions and cultural practices in terms of which these objects are made to mean. Only in this way, it was argued, can the study of cultural transfer be more than simply a rebaptized form of disembodied intellectual history.

Espagne and Werner focused on cultural exchanges between France, Germany and the German-speaking lands. But their analyses were not cast exclusively in terms of the national. Or rather, for them 'the nation' possessed no privileged explanatory power with regard to cultural production, the 'nation' being but one space – be it geographical, discursive or imaginary – among others, spaces such as states, ethnic groups or linguistic and denominational communities. To some extent, the notion of cultural transfer corresponds to a 'post-national' way of understanding cultural production, of thinking beyond the national as master narrative, aiming instead to account for forms of movement between national spaces, movement that involves objects, individuals, populations, words, ideas, memories and concepts. Cultural transfer also involves what lies between these spaces, within the intercultural, in areas made up of frontier zones and mixed spaces of *métissage* where border crossings occur between cultures, languages, political systems and aesthetic forms in ways that cannot adequately be captured in terms of the dominant national narrative.

The study of cultural transfer implies a theory of influence as cultural transformation, insofar as the passage from one cultural space to another brings about change. As Espagne notes, 'les besoins spécifiques du système d'accueil opèrent une sélection: ils refoulent des idées, des textes ou des objets, qui demeurent désormais dans un espace où ils restent éventuellement disponibles pour de nouvelles conjonctures' ('the particular needs of the host system produce a selection: they repress ideas, texts or objects, which then stay in a space where they remain potentially available for new situations').[10] These ideas, texts or objects circulate in the world, yet stripped of their context, disconnected from the field of production of which they are a product. Receivers of these ideas, texts or objects belong to a different field of production, reinterpreting them according to their own field of reception, which is characterized by a number of social operations. For Pierre Bourdieu, this reception or appropriation can be defined in terms of interests: 'Mais je pense que celui qui s'approprie, en toute bonne foi, un auteur et s'en fait l'introducteur a des profits subjectifs tout à fait sublimés et sublimes, mais qui sont néanmoins déterminants pour comprendre qu'il fasse ce qu'il fait' ('anyone, no matter how well intentioned, who appropriates an author for him- or herself and becomes the person who introduces that author to another country inevitably has some ulterior motive. It may be sublime, or it may be sublimated, but it should be revealed, as it is clearly a determining factor in what is being done').[11] Turning Bourdieu's insight back on the question of influence as a form of cultural transfer, we can stress the importance of keeping in view the notion of influence as designating a mode of interest and indeed of desire.

A third aspect of influence involves time, considered in particular from the perspective of history and memory. In what we say and write about literature, the term 'influence' serves as a temporal operator, organizing the relation between texts, and with them between subjects, either as writers or as readers. In addition, and borrowing a term from François Hartog, one could say that the temporal operator of influence establishes a *régime d'historicité*, a specific way of relating past, present and future. One such *régime* is a classical one, in which there is no break between past, present and future, only the possibility of perfect imitation, seamless and complete repetition and timeless and total recall. Jorge Luis Borges illustrates this situation in a short story entitled 'Funes, His Memory' (also translated as 'Funes the Memorious'), the story of a young man who, following a horse-riding accident, cannot forget. At one point, to pass the time, he sets about to reconstruct all the details of a past day; his memory is so complete that this venture takes him an entire day. Only a few years after his accident Funes dies, as if his ability for total recall had lodged within it a certain mortality. At the other extreme of this classical, even antiquarian *régime* lies another, which aims at freedom from the past not through oblivion to the past but through its destruction. Filippo Tomaso Marinetti's 'Manifeste initial du futurisme', published in *Le Figaro* on 20 February 1909, illustrates such a *régime*. Addressed to youth to whom the future is barred, and refusing the past, which offers solace only for the moribund and the sickly, Marinetti compares museums to cemeteries and scholarly academies to 'ces calvaires de rêves crucifiés' ('those Calvaries of crucified dreams'). 'Viennent donc' ('Come on'), he calls to 'les bons incendiaires aux doigts carbonisés!' ('sooty-fingered arsonists'), 'Et boutez donc le feu aux rayons des bibliothèques! Détournez le cours des canaux pour inonder les caveaux des musées! [...] Oh qu'elles nagent à la dérive, les toiles glorieuses! [...] A vous les pioches et les marteaux! Sapez les fondements des villes vénérables!' ('Set fire to the library shelves! Turn aside the canals to flood the museums! [...] Oh, the joy of seeing the glorious old canvases bobbing adrift on those waters, discoloured and shredded! [...] Take up your pickaxes, your axes and hammers and wreck, wreck the venerable cities, pitilessly!').[12]

In addition to the classical *régime* and the futurist one, we might add that of modernism, post-modernism and others. Rather than construct categories, though, let me simply note a characteristic often attributed to contemporary culture; namely, its thoroughgoing denial of the past, a 'presentism' founded on nostalgia, marked by trauma and bordering on willed amnesia. However, as much contemporary literature so palpably shows, this being in the present entails a repeated and obsessive return to particular past events. Associated with some of the most painful moments of the twentieth century, on both individual and collective levels, these events include World War II and the entwined episodes of the Occupation and the Holocaust, the Algerian War, colonialism and decolonialization, and life in the post-colony. Through literature and through film, the means to account for these events has been sought by elaborating ways to recount them. And frequently, these narrative, theatrical, fictional, figural, filmic and symbolic accounts represent the events of the past according to a psychic logic defined by catastrophe, painful trauma, violent breach and loss, as well as ongoing and seemingly irredeemable suffering. The past is phrased in terms of negativity and death, and the relation to that past is one of unceasing melancholy for unbearable loss, a melancholy that seems to beckon towards a survivalist, restorative mourning, a putting together of the past in order to put it away.

As Slavoj Žižek observes, the dead return only when they were not adequately buried; if they are not assured of an appropriate memorialization by those who survive them, these spectres will continue to haunt until the trauma of their death is integrated into historical memory.[13] Michel de Certeau says much the same thing concerning the writing of history:

> D'une part, l'écriture joue le rôle d'un *rite d'enterrement*; elle exorcise la mort en l'introduisant dans le discours. D'autre part, elle a une fonction *symbolisatrice*; elle permet à une société de se situer en se donnant dans le langage un passé, et elle ouvre ainsi au présent un espace propre.

> (On the one hand, writing plays the role of a *burial rite*, in the ethnological and quasi-religious meaning of the term: it exorcises death by inserting it into discourse. On the other hand, it possesses a

symbolizing function; it allows a society to situate itself by giving itself a past through language, and it thus opens to the present a space of its own.)[14]

The writing of history and history's writing possess a ritualistic, sepulchral function, a function that defines precisely what is historical about writing the past, what presents the historicity of the past, giving the past over to the interment of history. Literature is thus as much involved in the writing of history as is historiography.

It is in this sense that literary studies have taken an historical turn. Literary studies have sought to gauge the influence of history by examining post-World War II writing to reveal how that writing plays out the traumatic negativity of pain, suffering and death, through the dialectic of remembrance and forgetting, recall and release. Post-war culture may well be characterized by a crisis of memory, marked by a symptomology whose temporality is more psychic than chronological, as Henry Rousso's notion of a 'Vichy syndrome' suggests.[15] However, that crisis also involves finding ways to testify to the events of the past, if at all possible, to provide witness to these events and their legacy, even if the only testimony possible must ultimately be to the impossibility of witnessing.

Literary studies thus find its historical place after the fact, *après-coup*, in a post-catastrophic moment. Yet behind one catastrophe may well lie another. Writers in the early nineteenth century expressed their own period's wary fascination with catastrophe, a fascination that expressed a new, modern relation to catastrophic history, to fractured, disjointed time that was its result, and to those symbolic archives, such as the literary text, in which the perishable, all-but-destroyed past was preserved as anachronistic imprint and trace.

By way of conclusion, I would like to raise one last question concerning influence, namely, whether influence can be understood in terms of ethics. Can there be an ethics of influence? I propose to approach this question via Martha Nussbaum's recent book, *Not for Profit: Why Democracy Needs the Humanities*. Nussbaum argues here in support of the humanities by claiming that if the faculties of thought and the imagination render us human, they do so by making our relations with others rich and full relationships, and not ones that are determined by mere use and manipulation, the latter being mediated by what she calls 'the thin norms of market exchange in which human lives are seen primarily as instruments for gain'.[16] Market exchange, and the economic paradigm more broadly, do not provide sufficient models for imagining and realizing human relationships in a fundamentally ethical way. As a corollary, Nussbaum notes, it is far from certain that economic growth results in the goals sometimes ascribed to it, such as economic and social equality, the preconditions of a stable democratic system, enhanced quality of race and gender relations. Fostering economic growth does not mean fostering democracy.

What does contribute to democracy, argues Nussbaum, is 'positional thinking', that is, the ability of thought to open out of what she calls 'the soul' and to connect the person to the world in a rich, subtle and complicated manner. Positional thinking promotes approaching another individual as a full person rather than as a mere usable instrument or an obstacle to one's own plans. The humanities encourage positional thinking, moreover, promoting 'the ability to think well about a wide range of cultures, groups and nations in the context of a grasp of the global economy and of the history of many national and group interactions'.[17] The humanities can promote 'the ability to feel concern and to respond with sympathy and imaginative perspective'. The partisans of economic growth will not support the humanities, which they may even fear, Nussbaum adds, noting that 'a cultivated and developed sympathy is a particularly dangerous enemy of obtuseness, and moral obtuseness is necessary to carry out programs of economic development that ignore inequality. It is easier to treat people as objects to be manipulated if you have never learned any other way to see them'.[18]

Nussbaum is quick to note, however, that this empathic view offers no ethical guarantee in and of itself. Empathy is not morality, and compassion alone, she observes, 'is not sufficient to overcome the forces of enslavement and subordination, since compassion can become an ally of disgust and shame, strengthening solidarity among elites and distancing them further from the subordinated'.[19] Nonetheless, the cultivation of sympathy has played a key role in the best modern ideas of democratic education. At that historical moment when citizens required democratic self-governance, education was remodelled to produce the sort of student who could function well in this demanding form of government. No longer was education geared to producing the cultivated gentleman, but rather, as Nussbaum puts it, to producing 'an active, critical, reflective and empathetic member of a community of equals, capable of exchanging ideas on the basis of respect and understanding with people from many different backgrounds'.[20] If the influence of our institutions of higher education should be to 'produce' a certain kind of student, it is this kind of critical-ethical subject, and not a merely economic subject who has learned better how to make a profit.

Beginning with formal issues, we have seen that the question of influence involves the ways the text is open, both exposed to and traversed by other texts, other voices, other media. As a result, writing and reading can never be exercises in monological autonomy, involving as they do various kinds of multivoiced interconnectedness. We have also seen that these practices cannot be cut off from questions of will, interests and desires, flows of affect that define subjects in multiple ways, subjects of influence who are located in specific moments and contexts, be they historical, cultural, institutional or disciplinary. And with the question of the influence of texts on persons, and the influence that persons exercise through texts, we come to the possibility of envisioning an ethical turn in literary studies, a moment when we can reimagine the discipline of literary studies, or continue to imagine it, as involved not just with elaborating beautiful new forms and with performing complex new identities, but more crucially with acting ethically.

Notes

1. A recent and compelling contribution to the UK version of that history is *French Studies in and for the Twenty-First Century*, ed. by Philippe Lane and Michael Worton (Liverpool: Liverpool University Press, 2011).
2. François Dosse, *Histoire du structuralisme*, 2 vols (Paris: La Découverte, 1991–92).
3. Julia Kristeva, *La Révolution du langage poétique: l'avant-garde à la fin du XIXe siècle, Lautréamont et Mallarmé* (Paris: Seuil, 1974), p. 60; translated by Thomas Gora, Alice Jardine and Leon S. Roudiez as *Desire in Language: A Semiotic Approach to Literature and Art*, ed. by Leon S. Roudiez (New York: Columbia University Press, 1980), p. 66.
4. Roland Barthes, 'Texte (théorie du)', *Encyclopaedia universalis*, available at http://asl.univ-montp3.fr/e41slym/Barthes_THEORIE_DU_TEXTE.pdf (accessed 31 August 2012).
5. See Vincent Descombes, *Le Même et l'autre: quarante-cinq ans de philosophie française (1933–1978)* (Paris: Minuit, 1979).
6. In a 17 April 2010 *Le Monde* article, Roudinesco critiques Michel Onfray's *Le Crépuscule d'une idole: l'affabulation freudienne*, a defence of Freud she pursues in *Mais pourquoi tant de haine?* (Paris: Seuil, 2010).
7. Étienne Balibar, *Nous, citoyens d'Europe? Les frontières, l'État, le peuple* (Paris: La Découverte, 2001).
8. Louis Menand, *The Marketplace of Ideas: Reform and Resistance in the American University* (New York and London: W. W. Norton, 2010).

Influence: Form, Subjects, Time   17

9. *Transferts: les relations interculturelles dans l'espace franco-allemand (XVIIIe–XIXe siècles)*, ed. by Michel Espagne and Michael Werner (Paris: Éditions Recherche sur les civilisations, 1988), p. 5. My translation.
10. Espagne, *Transferts*, p. 286. My translation.
11. Pierre Bourdieu, 'Les Conditions sociales de la circulation internationale des idées', *Actes de la recherche en science sociales*, 145 (December 2002), 3–8 (p. 5); translated by J. P. Murphy as 'The Social Conditions of the International Circulation of Ideas', in *Bourdieu: A Critical Reader*, ed. by Richard Shusterman (Oxford: Wiley-Blackwell, 1999), pp. 220–28 (p. 222).
12. See http://www.unknown.nu/futurism/manifesto.html (accessed 9 September 2012).
13. Slavoj Žižek, *Looking Awry* (Cambridge, MA: MIT Press, 2000), p. 23.
14. Michel de Certeau, *L'Écriture de l'histoire* (Paris: Gallimard, 1975), p. 118; translated by Tom Conley as *The Writing of History* (New York: Columbia University Press, 1975), p. 100. Emphasis in original.
15. Henry Rousso, *Le Syndrôme de Vichy* (Paris: Seuil, 1987).
16. Martha C. Nussbaum, *Not for Profit: Why Democracy Needs the Humanities* (Princeton, NJ: Princeton University Press, 2010), p. 80.
17. Ibid., p. 10.
18. Ibid., p. 23.
19. Ibid., p. 38.
20. Ibid., p. 141.

1
Voltaire, Dante and the Dynamics of Influence

Russell Goulbourne

Writing in 1927 about the influence of Stéphane Mallarmé's poetry on his own, Paul Valéry remarks: 'Il n'est pas de mot qui vienne plus aisément ni plus souvent sous la plume de la critique que le mot d'*influence*, et il n'est point de notion plus vague parmi les vagues notions qui composent l'armement illusoire de l'esthétique' ('No word comes more easily nor more often from the pens of critics than the word *influence*, and there is no vaguer notion among the vague notions that make up the illusory arsenal of aesthetics').[1] The aim of this chapter is to interrogate and clarify a little that vague notion by considering, as a possibly rather perverse test case, the relationship between Voltaire and a writer who, critics essentially agree, did not influence Voltaire at all: Dante. In exploring at once the limits and the possibilities of what we call influence, this chapter will also cast new light on the specific question of the relationship between Voltaire and Dante.

That relationship does not appear to have been a particularly close, let alone fruitful one. Voltaire seems to have been very much of his time in having all but no time for Dante. For Dante did not enjoy very much popularity in the eighteenth century: in the whole of Voltaire's lifetime, only 16 editions of the *Commedia* were published in Europe, compared to 14 in the first decade of the nineteenth century alone. Dante appealed more to the Romantics than to the rationalists of the Enlightenment. Voltaire, for his part, is normally thought to have engaged very little with the *Commedia*. It is true that he read Dante and that he did so in the original Italian: he owned and annotated a copy of the 1536 Venice edition of the *Commedia*.[2] But in his writings Voltaire comments on Dante relatively rarely, and the burden of those occasional remarks seems to be overwhelmingly negative, dismissing the *Commedia* as a bizarre, badly written and barely intelligible work. And perhaps even more striking than what he says is what he does not say. In his vast *Questions sur l'Encyclopédie* (*Questions on the Encyclopédie*) of 1770–74, Voltaire includes articles entitled 'Enfer', 'Paradis' and 'Purgatoire', yet in none of them does he refer to Dante, nor does he in the *Dictionnaire philosophique* (*Philosophical Dictionary*) article 'Enfer' ('Hell') of 1764. Dante is yet more conspicuous by his absence from Voltaire's 1727 *Essai sur la poésie épique* (*Essay on Epic Poetry*), his comparative study of what he considered to be the greatest examples of European epic poetry from Homer to Milton. And, lastly, we look in vain for thematic, stylistic or structural echoes of the *Commedia* in Voltaire's epic *La Henriade (The Henriade)* and his mock-epic *La Pucelle d'Orléans* (*The Maid of Orleans*).

If influence is understood in terms of X's power over Y, where Y comes temporally after X, the great forebear, and if that influence is normally considered to be discernible in identifiable details, images, borrowings or sources, then we might reasonably conclude that Dante had no influence on Voltaire. However, there are two interrelated problems with such an argument: first, it relies on a limited, inherently hierarchical, monodirectional, even negative understanding of influence, where the earlier text wields power over the later author; and secondly, it takes no account of what influence meant to Voltaire and his contemporaries. Addressing what the term meant in the eighteenth century in fact points us towards a more fruitful, and inherently more positive, understanding of influence.[3]

If we start with the term 'influence' itself, it is worth bearing in mind that Voltaire, in common with his fellow eighteenth-century French writers, does not use it in a literary, artistic or cultural sense. Rather, he and they use the term primarily in its physical as well as in its moral sense. For example, the fourth edition of the *Dictionnaire de l'Académie française* (1762) gives, firstly and somewhat sceptically, the traditional, astrological definition of influence: 'Qualité, puissance, vertu qu'on prétend qui découle des astres sur les corps sublunaires' ('Quality, force, virtue that is said to be exercised by the stars on the sublunary bodies'). It then gives a figurative definition by means of two examples: 'Les premières démarches qu'on fait dans le monde ont beaucoup d'influence sur le reste de la vie. Il a eu beaucoup d'influence dans cette affaire' ('The first steps one takes in the world have a great deal of influence on the rest of one's life. He had a great deal of influence in this matter'). In a similar vein, Voltaire's *Questions sur l'Encyclopédie* article on influence (1771) begins with a clear and characteristic definition of the term: 'Tout ce qui vous entoure influe sur vous en physique, en morale; vous le savez assez' ('Everything around you has an influence on you physically and intellectually; you already know that'). He goes on to place particular emphasis on direct contact as a defining feature of influence:

> Peut-on influer sur un être sans toucher, sans remuer cet être? On a démontré enfin cette étonnante propriété de la matière, de graviter sans contact, d'agir à des distances immenses. [...] Il me semble que nous ne devons admettre en physique aucune action sans contact, jusqu'à ce que nous ayons trouvé quelque puissance bien reconnue qui agisse en distance, comme celle de la gravitation, et comme celle de vos pensées sur les miennes quand vous me fournissez des idées. Hors de là, je ne vois jusqu'à présent que des influences de la matière qui touche à la matière.
>
> (Is it possible to influence a being without touching or moving that being? Finally, we have seen demonstrated the surprising property of matter to gravitate without contact, to act over immense distances. [...] It seems to me that we cannot accept in physics any action without contact until we have discovered some well-recognized force which acts over a distance, like that of gravity and like that of your thoughts over mine when you give me ideas. Beyond that, I have hitherto only seen the influence of matter touching matter.)[4]

Influence, according to Voltaire, is about a direct effect produced by one thing on another by dint of their coming into contact. Apart from that, he is prepared to admit of only two kinds of influence operating at a distance; namely, the gravitational and the intellectual. But while both of these may be intangible, Voltaire seems to imply that the influence of one person's ideas on another's is more arbitrary than the influence of gravity, which has been scientifically demonstrated. This very arbitrariness, of course, allows for the creative, dynamic and unexpected interaction and interrelation of ideas and, by extension, works of art.

It is precisely this kind of relationship between works of art that Voltaire analyses elsewhere with great clarity. In 1757, for example, he reflects on the relationship between artists of different generations in his *Encyclopédie* article 'Goût' ('Taste'):

> Le *goût* peut se gâter chez une nation; ce malheur arrive d'ordinaire après les siècles de perfection. Les artistes craignant d'être imitateurs, cherchent des routes écartées; ils s'éloignent de la belle nature que

leurs prédécesseurs ont saisie: il y a du mérite dans leurs efforts; ce mérite couvre leurs défauts, le public amoureux des nouveautés, court après eux; il s'en dégoûte bientôt.

(*Taste* can be spoiled in a nation; this misfortune normally comes about after those centuries in which the nation's sense had reached perfection. Artists, fearful of being imitators, seek out excentric paths; they distance themselves from the fine nature which their predecessors captured: there is merit in their efforts; this merit makes up for their failings, and the public, ever desirous of novelty, runs after them; but it soon loses its taste for them.)[5]

Voltaire diagnoses here what he sees as the misguided striving for novelty, or for what we might term originality, an aesthetic category that was taking shape in the middle of the eighteenth century, when Voltaire wrote this article.[6] Anticipating, in a sense, Harold Bloom, Voltaire sees this striving as a symptom of the desire on the part of some of his contemporaries not to be like their predecessors at all, to be free of their influence: in their struggle for supremacy, their relationship to the past is an antagonistic one, one characterized by fear in Voltaire's terms, in Bloom's terms, by anxiety.[7]

In part, Voltaire's critique of so-called originality informs his broader view of the eighteenth century as a period of artistic decline and decadence following the glories of the seventeenth.[8] But more than that, it is also part of an aesthetics that privileges cultural continuity and memory. For instance, seven years after his *Encyclopédie* article 'Goût', Voltaire notes in *La Défense de mon oncle* (*The Defence of My Uncle*): 'Les Muses filles de la Mémoire vous enseignent que sans mémoire on n'a point d'esprit et que pour combiner des idées il faut commencer par retenir des idées' ('The Muses, daughters of Memory, teach you that without memory one can have no mind and that, in order to arrange ideas, one has to start by remembering ideas').[9] And also in 1764, in his *Discours aux Welches* (*Speech to the Welches*), he sets out to counter the cultural narrow-mindedness of many contemporary writers: 'Les Muses enseignent tous les beaux-arts: elles sont filles de Mémoire, et leur naissance vous apprend que, sans la mémoire, l'homme ne peut rien inventer, ne peut combiner deux idées' ('The Muses teach all the fine arts: they are the daughters of Memory, and their birth teaches you that, without memory, humankind can invent nothing and cannot arrange two ideas').[10] Voltaire's argument rests in part on an allusion to classical rhetoric: *inventio* is the first of the elements of composition, and its etymology implies that the writer does not make up but rather uncovers material; that is to say, he draws on a pre-existing inventory. The writer writes with, through and in the light of previous writers.

That memory is the starting point for invention is the point that Voltaire also makes in his article 'Imagination', published in volume 8 of the *Encyclopédie* in 1765 but which d'Alembert had commissioned him to write as early as 1756:

> C'est le pouvoir que chaque être sensible éprouve en soi de se représenter dans son esprit les choses sensibles; cette faculté dépend de la mémoire. On voit des hommes, des animaux, des jardins; ces perceptions entrent par les sens, la mémoire les retient, l'*imagination* les compose; voilà pourquoi les anciens Grecs appelèrent les Muses *filles de Mémoire*.
>
> (It is the capacity that every sentient being feels to represent in his mind objects perceptible to the senses; this faculty depends on memory. One sees men, animals, gardens; these perceptions enter by means of the senses, memory retains them and the *imagination* puts them together; this is why the ancient Greeks called the Muses *the daughters of Memory*.)[11]

For Voltaire, these memories offer voices to converse with and examples to learn from. In particular, imitation of earlier writers is not something to be shunned, but something to be embraced, lest the imagination run wild.[12] In this respect he is fully in tune with the neo-classical aesthetics of his time. For example, in his article 'Imitation', published in the same volume of the *Encyclopédie* as Voltaire's article 'Imagination', the Chevalier de Jaucourt defines the term thus: 'l'emprunt des images, des pensées, des sentiments, qu'on puise dans les écrits de quelque auteur, et dont on fait un usage, soit différent, soit approchant, soit en enchérissant sur l'original' ('the borrowing of images, thoughts and feelings which one finds in the writings of a certain author and which one makes use of, either differing from, resembling or improving upon the original'). The original text is a starting point, a text to be used in a variety of different ways, for at the heart of imitation is appropriation and re-creation: 'La bonne imitation est une continuelle invention. Il faut, pour ainsi dire, se transformer en son modèle, embellir ses pensées, et par le tour qu'on leur donne, se les approprier, enrichir ce qu'on lui prend, et lui laisser ce qu'on ne peut enrichir' ('Good imitation is continual invention. One has, as it were, to transform oneself into one's model, embellish his thoughts and, by the turn of expression one gives them, appropriate them, enrich what one takes from him and leave behind that which cannot be enriched').[13] Imitation opens up a space for interpretation and innovation; imitation is liberating and empowering.

This kind of imitation and free reworking is a useful way of thinking about influence in general, and in particular about the question of the relationship between Voltaire and Dante. For Voltaire composed two free translations of passages from the *Commedia* in the 1750s, which allow us to see how influence can be understood as a positive and dynamic process, not negative and monodirectional, where authority can be dialogic and reciprocal, not monologic and hierarchical. In his translations, which modern critics have either simply ignored or dismissed, unhelpfully, as 'unfaithful' and 'inaccurate',[14] Voltaire engages with, adapts, draws on and responds to Dante's text in a richly creative and organic way.

The first of these translations is contained in the *Lettre à M. de **** (*Letter to M. de ****), published in 1753 as a kind of preface to the first volume of Voltaire's *Annales de l'Empire* (*Annals of the Empire*). Voltaire translates *Purgatorio* XVI. 106–11:

> Soleva Roma, che 'l buon mondo feo,
> due soli aver, che l'una e l'altra strada
> facean vedere, e del mondo e di Deo.
> L'un l'altro ha spento; ed è giunta la spada
> col pasturale, e l'un con l'altro insieme
> per viva forza mal convien che vada.

> (Once, Rome, which made this world for us pure good,
> Had two suns in its sky. And these made known
> Both roads to take, the world's and that of God.
> One sun has snuffed the other out. The sword
> Is joined now to the shepherd's crook. And ill
> Is bound to follow when force links these two.)[15]

His translation is a kind of imitation of, or poetic variation on, Dante's original:

> Jadis on vit, dans une paix profonde,
> De deux soleils les flambeaux luire au monde,
> Qui, sans se nuire, éclairant les humains,
> Du vrai devoir enseignaient les chemins,
> Et nous montraient de l'aigle impériale

Et de l'agneau les droits et l'intervalle.
Ce temps n'est plus, et nos cieux ont changé.
L'un des soleils, de vapeurs surchargé,
En s'échappant de sa sainte carrière,
Voulut de l'autre absorber la lumière.
La règle alors devint confusion,
Et l'humble agneau parut un fier lion
Qui, tout brillant de la pourpre usurpée,
Voulut porter la houlette et l'épée.

(In the past one saw, living in perfect peace,
The flames of two suns lighting up the world,
Each, without harming the other, enlightening man,
Teaching the paths of true duty,
And showing us the rights of the imperial eagle
And the lamb as well as the distance between them.
Those days are no more and our skies have changed.
One of the suns, freighted with fog,
Escaping from its sacred path,
Sought to absorb the other's light.
Order turned into confusion,
And the humble lamb became a proud lion
Which, resplendent in its usurped purple,
Sought to carry the crook and the sword.)[16]

It is remarkable that Voltaire has chosen a passage that is, structurally and intellectually, at the very heart of the *Commedia*, in the middle of the second part of this three-part work. *Purgatorio* XVI stands out as particularly important because it addresses two central issues in Dante's philosophy, namely the role of law and free will, with free will being in many ways one of the keys to the work as a whole. At this particular point in canto XVI, Dante is speaking through the historical figure of Marco Lombardo, a thirteenth-century minor Venetian nobleman who, in an angry and sometimes aggressive tone, champions the law as a means of safeguarding justice and freedom for all in a corrupt world: according to Dante, peace and order can be restored only by implementing imperial justice. So here, Dante flies in the face of medieval papal propaganda, which argued that the Empire was subject to the Papacy and stood in the same relation to the Church as the moon does to the sun. Dante, by contrast, believes that Church and Empire (or state) are equal agents of God's will, hence the image of the two suns: the city of Rome once had two suns in its sky – the Empire and the Papacy – but now it has only one, the power of the Pope, and the sword is united with the bishop's crook.

It is important to note that Dante's Marco is clearly a Christian; moreover, he is not attacking the idea of the Church per se, but rather the ways in which the Church has been corrupted by taking on the role of Empire and the ways in which the Empire has neglected its duties. But in Voltaire's hands, Dante's criticisms effectively shift focus: whereas Dante's criticisms of the Church always start from the idea that the Church ought to be giving spiritual leadership to the world, Voltaire's criticisms are more fundamental and radical insofar as he sees the Church as an inherent threat to society. That his attack goes further and deeper than Dante's is suggested by Voltaire's elision of any reference to Rome: by not mentioning Rome, he extends the frame of reference for his satire. Voltaire's critique of the Church is not the same as Dante's. In fact, their differing conceptions of the Church serve to highlight how translating Dante becomes, for Voltaire, a vehicle for a new attack in his ongoing battle against the whole gamut of religious corruption and intolerance in eighteenth-century France: Voltaire's free translation of *Purgatorio* XVI. 106–11 works at once with and against the original to achieve its distinctive satirical effect.

If Voltaire's first translation of Dante shifts the focus of the original, his second follows its structure quite closely, albeit making more explicit the targets of the satire and rendering Dante's violent language about them into a French that reinforces the satirical effect through its comic pithiness. This second translation appears in the *Lettre sur le Dante* (*Letter on Dante*) of 1756.[17] After a detailed summary of the *Inferno*, he offers a 63-line, decasyllabic version of the story of the Ghibelline warlord and politican Guido da Montefeltro (1223–98) from *Inferno* XXVII. 67–129,[18] a passage marked by a bookmark in Voltaire's copy of the *Commedia*. In Dante's poem, Guido recounts how, as an old man, having led a sinful life, he reconciled himself with the Church and became a Franciscan, only to find himself being lured out of his religious retirement by none other than Pope Boniface VIII, who sought his advice on how best to conquer the city of Palestrina, promising him, as his reward, eternal salvation.

Like *Purgatorio* XVI. 106–11, *Inferno* XXVII. 67–129 is critical of the Church: through Guido, Dante offers a scathing criticism of the corrupt Pope. Voltaire reinforces this criticism in his translation (ll. 1–5):

>Je m'appelais le comte de Guidon;
>Je fus sur terre et soldat et poltron;
>Puis m'enrôlai sous Saint François d'Assise

> Afin qu'un jour le bout de son cordon
> Me donnât place en la céleste église.
>
> (My name was Count Guido;
> On earth I was a soldier and a coward;
> Then I enrolled with St Francis of Assisi
> So that one day the end of his belt
> Would grant me a place in the celestial church.)

Whereas Dante's Guido, who refers to himself only allusively and describes himself as a soldier-turned-Franciscan monk (*Inf.*, XXVII. 26–8, 67), Voltaire's unashamedly names himself and promptly describes himself as a 'soldat et poltron', with 'poltron' rhyming tellingly with 'Guidon'. Voltaire also draws out the moral corruption of Dante's Guido: his stated motivation in Dante's text in turning to the Franciscans – 'credendomi, sì cinto, fare ammenda' ('believing, bound by cord, I'd make amends'; *Inf.*, XXVII. 68) – becomes in Voltaire a declaration of barefaced ambition. In addition, like Dante's, Voltaire's Guido revels in the irony of the Pope attacking fellow Christians (ll. 18–20; cf. *Inf.*, XXVII. 85–90); his Pope boasts about having the keys of Heaven at his disposal (ll. 29–32; cf. *Inf.*, XXVII, 103–5); and his devil is a better theologian than the Pope himself as he has a farcical tussle with St Francis over Guido's soul (ll. 47–53; cf. *Inf.*, XXVII. 118–23). However, Voltaire's Pope goes further than Dante's in making explicit his political ambitions, as Guido records (ll. 23–8):

> Frère, dit-il, il me convient d'avoir
> Incessamment Préneste en mon pouvoir.
> Conseille-moi, cherche sous ton capuce
> Quelque beau tour, quelque gentile astuce,
> Pour ajouter en bref à mes états
> Ce qui me tente, et ne m'appartient pas.
>
> (Brother, he said, it is right that I should have
> Palestrina under my control without delay.
> Advise me, look under your skull cap
> For some clever trick, some lovely ruse,
> To add, in short, to my states
> What tempts me but does not belong to me.)

Bringing under his control the fortress of Palestrina, and by extension the cardinals based there, Piero and Jacopo Colonna, with their followers, who denied the legitimacy of Boniface VIII's election as Pope, becomes just as much of a whim as offering eternal salvation to Guido in advance of his committing the sin of helping the Pope fight his personal battle (ll. 33–5):

> Si tu me sers, ce ciel est ton partage.
> Je le servis, et trop bien, dont j'enrage.
> Il eut Préneste, et la mort me saisit.
>
> (If you serve me, heaven will be your reward.
> I served him all too well, I am angry to say.
> He got Palestrina and death got me.)

The comic concision of these lines, unparalleled in Dante's original, serves to reinforce the characteristically Voltairean criticism of papal corruption. And to comic concision Voltaire adds, as a sting in the tail, a defiant refusal of periphrasis: whereas Dante's Guido refers to 'il gran prete' ('that sovereign priest') and 'lo principe d'inovi Farisei' ('the foremost lord of our new Pharisees'; *Inf.*, XXVII. 70, 85), Voltaire's names Boniface VIII by name at the end of his narrative in hell (ll. 56–9):

> Lors il [Belzébut] m'empoigne, et d'un bras raide et ferme
> Il applique sur ma triste épiderme
> Vingt coups de fouet, dont bien fort il me cuit;
> Que Dieu le rende à Boniface huit!
>
> (Then he [Beelzebub] grabbed me, and with a taut and
>   firm arm
> Applied to my sorry skin
> Twenty lashes, which made me smart;
> May God do the same to Boniface VIII.)

The torture is different in Dante – 'e quelli attorse / otto volte la coda al dosso duro' ('who then – / eight times! – coiled tail around relentless spine'; *Inf.*, XXVII. 124–25) – but the change allows Voltaire, by dint of the comic rhyme between the Pope's name and the torture meted out to Guido, to foreground Guido's hope that Pope Boniface VIII will get his just deserts.

Crucially, then, in and through these two translations Voltaire foregrounds the satirical in Dante. And herein lies the crux of the dynamics of influence between Voltaire and Dante. For Dante does have an influence on Voltaire, and it is precisely in terms of satire: through reading and translating Dante, Voltaire adds a new voice to his polyphonic discourse of religious satire in the 1750s, at the very time when the struggle of the *philosophes* against their enemies is gathering pace, leading up to the launch of Voltaire's famous campaign in the 1760s to 'écraser l'Infâme' ('crush the despicable'), where 'l'Infâme' stands for superstition, intolerance and irrational behaviour of any kind. Voltaire appropriates Dante, in other words, and gives at least some of his text a new currency, thus effectively illustrating his homely account of the art of imitation in an addition made in 1756 – the same year as the *Lettre sur le Dante* – to what was previously the 22nd of the *Lettres philosophiques* (*Philosophical Letters*): 'Ainsi presque tout est imitation [...]. Il en est des livres comme du feu dans nos foyers; on va prendre ce feu chez son voisin, on l'allume chez soi, on le communique à d'autres, et il appartient à tous' ('Thus almost everything is imitation [...]. Books are like the fire in our hearths; we use our neighbour's fire to light our own, we pass it on to others, and it belongs to everyone').[19]

Moreover, the relationship between Voltaire and Dante is dynamic and reciprocal insofar as Voltaire's reading necessarily influences our own reading of Dante's text: the meaning of any text is produced by a series of interpretive acts; Voltaire's reading of the *Commedia* is one such act, and so it influences the reception of it.[20] Voltaire's Dante was above all a satirical poet, and specifically a critic of the Church. He implicitly presents Dante in this way in his *Lettre sur le Dante*, for example, when he observes of the *Commedia*: 'Un poème d'ailleurs où l'on met des papes en enfer, réveille beaucoup l'attention' ('Moreover, a poem in which popes are dispatched to hell arouses lots of interest').[21] This reading of Dante was unusual and subversive: much of the early modern reception of Dante focused on genre, and specifically on the question of whether or not the *Commedia* fitted the classical category of comedy. Consequently, champions of the work tended to downplay considerably the attacks on the Church, while opponents of it, if they mentioned Dante's attacks on the Church at all, saw them simply as further evidence of his bad taste.[22] Voltaire, by contrast, brings satire to the foreground in his encounter with Dante. In this context, then, the very partial nature of Voltaire's response to the *Commedia* serves to highlight the importance of the influence that Dante had on him, for, as Valéry goes on to observe in his discussion of Mallarmé's influence, with which this chapter began: 'Quand un ouvrage, ou toute une œuvre, agit sur quelqu'un, non par toutes ses qualités, mais par certaine ou certaines d'entre elles, c'est alors que l'influence prend ses valeurs les plus remarquables' ('When a text, or an entire body of work, acts on someone, by dint not of all its qualities but of one or some of them, then influence takes on its most remarkable value').[23] Dante's *Commedia* and Voltaire's free translation of two passages from it exist side by side, but together create more meaning than either could generate in isolation or mere sequence: Voltaire's verse gains from being read with Dante's, and Dante's gains from being read in the light of Voltaire's reading, rewriting and reactivation of it. There is a kind of 'interanimation', to borrow, as George Steiner does,[24] John Donne's term – an interanimation that signals a very lively, dynamic and positive kind of influence. And perhaps, ultimately, what the example of Voltaire and Dante points us towards is the possibility that it is above all translation that holds out to writers a way of making influence beneficial, a way of dealing with influence without fear or anxiety.

Notes

1. Paul Valéry, 'Lettre sur Mallarmé' (*Revue de Paris*, 1 April 1927), in *Œuvres*, ed. by Jean Hytier, 2 vols (Paris: Gallimard, 1957–60), I, p. 634. Emphasis in original. Unless otherwise indicated, translations are my own.
2. *Commedia del divina poeta Danthe Alighieri, con la dotta e leggiadra spositione di Christophoro Londino* (Venice: G. G. da Trino, 1536): see *Bibliothèque de Voltaire: catalogue des livres*, ed. by M. P. Alekseev and T. N. Kopreeva (Moscow: Éditions de l'Académie des Sciences de l'URSS, 1961), n° 940. For the evidence of Voltaire's reading of this copy, which is now in St Petersburg, see *Corpus des notes marginales de Voltaire*, ed. by O. Golubiéva *et al.* (Berlin: Akademie-Verlag, 1979–), III, pp. 44–5. For a detailed analysis of Voltaire's writings on Dante, see Russell Goulbourne, '"Bizarre, mais brillant de beautés naturelles": Voltaire and Dante's *Commedia*', *La parola del testo*, 17 (2013), 31–44.
3. For a useful discussion of the potential of the concept of influence in modern critical theory and practice, see Mary Orr, *Intertextuality: Debates and Contexts* (Cambridge: Polity Press, 2003), pp. 60–93.
4. Voltaire, *Œuvres complètes*, ed. by Louis Moland, 52 vols (Paris: Garnier, 1877–85; henceforward *M*), XIX, pp. 462–64. Voltaire's article represents an implicit response to the three articles on influence published in the *Encyclopédie* in 1765: see *Encyclopédie, ou Dictionnaire raisonné des sciences, des arts et des métiers*, ed. by Denis Diderot and Jean Le Rond d'Alembert, 17 vols (Paris: Briasson, David, Le Breton, Durand, 1751–65), VIII, pp. 728–38.

5. *Les Œuvres complètes de Voltaire*, ed. by Theodore Besterman *et al.* (Oxford: Voltaire Foundation, 1968–; henceforward *OCV*), XXXIII, p. 131. Emphasis in original.
6. See Roland Mortier, *L'Originalité: une nouvelle catégorie esthétique au siècle des Lumières* (Geneva: Droz, 1982).
7. See Harold Bloom, *The Anxiety of Influence: A Theory of Poetry* (Oxford: Oxford University Press, 1973).
8. See Roland Mortier, 'L'Idée de décadence littéraire au XVIIIe siècle', *Studies on Voltaire and the Eighteenth Century*, 57 (1967), 1013–29.
9. *OCV*, LXIV, p. 256.
10. *M*, XXV, p. 246.
11. *Encyclopédie*, VIII, p. 560; *OCV*, XXXIII, p. 204. Emphasis in original. The idea that the muses are the daughters of memory, or Mnemosyne, goes back to Hesiod's *Theogony*: see Hesiod, *'Theogony' and 'Works and Days'*, ed. and trans. by Martin L. West (Oxford: Oxford University Press, 2008), pp. 4, 30.
12. On the distinction between imitating the ancients and letting one's imagination run wild, see also Voltaire's 1750 *Dissertation sur les Électre*, in *OCV*, XXXI^A, pp. 565–616 (p. 592).
13. *Encyclopédie*, VIII, pp. 567–8.
14. According to Arturo Farinelli, for instance, Voltaire's translations betray 'son manque de compréhension' ('his lack of understanding') and 'ses erreurs d'interprétation, provenant de sa connaissance limitée de la langue' ('his errors of interpretation, caused by his limited knowledge of the language'): see 'Voltaire et Dante', *Studien zur vergleichenden Literaturgeschichte*, 6 (1906), 86–128 (p. 96).
15. Dante, *Purgatorio*, ed. and trans. by Robin Kirkpatrick (London: Penguin, 2007), pp. 150–51.
16. *M*, XXIV, p. 31. Voltaire also uses this translation in Chapter 82 of the *Essai sur les mœurs* and in the chapter on the arts: see *Essai sur les mœurs*, ed. by René Pomeau, 2 vols (Paris: Garnier, 1963), I, p. 764; II, p. 823.
17. *OCV*, XLV^B, pp. 216–18.
18. See Dante, *Inferno*, ed. and trans. by Robin Kirkpatrick (London: Penguin, 2006), pp. 240–43.
19. Voltaire, *Lettres philosophiques*, ed. by Gustave Lanson and André-Michel Rousseau, 2 vols (Paris: Didier, 1964), II, p. 136.
20. For a variation on this idea, see Jorge Luis Borges's essay 'Kafka and his Precursors' (1951), in which he argues that we read literary texts in a different way with the knowledge of subsequent writers, hence his example of how our reading of Franz Kafka changes our reading of Robert Browning: 'The poem "Fears and Scruples" by Robert Browning prophesies the work of Kafka, but our reading of Kafka noticeably refines and diverts our reading

of the poem. Browning did not read it as we read it now. [...] Each writer *creates* his precursors. His work modifies our conception of the past, as it will modify the future' (Borges, *The Total Library: Non-Fiction, 1922–1986*, ed. by Eliot Weinberger and trans. by Esther Allen *et al.* [Harmondsworth: Penguin, 1999], p. 365). A similar argument is developed by Pierre Bayard in *Le Plagiat par anticipation* (Paris: Minuit, 2009), pp. 61–9.

21. *OCV*, XLV^B, p. 216. See also the chapter on the arts intended for the *Essai sur les mœurs*, in which Voltaire observes of Dante: 'Ce qui contribua le plus à sa vogue, ce fut le plaisir malin qu'eurent les lecteurs de trouver dans un ouvrage bien écrit la satire de leur temps' ('What contributed the most to his renown was the naughty pleasure that readers took in finding in a well-written work a satire of their times') (*Essai sur les mœurs*, II, p. 823).

22. In *L'Académie de l'art poétique* (Paris: J. de Bordeaulx, 1610), for example, Pierre de Deimier remarks that a number of respectable individuals 'ne devaient point être ainsi diffamées par ce poète, à se voir décrire parmi le nombre des misérables qui sont enchaînés en ces peines infernales' ('should not have been so defamed by the poet as to see themselves described amongst the wretched souls who are chained up in hell'; p. 525). Voltaire also contradicts eighteenth-century Italian critics of Dante like Giuseppe Baretti, who takes Dante to task for 'having ridiculed and satirized, with as much bitterness as Luther himself, the priests and friars, and generally all the supporters of the Church in which he lived', thereby setting an 'imprudent and dangerous example' to later poets (*Dissertation upon the Italian Poetry* [London, 1753], pp. 63–4).

23. Valéry, 'Lettre sur Mallarmé', p. 635.

24. George Steiner, *After Babel: Aspects of Language and Translation* (Oxford: Oxford University Press, 1975), pp. 452–3.

2
Post-Revolutionary Uses of Pascal
Philip Knee

I propose to explore a convergence of influences in the period following the French Revolution, when Christian discourse weakens in some respects and is renewed in others. At the dawn of the nineteenth century, counter-revolutionary and neo-Catholic writers acclaim religious and political authority and decry the Enlightenment, whose contribution to the Revolution and effects on social life (as seen from their viewpoint) they denounce. And so the Enlightenment is blamed for the Terror, the persecution of the clergy and the corrosion of society by an all-pervasive scepticism. This denunciation is fed by a revisiting of the great figures of tradition – Montaigne, Descartes, Bossuet, Rousseau – with a view to finding, in given aspects of their thought, explanations or arguments in the struggle to defend authority from dissolution. The place of Pascal within this historical context is a decisive one, recently highlighted by Antoine Compagnon, who identifies in the movement from Rousseau to Pascal the 'usual route' taken by 'antimodern' writers.[1] Having been influenced by reading the philosophers of the Enlightenment, especially Rousseau, to an important extent the counter-Revolutionaries use their own arms against them.

This explains why the Pascal invoked by such thinkers is a Pascal modified by the eighteenth century; a Pascal who meets the needs of the new, post-Revolutionary spirit, even if the project that he is supposed to serve is resolutely hostile to that spirit. Space does not permit a discussion of the general influence of Pascal on these writers, for it can be found everywhere in their texts; rather, we will observe some of the variations and internal tensions of that influence.

Pascal's presence loomed large throughout the eighteenth century, but in the form of a figure to be refuted. Two reference points are key to showing the context in which the counter-Enlightenment will be deployed: Voltaire's critique of Pascal in the *Lettres philosophiques* (*Philosophical Letters*) of 1736,[2] and Condorcet's judgement, especially in his edition of the *Pensées* in 1776.[3] In a text that has entered the canon, Voltaire pours scorn on Pascal's pessimistic anthropology by defining man, not by the Fall, but by his agency in the world. Even if man's projects remain partial, inconstant and relative, it is possible to aim for happiness via knowledge of nature, the creation of wealth and the free exchange of ideas. Such a route towards happiness is lit by many sources that converge and modify each other, forming what might be called concentrations of enlightenment. By contrast, Pascal's vision suggests that all man's striving for happiness is a wild goose chase, which exhausts all his efforts but produces no worthwhile results. To become rich, to seduce, to gain knowledge, to amuse oneself cannot afford access to meaning, and those who believe otherwise are rapidly disabused when they face illness or death. For Pascal, only the love of God and accepting to exist as part of the great Whole can give rise to meaning. It is the Whole that enlightens the world; the Whole is the light that precedes and envelops man, a light to which he is supposed to submit.

While Voltaire takes the side 'de l'humanité contre ce misanthrope sublime' ('of humanity against this sublime misanthrope')[4] by concentrating on Pascal's moral and religious thought, Condorcet's approach is more nuanced, at least to start with. As a mathematician, Condorcet opens by emphasizing his esteem for Pascal's scientific thought. For instance, of his *Traité de la roulette* (*Treatise on the Game of Roulette*) Condorcet writes that it will be 'regardé comme un monument imposant de la force de l'esprit humain' ('looked on as an imposing monument of the strength of the human mind').[5] He also expresses his admiration for Pascal the polemicist, author of the *Lettres Provinciales* (*The Provincial Letters*), 'livre de tous les états, de tous les esprits, de tous les âges' ('a book for those in all stations in life, all minds, all ages'), who manages to transcend his era.[6] But as far as morality and religion are concerned, Condorcet's position gradually converges with Voltaire's judgement on the *Pensées*: in spite of the subtlety with which they analyse the human heart, they eloquently proffer 'des injures au genre humain' ('insults to the human race'), and their 'plaidoyer contre l'espèce humaine' ('case against human nature')[7] can be likened to that of Hobbes.[8] Ultimately, since he seeks less to understand man than win his reader round, Pascal does not deserve to be called a philosopher, for he is sworn to defend Jansenism's (fanatical) cause.

The general intention of the counter-Revolutionaries is, obviously, to fight against this negative, eighteenth-century view of Pascal, but they do not merely aim to negate that earlier negation. When we read the works of the principal figures within this tendency – Chateaubriand, Bonald, Lamennais and Maistre – we see that they are far from forming any kind of united front in their approach to Pascal. Beneath the surface where all may appear smooth, Pascal's influence on counter-Revolutionary writers is in fact a tangle of citations and displacements, of impassioned appeals and provisos.

I

Among the writers to be discussed here, Chateaubriand is the best known and the most influential in his own right, for he sketched a likeness of Pascal that has remained with us for two centuries. He explicitly places his work *Génie du christianisme* (*The Genius of Christianity*) under the aegis of the *Pensées*, undertaking to complete the apologetics that Pascal had begun.[9] However, we should add nuance to this apparent convergence, in two respects.

First, the two authors' respective approaches to apologetics are clearly opposed. Admittedly, like the *Pensées*, the *Génie du christianisme* is designed to persuade readers in ways that the use of logical proofs cannot achieve. Nevertheless, where Pascal relies on creating fear and sapping intellectual confidence, Chateaubriand has recourse to beauty. He celebrates the marvels of nature and art as so many manifestations of God. Pascal sets out the corruption of earthly existence and undermines his libertine reader by holding up a mirror to his concupiscence. Admittedly, certain fragments of the *Pensées* lend a theological dimension to Chateaubriand's appeal to the 'evidence of our eyes' in the *Génie du christianisme*; for Pascal maintains that God sometimes manifests himself to men in the beauties of nature.[10] Still, such beauties do not announce God always and everywhere. The spectacle of nature, however beautiful, is not in itself a source of reassurance, and is quite powerless when it comes to persuading the unfaithful to find their way to God.

Expressed in broad terms, Chateaubriand's Christianity is indebted to the idea of sin attacked by the Enlightenment, being mocked (by Voltaire) and expelled from history (by Rousseau). Of course, religion as depicted in the *Génie du christianisme* is more historically based and positive than Rousseau's purely spiritual and otherworldly version, expressed in the *Profession de foi d'un vicaire savoyard* (*Profession of Faith of a Savoyard Vicar*). Nevertheless, the tone of Chateaubriand's work is a Rousseauistic one, and nowhere more so than in his peculiar eulogy of Pascal, which praises Pascal's character and actions far more strongly than his thought.[11] For the Pascal Chateaubriand describes is not true to the seventeenth-century original; or rather, if he resembles that original, it is as having been lost from sight then rediscovered; seen from a distance, or from Chateaubriand's nineteenth-century perspective, he is a *Romantic* figure, as we might put it now, having been endowed with aspects of the inward-looking religion that Rousseau had done more than any other thinker to promote. Pascal's influence on Chateaubriand and the latter's nineteenth-century readers is mediated by this other great influence: the Pascal we find in the *Génie du christianisme* is a Rousseauized one.

On the other hand, Pascal and Chateaubriand have a great deal in common when we consider their views on the political sphere. Chateaubriand laments the extent to which France has been 'contaminated' by the liberal ideas of the eighteenth century, which culminated in the Revolution. But he adds nuance: it is not these ideas in themselves that were harmful, but the way in which Enlightenment thinkers had expressed and publicized them, without due caution. Christian thinkers of the seventeenth century had, it seems, already discovered the basic principles that their eighteenth-century successors were to develop, but the earlier period knew to veil them sufficiently to contain their destructive potential. Chateaubriand finds in Rousseau, 'presque mot pour mot' ('almost word for word') certain of Pascal's ideas: 'le penseur le plus hardi du [18ᵉ] siècle, l'écrivain le plus déterminé à généraliser les idées pour bouleverser le monde, n'a rien dit d'aussi fort [que Pascal] contre la justice des gouvernements et les préjugés des nations' ('the most audacious thinker of the [eighteenth] century, the writer with the greatest determination to generalize [new] ideas and so change the world, said nothing as strong [as Pascal] against the justice of governments and the prejudices of nations'). However, 'en connaissant comme nous, et mieux que nous, la nature des choses, [les Bossuet, Fénelon et Pascal] ont senti le danger des innovations' (while knowing as well as us, or better than us, the nature of things, [a Bossuet, a Fénelon or a Pascal] sensed the danger contained in the new', because their perspicacity reached 'jusqu'au fond' ('to the bottom of things'). This, for Chateaubriand, explains why the seventeenth century was a stable one. Nothing had escaped the understanding of its great thinkers, but 'contemplant les objets de plus haut que nous [...] ils ont dédaigné les routes où nous sommes entrés, et au bout desquelles leur œil perçant avait découvert un abîme' ('contemplating objects from a greater height than us, they disdained the routes we were to take, for their piercing eye had already seen the abyss to which they lead').[12] Criticizing organized religion and political authority in the name of their brave new world, the Enlightenment *philosophes* proved to be imprudent and indiscreet, and so undermined spiritual life and traditional values. In a word, they marked the coming of those whom Pascal calls the 'demi-habiles' ('the half-clever'):[13] those who demystify existing beliefs and call for their overthrow in the name of supposed transparency.

Chateaubriand thus carries forward Pascal's idea that politics does nothing to help us towards salvation, but that it is nevertheless an arena in which men's passions are pursued without restraint, and this means that they need to be helped in spite of themselves: some need to be protected against others, some against themselves. Those who wish to neutralize the passions, those who adopt a suspicious attitude towards the 'hôpital des fous' ('madhouse') of politics, like Pascal, need to use 'pensée de derrière' ('a rearguard strategy'), which is to say they must proceed by stealth.[14] By contrast, those such as Voltaire or Condorcet who rehabilitate the will and see human agency as the means to achieve justice, and so lead men to hope for redemption at a political level, lose the transcendent authority that allows a true regulation of politics, including a definition of its limits and a critique of its folly. For Chateaubriand, it is precisely this illusion of political redemption, which bypasses the very concept of *evil*, that was played out in the Terror.

This, then, is the tension in Chateaubriand's treatment of Pascal. The praise he offers Pascal in the realms of theology and ethics serves as a cover for the way in which he 'modernizes' him. For the later writer's sentimental version of Christianity is nourished by the fact that the Enlightenment had broken with the concept of sin. At the same time, that breaking with sin led, in Chateaubriand's view, to the voluntarism of the Revolution; and he turns to Pascal's thoughts on politics to find a way to counteract this. Even if Chateaubriand's double use of Pascal may be shown to be consistent on its own terms, it brings the coherence of the *Pensées* into question.

II

Less artistic and more philosophical than Chateaubriand, Bonald owes more to the rationalist than the sentimental tendency of the eighteenth century. In spite of this, and in spite of the scarcity of explicit references by Bonald to Pascal, his reaction to Enlightenment philosophy can be qualified as Pascalian. Indeed, one could summarize it in the famous formula of the *Pensées*, according to which the true philosopher dismisses philosophy.[15]

The rationalist tendency of the Enlightenment, which emerges from the Cartesian method, consists in locating within each (reasoning) man the 'point fixe' ('fixed point') that guarantees true knowledge. According to Bonald, this cannot lead to truth, for such a man connects the 'first link' of the chain of knowledge and its extension. However, this is not, as man hopes and believes, a way of developing certain knowledge. All new links are made in the image of man; believing he is understanding the world, he is only seeing himself, and his mind becomes sterile.[16] Man's illusion consists in the belief that one can divide oneself to acquire knowledge; one 'self' would then act, while a second 'self' would observe and analyse the first. To escape this illusion, man must embrace belief as the means to knowledge, as recommended by Augustine; he should not begin by seeking within himself what is open to doubt and (by elimination) beyond doubt. Rather, he must begin by what properly precedes such judgements; for the only true proofs can be derived from the submission of the individual consciousness to an external will. Bonald recognizes that the human being is endowed with reason, and might therefore aspire to take reason alone as its guide. Yet reason, according to Bonald, is not immediately accessible to itself: it only comes into being through that which precedes it; belief must come first, in order for reason to be formed and to operate. Moreover, Bonald admits, like Pascal the scientist, that it is entirely possible to set aside previous traditions in order to understand nature (for nature does not cease to function while it is being examined), but to do the same in the realms of morality, politics and/or religion leads only to the destruction of true knowledge.

The divine will, therefore, is not manifested to men through philosophy, which consists in constantly seeking and questioning. No society, no people can survive by questioning alone; survival requires true knowledge.[17] This is why the philosophy of (successful) Christian societies tends towards the praise of religion, and this is the perspective adopted by the great philosophers of the seventeenth century such as Pascal. Outside this framework, the very diversity of philosophical schools betrays their essence; they express the activity of this or that individual understanding, and they provide no way for man to escape from ceaseless wandering in his maze of uncertainties and mere opinions. Above and beyond the specific content of each discrete school of thought, the fact that (secular) philosophy in general promotes speculation on man and presumes to suspend belief as a means to knowledge, it serves the cause of atheism – and in that sense, the Revolution realized philosophy's general project.

This critique of philosophy echoes the great detour into scepticism (especially as represented by Montaigne) that Pascal takes in the *Pensées*, with the aim of undermining the freethinker's belief in reason. Pascal's 'espaces infinis' ('infinite spaces') becomes, in Bonald, an 'océan d'incertitudes' ('an ocean of uncertainties'), in which we cannot drop anchor. However, Bonald does not follow Pascal in dramatizing this experience, nor does he have recourse to theology to find a way out. He seeks to identify a foundation for moral and political life based on '[les] faits publics' ('public facts'), so that it might win 'l'approbation générale' ('general approbation').[18] This foundation cannot consist in any individually held opinion or truth; it must be a social fact agreed on by all. Bonald considers God-given language, the 'don primitif et nécessaire fait au genre humain' ('primitive and necessary gift made to the human race'), to be the foundation of social life.[19]

Here, we notice that Bonald has recourse to Enlightenment rationality in order to critique that very tradition. He works in Pascal's 'anti-modern' spirit to the extent that he dispossesses man, but that dispossession cannot be entirely explained by an Augustinian metaphysics of sin.[20] Bonald breaks with this tradition by seeing divine order manifested in the way society forms men. In post-Enlightenment vein, the powerlessness of men is rethought as a dependence of each individual will on a collective will, which Bonald terms 'la volonté générale' ('the general will'), a distinctly eighteenth-century term. For Bonald, the general will is clearly that of God revealed through the Christian religion, but his conceptualization of man's dispossession goes beyond Pascal's resistance to the modern. Pascal's strategy was (we have seen) to discredit reason to make place for the heart; in Bonald's view, this does not suffice to win round sceptical minds. For him, the 'preuves de sentiment' ('proofs derived from feeling') are like the ever-receding proofs of history, or objects at a distance: the longer one lives, the less distinct they become. But *rational* proofs increase with time and distance. Nothing could therefore be further from Pascal than Bonald's method of proof: dogged, repetitive, dense to the point of obscurity, he is entirely focused on demonstrating providential necessity at work in the organization of society.

III

When Lamennais refers to Pascal, he too displays ambivalence concerning the ideas bequeathed by the Enlightenment. At first, he uses the term 'indifférence' to reject Enlightenment ideas, and Pascal seems to be his main inspiration in this.[21] In Lamennais's eyes, the eighteenth century deployed its considerable energies to rebel against Church and Monarchy, but since the Revolution there has been no will to resist the winds that blow humanity in different directions. According to Lamennais, the Enlightenment sought to achieve understanding rather than belief, but without belief understanding is rudderless; it never reaches a conclusion, preferring to take a distance from any strongly held belief; it is a feverish, restless version of knowledge; it leads nowhere. The indifference of post-Revolutionary society is the result, Lamennais argues, of such epistemological hesitation, repeated over time.

Lamennais's choice of the term *indifférence* is probably based on a fragment of the *Pensées* concerning the freethinker's indifference towards the immortality of the soul.[22] Lamennais's critique draws on a characteristically Pascalian anthropology, which posits a contradiction in the human heart. Man is supposedly torn between the desire to know the truth and a refusal to recognize it, for the truth tells him he is wretched. Thus man wants truth, but is distressed by truth; his hunger for truth never abates, but in his quest to find it, he wears himself out and becomes confused; he presumes he can succeed and yet he despairs because he must fail.[23] And so indifference results when the soul is denied the true, religious answer and disperses its energy pursuing false directions (e.g. art or worldly glory).

According to Lamennais, the only adequate response to such sceptical indifference begins by saying, in effect: so be it! Let us follow scepticism to its ultimate conclusion, and see where it takes us. This is Pascal's method. Reason orders man to doubt everything; but nature orders him not to, and prevents him 'd'extravaguer jusqu'à ce point' ('from taking things to such insane lengths').[24] For in fact, men always assume certain things to be certain in order to lead their lives, and they do not do so on the basis of their individual reason; they naturally submit to the transcendent principle that is offered by religion. For religion constitutes the body of beliefs that man needs in order to use his reason and discover its limits, without which he cannot escape from uncertainty. The reference to Pascal charts a course between the Scylla and Charybdis that are the disheartening uncertainty of scepticism and the false certainty of the Enlightenment.

However, even if Lamennais asserts 'la parfaite conformité' ('the perfect conformity') of his doctrine with that of Pascal,[25] he goes beyond dismissing scepticism and Enlightenment and simply using their common failure as an argument in favour of religion. He tries to identify an authority that might meet his era's need for rationality, and this is where he takes his distance from Pascal.[26] In his view, it is not enough to legitimate authority per se against individual reason; men must submit to the right authority; and on this point he finds Pascal's critique of scepticism inadequate as far as winning round the undecided reader of the early nineteenth century is concerned. Pascal sought to lead the freethinker to react to his natural need to believe by entering into a wager, but the wager he proposed was precisely to take the leap of faith that the freethinker insisted he could not bring himself to do. Lamennais considers such a wager to be still more difficult in 1820 than it had been in 1660. He believes that Pascal's method for inducing submission to the authority of Christianity is a case of preaching to the converted. The rest remain trapped between complete doubt (which is, in Lamennais's view, impossible to sustain and which any sincere freethinker will naturally reject) and belief in Revelation (which is too far removed from the freethinker's tendencies and his requirement for belief to be based on facts). Lamennais is therefore not content to give systematic form to Pascal's critique of indifference; he aims to provide a criterion allowing man to escape the dichotomy of faith versus doubt. But how to speak to those among the undecided who wish to believe, without finding an insuperable obstacle in their adherence to the critical-rationalist tendency that they have inherited from the Enlightenment? How to buttress Christian authority with a proof in tune with the historical consciousness of the post-Revolutionary period?

Lamennais answers by invoking a 'raison supérieure à celle de l'individu' ('reason superior to that of the individual'), which consists in finding where judgements and factual evidence meet, throughout history and across the world. And so he strives to renew the appeal of religion by showing, patiently and laboriously, that Christian authority is consonant with what can be known of humanity throughout its history. This approach recalls that of Bonald, but they diverge in the political realm. For Bonald, individual freedom only has meaning as submission to a general will manifested in the language that God imparts to man; that is why he remains faithful to the strict respect for authority that Pascal recommends. By contrast, Lamennais identifies humanity with the struggle for freedom that forms the pulse of the 'peuple'. For him, the people is a substantial reality in which individual existence is realized, and the study of history reveals the links between that struggle and the Christian religion that lends it expression. Lamennais thus moves to the position that Catholicism can detach itself from the Ancien Régime and espouse the popular will. This in turn leads him to embrace a political position bordering on Republicanism, or even Socialism, without a backward glance at Pascal's recommendation of prudence; it also implies a break with the Roman Catholic Church.

IV

If Lamennais takes his distance from Pascal's political thought in the name of the popular struggle for freedom, Maistre does the same, but from a quite different motive. For he decides that Jansenism's persistent refusal to submit to official Church doctrine leads it into self-contradiction. Troubled by this dissidence on the part of Jansenists, Maistre is compelled to juggle with the meanings of Pascal's texts: while he approves of the eulogy of Roman Catholic authority in the *Pensées*, he laments the more adventurous *Provinciales*, which effectively defy the authority of the Pope.[27] In this respect, the fierce criticisms that Maistre levels against Protestantism are partly applicable to the radical stance adopted by the Jansenists in spite of their belonging to the Roman Catholic Church.[28] It may well be that, writing after the Revolution, Maistre saw this split within the Church as a forerunner of the pluralist tendency of the modern age, which is to say its tendency to engage in continual debates fuelled by a wide diversity of customs and laws practised in different cultures; and this without any shared recognition of an overarching authority capable of settling any given question or providing, more generally, stability and legitimacy. In Maistre's view, those who weaken traditional beliefs and attitudes are contributing to the placing of moral and spiritual uncertainty at the heart of religion, making (true) religion impossible.

Still, Maistre's apologetics echoes what might be termed the method of 'argument by fear' deployed in the *Pensées*, and it is probable that his violent rhetoric makes him the author who most closely resembles Pascal in the period. Like Chateaubriand, Bonald and Lamennais, Maistre refers to Providence to explain the degradation of the general will at work in society, especially in the Terror, which he presents as God's lesson to humanity, reminding us of our weakness. But for Bonald this is above all an intellectual lesson: God reminds men of the social principles and the collective order that correspond to his great plan. For Lamennais and Chateaubriand the Revolution reveals, despite its excesses, a political dimension to the Gospel message – that of equality – that was neglected for too long by the Church. For Maistre, by contrast, the Terror contains a moral message: God punishes men for their madness by making them suffer in the political realm into which they had blundered with the presumption of mastering it.[29] In Maistre's vision, Providentialism operates through punishment and suffering, so that man is forced to confront his own sinfulness and can only gain succour through prayer. Moreover, Maistre pursues this call to order so vigorously that it is scarcely possible to speak of his apologetics, since 'holy rage' seems better suited to characterize his approach.

Surprisingly enough, Maistre's Pascalian dramatization of man's situation leads him to echo Voltaire as well. At first glance, the two authors are opposed in every respect: Maistre's depiction of Voltaire is an excoriating one;[30] in one passage praising Pascal, he denounces the *Lettres philosophiques* as a 'sacrilegious' work.[31] However, we should remember that *Candide* was designed to distance the reader from the easy comforts of a divine order that negates evil, recuperating each and every horror within a Providential order in which 'tout est bien' ('all is well'). And Voltaire's attack on the resigned, Optimist version of Christianity converges with Maistre's approach, even if the two authors diverge in terms of the ramifications of their respective arguments. Maistre seeks to prove that our experience of suffering must push us towards a Providentialist view of the world. The sacred terror that evil produces in men is designed to show them the necessity of finding a supernatural explanation for the course of human history. For Maistre effectively asks: How can we conceive of the fact that men have been abandoned to history's horrors if they cannot be explained in terms of a divine plan? This echoes Pascal's radical judgement that rational proofs of religion, together with those based on the spectacle of nature, were insufficient, and that only a sense of terror created by the perspective of a life without God could lead to a state of mind compatible with salvation.[32] Similarly, Maistre refuses to look away from the horrors of history. Of course, he refuses to take refuge in Voltaire's rational ethics, which involves seeing the world through secular eyes. But more than this, he refuses to take refuge in a facile Christian optimism – of the type denounced by Voltaire – that denies the existence of evil in the best of all possible worlds. If the world is simply as it should be, the problem of evil collapses, along with its particular manifestation during the Revolution; and we need not strive to square divine justice with the experience of suffering in the world.

V

It is difficult to overstate Pascal's influence on the thinkers discussed above. Their horizon is undeniably Pascalian, since they wish to reverse the direction of Enlightenment thought inaugurated by Voltaire. Opposition to Enlightenment morality and Revolutionary politics begins, for them, with the rehabilitation of the rhetorical force of the *Pensées*, with a view to making men submit (again) to the authority of Church and King. Yet at the same time, these writers sense that such 'counter-Enlightenment' only becomes possible if they embrace, at least in part, the evolution of mentalities in the course of the eighteenth century, including their demand for rationality but also the value they placed on sentiment.

Doubtless, the counter-Revolutionary writers also revive the spirit of resistance to be found in the *Pensées*: resistance, that is, to the context of nascent scientific modernity in the seventeenth century, by recourse to Christian apologetics. It is reasonable to assert that Pascal was already speaking to freethinkers in the way in which later traditionalist writers would speak to sceptics and doubters after the Revolution. Those later writers, like Pascal, would hold the Christian torch aloft to expose the dangers of disbelief. Pascal is therefore, in one sense, the first 'anti-modern' thinker. But it is difficult to deny that each 'anti-modern' is always, willy-nilly, a modern. This explains why, around 1800, traditionalists turn to Pascal yet betray his apologetic method and make a Romantic of him. They claim that his political thought, which has entirely Christian roots, helps to explain the Terror, and they assume the task of correcting him, selectively and reluctantly, in the name of the socially aware Catholicism and the new humanitarianism that are in the process of emerging. This is the paradoxical destiny of great thinkers: their influence is proclaimed all the more vigorously as they are harnessed to causes that were never theirs.

Notes

This chapter, including English versions of quotations from Pascal, was translated from French by James Fowler, in consultation with the author.

1. Antoine Compagnon, *Les Antimodernes: de Joseph de Maistre à Roland Barthes* (Paris: Gallimard, 2005), p. 46.
2. Voltaire, *Lettres philosophiques* ('Sur les *Pensées* de M. Pascal'), in *Mélanges*, ed. by J. Van Den Heuvel (Paris: Gallimard, 1961), pp. 1–133 (pp. 104–33).
3. Nicolas de Condorcet, *Éloge de Blaise Pascal*; *Remarques sur les Pensées de Pascal*; *Préface aux Remarques de Voltaire sur les Pensées de M. Pascal*, in *Œuvres*, ed. by A. Condorcet O'Connor and F. Arago, 12 vols (Paris: Firmin Didot Frères, 1847), vols III and IV.
4. Voltaire, *Lettres philosophiques*, p. 104.
5. Condorcet, *Œuvres*, III, p. 632.
6. Ibid., p. 599.
7. Condorcet, *Œuvres*, IV, p. 292.

8. Condorcet, Œuvres, III, p. 643.
9. See François-René de Chateaubriand, Génie du christianisme, ed. by M. Regard (Paris: Gallimard, 1978), Part 3, Book II, Chapter 6.
10. 'Dieu, voulant faire paraître qu'il pouvait former un peuple saint d'une sainteté invisible et le remplir d'une gloire éternelle, a fait des choses visibles. Comme la nature est une image de la grâce, il a fait dans les biens de la nature ce qu'il devait faire dans ceux de la grâce, afin qu'on jugeât qu'il pouvait faire l'invisible, puisqu'il faisait bien le visible [...]. Dieu a donc montré le pouvoir qu'il a de donner les biens invisibles, par celui qu'il a montré qu'il avait sur les visibles' ('God, wishing to show that He could form a people that was holy with an invisible holiness and fill it with eternal glory created visible things. As Nature is an image of [divine] grace, He did through Nature's riches what he was to do through those of grace, so that we might understand that he could do things invisibly, since he did things visibly [...]. Therefore God showed the power He has to give invisible blessings by the power he had to bestow visible ones'; Blaise Pascal, Pensées, in Œuvres complètes, ed. by L. Lafuma [Paris: Seuil, 1963], pp. 493–641 [L. 275]).
11. Although he is not named, Rousseau is clearly the opponent targeted in these passages of the Génie du christianisme (see especially p. 827).
12. Chateaubriand, Génie du christianisme, pp. 826–9. Here, 'nous' or 'we' are men and women of the nineteenth century who were raised in the ideas of the eighteenth.
13. Pascal, Pensées, L. 90.
14. Ibid., L. 533.
15. 'Se moquer de la philosophie c'est vraiment philosopher' (ibid., L. 513).
16. Louis Gabriel Ambroise de Bonald, Recherches philosophiques sur les premiers objets des connaissances morales, in Œuvres complètes, ed. by J. P. Migne, 3 vols (Paris: Migne, 1859), III, pp. 34–6.
17. Ibid., p. 38.
18. Ibid., p. 42.
19. Ibid., p. 45.
20. For Pascal, it is through the heart that divine grace operates on man, and therefore it is through the heart that one accedes to the first principles: 'Car les connaissances des premiers principes: espace, temps, mouvement, nombres sont aussi fermes qu'aucune que nos raisonnements nous donnent et c'est sur ces connaissances du cœur et de l'instinct qu'il faut que la raison s'appuie et qu'elle y fonde tout son discours' ('For the knowledge of first principles [space, time, movement and numbers] is as firm as any that we derive from our reasoning, and it is on such knowledge of the heart and of instinct that reason must depend and must found its whole discourse'; Pascal, Pensées, L. 110).

21. Félicité Robert de Lamennais, *Essai sur l'indifférence en matière de religion*, in *Œuvres complètes*, ed. by L. Le Guillou, 11 vols (Geneva: Slatkine, 1980), vols I–IV. This edition is a reprint of the Paris editions of 1836–56.
22. Pascal, *Pensées*, L. 427.
23. Lamennais, *Essai*, I, pp. vi, 258–9.
24. Pascal, *Pensées*, L. 131.
25. Lamennais, *Défense de l'essai* in *Essai sur l'indifférence*, III, pp. 1–325 (p. 56).
26. Ibid., pp. 67–8.
27. 'Lorsque Pascal défend sa secte contre le Pape, c'est comme s'il ne parlait pas' ('When Pascal defends his sect against the Pope, it is as if he were saying nothing'; Joseph de Maistre, *Du Pape*, ed. by J. Lovie and J. Chetail [Geneva: Droz, 1966], p. 62).
28. Maistre, *Sur le protestantisme*, in *Œuvres*, ed. by P. Glaudes (Paris: Robert Laffont/Bouquins, 2007).
29. Maistre, *Considérations sur la France*, in *Œuvres*, especially Chapters 2 and 3.
30. Maistre, *Les Soirées de Saint-Pétersbourg*, in *Œuvres*, pp. 555–7.
31. Ibid., p. 635.
32. According to Pascal, we must 'faire croire nos deux pièces' ('make both our parts believe') at the same time: 'l'esprit' ('the mind') and 'l'automate' ('the automaton'). See *Pensées*, L. 821.

3
The Survival of Sade in French Literature of the 1950s

Perrine Coudurier

Today, almost two centuries after his death, Sade still stands for absolute evil. He cannot, however, be reduced to this role. In various ways, he makes his presence felt in literature and philosophy. He is at once a man, a body of work and a symbol. Critics have remarked that he often resurfaces during great, nihilistic crises, or at times when civilization seems to lose its bearings. Michel Delon writes that Sade is 'une des figures centrales de notre modernité et même de notre postmodernité' ('one of the central figures of our modernity and indeed of our postmodernity').[1] He acts as a historical reference point, while disturbing diachrony as such; he functions as a syntagm always questioning any given ideology and any definition of 'man'.

This phenomenon can be observed immediately after World War II and throughout the 1950s. As he re-enters the scene, Sade stimulates thinkers and writers to take up various positions, and to ask questions that extend beyond the literary and into the truly anthropological. In France, before the 1950s, the figure of Sade was rejected, as indeed he was during the main part of the nineteenth century, but now as an isolated oddity, a marginalized 'libertine' in the sense not of a freethinker but of a ('free-living') debauchee (during this phase, people are interested in Sade's 'sadism' rather than his writing). Subsequently, he is praised, by the Surrealists, as the ultimate figure of transgression. Thus, our relation to Sade has oscillated since the eighteenth century between reading and censoring his works, praising him and seeing him as a threat. Sade ceaselessly polarizes opinion.

After a period during which attention was focused on Sade as a flesh-and-blood individual (the 'Divine Marquis', according to the surrealists), the 1950s witness a return to Sade the writer. Though we do not propose to adopt a purely chronological approach, three dates are particularly important here: in 1947, there is a spike in books and articles that take Sade as their subject; 1954 sees the publication of Pauline Réage's *Histoire d'O* (*Story of O*), a text whose story is sadistic while its style is Sadean; and in 1956 begins the trial of Jean-Jacques Pauvert, who is accused of promoting obscenity by publishing Sade. These three reference points suggest the forging of a link, in the relevant period, between absolute evil (as enacted in World War II and the Holocaust) and Sade's novels. Sade becomes the precursor, the echo and the philosopher of the extreme of evil that is Nazism. Indeed, many links are posited. In the midst of this profoundly Hegelian period, Sade becomes Hegel's Other; in his novels, the master eclipses the slave, annihilating him at will.[2] Thus, Sade brings into question not only Hegelian dialectics but the very idea of the whole. He incarnates absolute negation: negation of the Other, negation of Man.

This is why we do not propose to examine Sade purely in terms of sources or intertextuality. We wish instead to relate his constant return to 'survival' – by which I mean the *Nachleben* of Aby Warburg as discussed by Georges Didi-Huberman: the afterlife of the repeat survivor.[3] Whether we speak of Sade's 'survival' into the twentieth century, his 'haunting' or his 'remanence', his case illustrates Didi-Huberman's assertion that what makes sense in a given culture is precisely what fails to 'fit' in chronological terms. Below, we will set out the various ways in which a writer of the eighteenth century 'impregnates' the culture of the twentieth, and will assess what is at stake in the process. This will be done by distinguishing between the following phenomena: the (intertextual) trace, the (editorial) phantom and the (ontological) symptom.[4]

Sade's Trace

Sade impregnates French culture of the 1950s first and foremost by offering a repository of themes. He is unambiguously present in the most scandalous novel of the time: *Histoire d'O* by Pauline Réage (alias Dominique Aury, secretary at the *Nouvelle Revue Française* and mistress to Jean Paulhan, who was at the heart of Gallimard's operations in the 1950s), which was published by Jean-Jacques Pauvert in 1954.[5] In her thesis partly devoted to the reception of *Histoire d'O*, Alexandra Destais writes:

> Après une longue période de purgatoire au XIXe siècle et à la faveur de l'intense phase de redécouverte du XXe siècle, l'œuvre sadienne

est désormais devenue le paradigme de la littérature érographique. L'écriture de Sade illustre un cas-limite de la représentation du corps, témoigne d'un 'seuil d'intensité maximale' par rapport auquel sont évaluées des œuvres contemporaines.

(After a long stay in purgatory during the nineteenth century and thanks to the intense phase of rediscovery that occurred during the twentieth, Sade's work has become the paradigm of 'erotographic' literature. His writing illustrates an outer horizon as far as representing the body is concerned, and bears witness to a 'threshold of maximal intensity' by which the works of our time are measured.)[6]

Thus, as Sade reappears he becomes the model for 'erotographic' writing, an inspiration and yet a horizon that can never be reached. His representation of the body in pleasure (according to the libertine) and in pain (according to the victim) will inspire a considerable number of erotic texts through the 1950s; besides Réage, famous examples are produced by Georges Bataille, André-Pieyre de Mandiargues and Pierre Klossowski.

The plot of *Histoire d'O* is widely known. It relates the adventures of a female character 'O' (short for Odile) who entirely submits to her lover's will, and so becomes the lover of characters named and unnamed, who abuse and/or rape her in a château at Roissy. The young woman accepts her subjugation to please her lover (as Réage writes the *Histoire d'O* to please Jean Paulhan, who is increasingly showing signs of wanting to end their connection, while remaining a fervent admirer of Sade). Perhaps no more accurate description of the work can be found than the following extract from the report of the consultative body that pressed for *Histoire d'O* to be the object of a court case:

Considérant que ce livre entend retracer les aventures d'une jeune femme qui, pour complaire à son amant, se soumet à tous les caprices érotiques et à tous les sévices. Considérant que ce livre violemment et consciemment immoral, où les scènes de débauche à deux ou plusieurs personnages alternent avec des scènes de cruauté sexuelle, contient un ferment détestable et condamnable, et que par là même il outrage les bonnes mœurs. Émet l'avis qu'il y a lieu à poursuites.

(Considering that this book undertakes to relate the adventures of a young woman who, to please her love, submits to all kinds of erotic whims and sexual abuse; considering that this book, which is violently and deliberately immoral, and contains scenes of debauchery between two or more persons in alternation with scenes of sexual cruelty, and possesses an intrinsic tendency that is to be detested and condemned, and thereby is an affront to good morals; [the Committee] concludes that there is a case to answer.)[7]

Réage clearly uses Sadean elements in her descriptions and in the events of the narrative: an isolated château; scenes of torture that vividly foreground the bodies being tortured; masks. In interview, Réage will confess her predilection for the world of secret societies while emphasizing their preference for disguise: 'il existe une panoplie classique (corset ou guêpière, porte-jarretelles, bas noirs), très troublante à porter. C'est un fantasme que je partage sans doute avec beaucoup de femmes. Dans les grands uniformes érotiques, il y a aussi pour moi les robes du XVIIIe siècle, avec un long busc' ('There exists a classic combination of elements – a corset or basque, garters and black stockings – which does something to the person wearing it. I probably share this fantasy with many women. For me, the great erotic outfits include dresses of the eighteenth century with a long busk').[8] However, over and above such elements, *Histoire d'O* is all the more scandalous for employing the kind of writing that is truly characteristic of Sade (and distinguishes him from pornographic texts normally included in the despised category of 'para-literature'): a measured, intellectualized writing. The latter contrasts with purely narrative passages and stresses the way the text affects the reader: Sade thus mixes the rational and the sensual in his novels. Réage does the same by treating pornographic themes with a certain decency: 'On peut tout dire, il faut le dire décemment. Parce que, sinon, c'est gênant, c'est grossier, c'est vulgaire' ('One can say everything, but decently. Because otherwise, it's embarrassing, crude, vulgar').[9]

We might even say that while Réage is influenced by Sade, she seems to outstrip him. She reaches a kind of climax in evil because while Justine and even Juliette are subjugated by the desire of men, sexual slavery is voluntary in *Histoire d'O*. In this way, Réage inverts Hegelian dialectics, because in her narrative the slave wants to remain a slave. This is reinforced by the device of doubling: O is in thrall to René, who is in thrall to Sir Stephen. Besides, Pauline Réage is a *feminine* pseudonym. In the 1950s, it is unthinkable that a woman should write an erotic tale; when *Histoire d'O* appeared, Camus apparently said: 'A woman? Never! This was not written by a woman.' Réage is the founder of a feminine *ars erotica*;[10] by following in Sade's footsteps, she opens up a new literary avenue.[11]

Literary critics have found other traces of Sade in Réage's writing. As soon as the novel appeared, connections were made with recent history.

We will find this same connection between history and fiction being made in a range of writers who offer interpretations of Sade's 'return' during the turbulent *après-guerre* in France.[12] Having read *Histoire d'O*, Pierre de Boisdeffre speaks of a 'musée [d']horreurs' ('museum of horrors') and a 'univers concentrationnaire' ('world in the image of the concentration camps').[13] Similarly, when Just Jaeckin brings out his cinematic adaptation in 1975 (*Story of O*), François Chalais writes a *Lettre ouverte aux pornographes* (*Open Letter to Pornographers*), in which he asserts that *Histoire d'O* is 'la Gestapo dans le boudoir', and so parodies the title of Sade's famous work *La Philosophie dans le boudoir* (*Philosophy in the Boudoir*).[14] Thus, *Histoire d'O* is a Sadean text that arguably exceeds Sade himself, and that echoes the evil embodied in Nazism. If Sade brought the perverse individual out of the brothel, as Klossowski puts it,[15] certain novelists of the 1950s do as much. What is more, literary criticism wastes no time in linking the perverse character to the S.S.

Influence through Publication, or Sade's Phantom

Sade's influence is manifested on another level during the 1950s. Sade raises in fact a problem that cuts across literary sociology and genre: What happens when evil is 'allowed' into the novel and, more broadly, into literature? No moral outcry met the relatively recent addition of the works of Casanova to the collection of the Bibliothèque Nationale, Paris; nor, it seemed, was anyone shocked by the appearance of Sade in the Pléiade edition (accompanied by the slogan 'Sade enters the Pléiade, Hell on Bible paper') in the 1990s. However, in the 1950s, any would-be publisher of Sade faced a formidable task. Nevertheless, a young publisher, Jean-Jacques Pauvert, rose to the challenge. Without providing details of the resulting court case here, it will be useful to examine the ethical questions raised by the accusation against Pauvert. But first, we should remember that the stakes of the prosecution went beyond the fate of one publisher. The problems raised were numerous: questions concerning evil, the definition of literature, freedom of the press and literary morality were at issue.

At the time of the trial, it was difficult to ignore Sade's seeming relevance for the 1950s, and the striking extent to which great writers of that decade saw in Sade a subject of interest for philosophers rather than publishers. Jean-Jacques Pauvert started publishing Sade's complete works in 1947. When the trial opened in 1956, 24 volumes had been produced. In 1954–55, the Commission du Livre declared that these works 'mêlaient à des propos sur la société du temps, des descriptions de scènes d'orgies, des cruautés les plus répugnantes, et des perversions les plus variées, et contenaient intrinsèquement un ferment détestable et condamnable pour les bonnes mœurs' ('combined statements on the society of the time with descriptions of orgies, acts of the most repugnant cruelty and the most varied perversions, and contained an intrinsic capacity to erode morals that is to be detested and condemned').[16] The resulting trial was brought before the 17th Chambre Correctionnelle de Paris on 15 December 1956.

Four famous writers testified in support of Pauvert: Jean Paulhan, Georges Bataille, Jean Cocteau and André Breton. The contributions of Paulhan and Bataille are significant given that both men were truly fascinated by Sade. Their testimonies describe not a writer of 'sadistic' novels but a perceptive analyst of humanity. Paulhan mitigates Sade's supposed excesses as a writer by arguing that all writers we especially associate with the nineteenth century – Lamartine, Baudelaire, Nietzsche – are the Marquis's literary heirs. Paulhan provocatively cites works that he claims are as dangerous as Sade's: Freud's writings, Baudelaire's poems and even the Bible. He argues that if human wickedness is portrayed in writing, the tendency to enact it in reality is obviated. Sade sets no dangerous example for, paradoxically enough, 'c'est un exemple qui se propose comme n'étant pas à suivre' ('he sets an example for others not to follow').[17]

As for Bataille, he argues that Sade is the first writer to have explained that man finds pleasure in contemplating pain and death. Bataille also insists that he does not recommend that we should all join in watching others suffer, but urges us to remember that (recent) history can only be understood in terms of this tendency. He demonstrates that Sade explained why we rebel against the promptings of reason, and suggests that 'cette désobéissance éclate dans les guerres et dans l'histoire' ('such disobedience erupts during wars and through history').[18] Representing Pauvert, Maître Maurice Garçon (a legal expert in the realm of publishing and a novelist in his own right) points to the value of Sade's pre-Freudian exploration of the unconscious. Garçon thus casts Sade in the role of physician. He also argues that, in order to understand humanity in all its complexity, it is necessary to read Sade precisely. Though initially the case went against Pauvert, the 1958 appeal cleared him and definitively recognized the value of Sade's writing, not in literary but in philosophical and anthropological terms. Consider the following extracts:

> Considérant que [...] Pauvert soutenant en effet que les ouvrages poursuivis constituent des documents qui seraient indispensables à

la compréhension de la philosophie du XVIIIème siècle en tant qu'ils contiennent un exposé du matérialisme et de l'athéisme dans son aspect absolu et qu'ils renferment en outre l'expression de l'angoisse d'un esprit tourmenté en face du problème du mal [...] qu'enfin la défense insiste sur le fait que Sade aurait été le génial précurseur de la pathologie sexuelle.

(Considering that [...] Pauvert [maintains] that the works under judgement constitute documents that are indispensable to an understanding of the philosophy of the eighteenth century given that they contain an exposé of atheistic materialism in its absolute form and, moreover, serve to express the anguish of a mind tormented by the problem of evil [...] and that, finally, the defence emphasizes that Sade's genius foreshadows [the science of] sexual pathology.)[19]

Interestingly enough, the Pauvert trial, which comes exactly 100 years after that of Flaubert (for *Madame Bovary*) and Baudelaire (for *Les Fleurs du mal*), rehearses a number of the nineteenth-century arguments for or against the idea that evil does not belong in literature. And Pauvert emerges victorious. Thanks to him, Sade is published and read during the 1950s, becoming available to all. Nevertheless, we should remember that Sade, the 'phantom' accused, is at the centre of this process, rather than Jean-Jacques Pauvert.

Ontological Influence: The Symptom

In this part of the discussion, the term 'symptom' will be used in Didi-Huberman's sense, as a 'complex serpentine movement', an 'irresolvable intrication', a 'non-synthesis'.[20] Nor should we lose sight of the psychological and medical aspect of the question. The term 'survival' seems particularly apt here, given that Sade's eighteenth-century analysis of evil enters into dialogue with comparable analyses of the post-war period; this gives rise to an exchange between two cultural instances.

And so Sade emerges as an essential philosophical reference point for any analysis of 'radical evil' as it was manifested during World War II.[21] Sade is a symptom; his survival in the 1950s makes sense in ontological terms; it allows those aspects of war, of evil, of humanity that seem to defy expression to be spoken of after all (if indirectly). Sade is the symptom of the difficulty facing those who attempt to stand at a critical distance from the historical evil associated with the war. In the study to which we have already referred,[22] Marty shows that the debates of 1947 and thereafter, in which an attempt was made to take the Nazism out of Sade or (to approach the problem from another angle) the Sade out of Nazism, end in an aporia. Thus, Adorno makes Sade the missing link between Kant and Auschwitz, by connecting the Marquis with Fascism and bourgeois reason. In all three cases, formal reasoning brings about a reification of the human.

Raymond Queneau and Michel Leiris (the latter in his *Journal*) also make a connection between Sade and Nazism. Queneau in particular makes Sade and Nietzsche the prophesiers of Nazi evil. However, according to Marty, the two writers who above all wanted to 'de-nazify' Sade (Georges Bataille and Maurice Blanchot) failed to do so. In Marty's view, Bataille's analysis, being focused on the question of language, may have seemed to allow him to take distance from the historical issues. Yet by contrasting real-life torturers and executioners, who do not speak of their violence, with Sade's characters, who do, Bataille cannot avoid the conclusion that the Sadean character occupies the position of the victim. Sade's discourse, then, brings him closer to the deportees of the Occupation than to the Nazis. As for Blanchot, the question of deportation resurfaces in his reflection on Kafka and Sade. Indeed, Marty shows that the two writers' approaches converge in the concentration camps, which present, on the one hand, a limitless destruction of the human (the Sadean perspective) and, on the other, the impossibility of dying, which constitutes a ceaseless death (the Kakfaesque perspective).

Sade thus becomes a metaphor expressing man's inhumanity to man. In the process, an emphasis on war and history shifts towards a literary one. It is all about finding new ways of speaking about (mass) extermination. Perhaps, too, it is a way of grappling with the unspeakable, the unimaginable.[23] The linking of Sade with history shows that the Marquis can occupy disparate roles, according to how his writing is interpreted: in readings like Bataille's, Sade speaks the language of the victim (who alone speaks of violence); therefore he speaks 'for' the deportee. But if one remains focused on the violent scenario in which one human being kills another, Sade stands for the S.S. Finally, if one casts Sade in the role of the aristocrat who believes he is above all human and social laws, he begins to resemble a member of the militia. Sade's function may be to verbalize historical evil, but this is not the same as explaining it; he allows us to know, but not to understand evil.[24] Speaking more broadly, Sade is the symptom of a society founded on evil. Here we return to the theory that

Warburg develops from Nietzsche, namely the idea that civilization is inhabited by an animal force, by the Dionysiac. As stated above, Sade's writing allows us to escape from Hegelian dialectics, to avoid an all-encompassing synthesis designed to account for reality and dissolve all contradictions. For thinkers in the 1950s, Sade suggests the possibility of taking from Hegel only the idea of negation as the freeing up of desire, as a way of avoiding entrapment in the movement from antithesis to synthesis. Still, with Sade, the opposite extreme beckons: the world seems on course towards cataclysm, and murder is the only project of which humans can conceive in relation to other humans. Sadism in this sense destroys paradigms and reference points, and makes a reality of evil. Maurice Blanchot analyses in detail the Sadean revelation of a transcendent negation, which fills the vacuum left by the death of God. The survival of Sade after World War II manifests French society's struggle to overcome its deep disenchantment.

For if Sade seems omnipresent in this period, it is because he fascinates the French intellectuals obsessed, in the *après-guerre*, by the problem of evil. Let us briefly take the example of Simone de Beauvoir. In her correspondence with Jean-Paul Sartre, we learn that having read *Justine* she became an enthusiast of Sade. When she publishes *Faut-il brûler Sade? (Must We Burn Sade?)* in 1955, or one year after the appearance of *Histoire d'O*, she has moved on: now she aims to emphasize the failure of the Sadean project.[25] While once she only wanted to see him from a political angle, henceforth she undertakes a precise description of his novels in terms of his portrayal of humanity, his philosophy of evil, his peculiar sexuality, his search for infinite *jouissance* and his literary goals. She seems, indeed, influenced by Sade; she is fascinated by the monstrous nature of being. In the course of *Faut-il brûler Sade?*, she diverges from the project she announces in the preface, with its emphasis on his work's (literary) coherence; the contents page implies a strong political orientation.[26] In her conclusion, she makes an explicit link between Sade and the twentieth century. At stake is the relationship of human to human: '[Sade] nous oblige à remettre en question le problème essentiel qui sous d'autres figures hante ce temps: le vrai rapport de l'homme à l'homme' ('Sade obliges us to question the essential question that haunts this era under other names: the true relationship of human to human').[27] Finally, the political issue recedes into the background; instead, attention is focused on the relation of self to other, which involves violence, but also a specific kind of communion made possible by debauchery. Consequently, it makes sense to ask: Should Beauvoir's title be understood as a rhetorical question, or as expressing a real fear aroused by the fascinating influence of Sade?

Sade after the 1950s

Our discussion shows that, in 1950s France, Sade is a great deal more than a passing fad or a random event in the publishing world. He is at once a worrying, haunting and symptomatic presence. He is a reference point for a century witnessing evil in an absolute, radical, unthinkable form, a century that turns to him as a way to explore such evil. This resonates with Didi-Huberman's comment on Warburg:

> Ce qui survit dans une culture est *le plus refoulé*, le plus obscur, le plus lointain et le plus tenace, de cette culture. *Le plus mort* en un sens, parce que le plus enterré et le plus fantomal; *le plus vivant* tout aussi bien, parce que le plus mouvant, le plus proche, le plus pulsionnel. Telle est bien l'étrange dialectique du *Nachleben*.
>
> (What survives in a culture is that which is *the most repressed*, the most obscure, most inaccessible and most stubborn within it. *The most dead* in a sense (the most buried, the most spectral); but equally, *the most alive* (the most mobile, the most accessible, the most instinctual. This is, indeed, the uncanny dialectic of the *Nachleben*.)[28]

Sade is one of the living dead who brings out the importance of the death wish in society. His 'unreadable' texts seemingly allow us not to understand but to express the (otherwise) inexpressible reality of the world that is ours after 1945.

It should be noted, finally, that Sade's survival does not cease with the end of Pauvert's trial. During the 1960s, for instance, eminent thinkers are intrigued by Sade, including Foucault, Deleuze, Sollers and Barthes, but the focus shifts once again, and cinematic treatments give rise to new interpretations of works by Sade or indebted to him. In 1975 the release of two films gives rise to a new 'Sadean Year': Just Jaeckin's *Story of O* and Pasolini's *Salo ou les 120 journées de Sodome* (*Salo or the 120 Days of Sodom*). At the same time, the visual medium may seem largely to reduce the texts to their pornographic aspect; certainly, the spectator of such adaptations cannot enjoy the linguistic subtleties of the original text. Even Dominique Aury apparently left the cinema disgusted by *Story of O*, which she found to be vulgar and obscene.

Notes

1. Michel Delon, *Les Vies de Sade* (Paris: Éditions Textuel, 2007), p. 5. All translations are my own.
2. Hegelian philosophy made a strong impact in 1950s France. The major authors of the time, including Georges Bataille, Brice Parain and Raymond Queneau, attended Alexandre Kojève's lectures on Hegel given at the École Pratique des Hautes Études, Paris, from 1933 to 1939. Queneau published these lectures in 1947, under the title *Introduction à une lecture de Hegel* (Paris: Gallimard, 1947).
3. See Georges Didi-Huberman, *L'Image survivante. Histoire de l'art et temps des fantômes selon Aby Warburg* (Paris: Minuit, 2002). Throughout this chapter, 'survival' (in French, 'survivance') will be used broadly in Warburg's sense, meaning the endurance of given signifying forms through the ages.
4. This scheme echoes that used by Didi-Huberman in *L'Image survivante*: 'l'image-fantome'; 'l'image-pathos'; 'l'image-symptôme'.
5. Dominique Aury is also a pseudonym. Pauline Réage's real name is Anne Desclos, as the author herself reveals in 1994, in an interview for the *New Yorker*. Incidentally, another 'scandalous' book that appeared in 1954 and served as something of a watershed is Françoise Sagan's *Bonjour tristesse* (Paris: Julliard, 1954).
6. Alexandra Destais, 'L'Émergence de la littérature érographique féminine en France: 1954–1975' (unpublished doctoral thesis, Université de Caen, 2006).
7. André Breton, Georges Bataille, Jean Cocteau and Jean Paulban, *L'Affaire Sade, compte rendu exact du procès intenté par le Ministère public* (Paris: Pauvert, 1957), p. 55.
8. Régine Deforges, *O m'a dit. Entretiens avec Pauline Réage* (Paris: Pauvert, 1995), pp. 36–8.
9. Ibid., pp. 29–31.
10. See Destais, 'L'Émergence'.
11. Having been awarded the Deux Magots prize in January 1955, *Histoire d'O* became a bestseller and has never been out of print; today it is freely available in paperback.
12. See Éric Marty, *Pourquoi le XXe siècle a-t-il pris Sade au sérieux?* (Paris: Seuil, 2011).
13. See Jérôme Garcin, 'Comment on a lancé les livres cultes: 1954, "Histoire d'O"', *Le Nouvel Observateur*, issue 1970 (8 August 2002), 58–61.
14. See François Chalais, *Lettre ouverte aux pornographes* (Paris: Albin Michel, 1975).
15. Pierre Klossowski, *'Sade mon prochain' précédé de 'Le Philosophe scélérat'* (Paris: Seuil, 1947).

16. Maurice Garçon, cited in *L'Affaire Sade*, p. 8.
17. Ibid., p. 52.
18. Ibid.
19. Jean-Jacques Pauvert, *La Traversée du livre, mémoires* (Paris: Viviane Hamy, 2004).
20. Didi-Huberman, *L'Image survivante*, p. 274.
21. The concept of radical evil was developed by Kant and revisited by Hannah Arendt, who coined the term 'the banality of evil' in 1963 (see *Eichmann in Jerusalem: A Report on the Banality of Evil* [London: Penguin, 2006]).
22. See note 12 above.
23. Georges Didi-Huberman writes: 'N'invoquons pas l'inimaginable' ('Let us not invoke the unimaginable'; *Images malgré tout* [Paris: Minuit, 2003], p. 11).
24. Primo Levi makes such a distinction between knowing and understanding in *Les Naufragés et les rescapés: quarante ans après Auschwitz* (Paris: Gallimard, 1989).
25. Simone de Beauvoir, *Faut-il brûler Sade?* (Paris: Gallimard, 1972).
26. Beauvoir's essays are supposed to answer the question: 'Comment les privilégiés peuvent-ils penser leur situation?' ('How can the privileged conceptualize their own situation?'; *Faut-il brûler Sade?* [back cover text]). This implies that Sade is to be primarily studied not as a novelist but as an aristocrat in a dominant position within (*ancien régime*) society.
27. Ibid., p. 82.
28. Didi-Huberman, *L'Image survivante*, p. 154. Emphasis in original.

4
Jules Laforgue, Hartmann and Schopenhauer: From Influence to Rewriting

Madeleine Guy

Like a number of his contemporaries, Jules Larforgue (1860–87) was open to the influence of Arthur Schopenhauer and the latter's disciple, Eduard von Hartmann. However, in Laforgue's particular case, this double influence went far beyond the borrowing of a few concepts. The fact of reading these two authors intensively from the age of 20, and especially his predilection for Hartmann's *Die Philosophie des Unbewussten* (*Philosophy of the Unconscious*), proved a truly formative influence. Indeed, Laforgue constructs his very Weltanschauung by combining the systems of both predecessors in his own particular way.

Small wonder, then, that Laforgue's first collections of poetry are full of references to Schopenhauer and Hartmann. Yet it is in his prose works that such references acquire their most surprising and interesting form. His collection of novellas, *Moralités légendaires* (*Moral Tales*), is presented explicitly as a parody of great artistic and literary myths (*Hamlet*, *Lohengrin*, Salome, etc.). It can also be read on another level, as a rewriting of the two philosophers who have especially influenced him. The integration of a truly philosophical system within a work of fiction is striking in itself. But the main originality of the procedure consists in the fact that Laforgue's parodic rewriting of myths is made possible and shaped by his reading of the philosophers in question (so that philosophy and myth are not simply co-present in the text). For Laforgue transforms various mythical figures into true disciples of Schopenhauer and Hartmann, as reflected in their actions as well as their precepts. He uses the thought of these philosophers as a prism through which he not only views the world but also reinterprets literature.

Below, we will show this complex intertextual practice at work in those novellas by Laforgue in which it is most strikingly deployed: 'Hamlet ou les suites de la piété filiale' ('Hamlet or the Consequences of Filial Piety'), 'Salomé' ('Salome') and 'Lohengrin, fils de Parsifal' ('Lohengrin, Son of Parzival'). However, first it is useful to establish, if briefly, the importance of Schopenhauer and Hartmann for Laforgue. In the relevant period, while Schopenhauer's thought was being vulgarized by a number of writers (including Théodule Ribot), only parts of his work were available in French translation.[1] Nevertheless, his thought had a wide impact. As for Hartmann's summing-up of his key ideas, *Die Philosophie des Unbewussten*, it was translated into French in 1877,[2] or several years before Laforgue began his writing career (circa 1880). At the age of 20, Laforgue was spending most of his time at the Bibliothèque Nationale, and very soon made both writers his intellectual guides.

This influence was not limited to the taking of notes, but was manifested in Laforgue's earliest works, in the form of creative rewriting. Indeed, at 20, he began to write a novel based substantially on the thought of his two predecessors:

> J'ai mon roman aussi. Un Chenavard disciple de Schopenhauer, qui se tue de se sentir devenir fou de ne pouvoir arriver à réaliser cette œuvre: l'épopée macabre de l'humanité (l'histoire et le XIXe siècle) en trois g[ran]ds cartons correspondant aux trois stades de l'Illusion de Hartmann.
>
> (I also have a novel. [It portrays a certain] Chenavard, disciple of Schopenhauer, who kills himself because he senses he is losing his sanity when he fails to achieve his great work: a macabre epic of humanity [through history and the nineteenth century] in three great paintings corresponding to Hartmann's three stages of Illusion.)[3]

However, above all, it is in the *Moralités légendaires*, the collection of novellas published posthumously in 1887, that Laforgue's reworking of philosophy is most fully manifest. The length of these texts allows him to deploy, in certain cases, a protocol that combines the rewriting of the 'primary intertexts' (as we might refer to the myths) with that of passages from Schopenhaueur and Hartmann. (This creates, as explained above, a prism through which the original works are reinterpreted.)

Of all the novellas, 'Hamlet ou les suites de la piété filiale' contains the greatest number of borrowings from the two philosophers, and in this case only they are distributed across the whole narrative. We will now discuss a range of examples that illustrate Laforgue's process of rewriting particularly well. Like his Shakespearean model, Laforgue's Hamlet struggles to come to terms with the murder of his father, and often loses himself in long, inconclusive monologues. Laforgue's Hamlet concludes his first meandering speech with the following words, which clearly echo Schopenhauer and Hartmann:

> Méthode, Méthode, que me veux-tu? Tu sais que j'ai mangé du fruit de l'Inconscience! Tu sais bien que c'est moi qui apporte la loi nouvelle au fils de la Femme, et qui vais détrônant l'Impératif Catégorique et instaurant à sa place l'Impératif Climatérique!
>
> (Method, Method, what dost Thou want of me? Thou knowest well that I have eaten the fruit of the Unconscious! Thou knowest well that it is I who bring the new law to man who is born of Woman, it is I whose business it is to unseat the Categorical, and install in its place the Climacteric Imperative!)[4]

In spite of the complexity of the process of rewriting and the embedding of the various hypotexts, Hamlet here makes a clear statement of belief in the new philosophy; indeed, he declares himself its fervent disciple. The highlighting of the term 'Inconscience' ('Unconscious'), written with a capital 'I', immediately calls for these lines to be read via Hartmann. In the first sentence, the term 'Méthode', with its capital 'M', has a similarly intertextual function, since it seems to point towards the *Discours de la méthode* (*Discourse on Method*), or more broadly towards Descartes's system as a whole. And when we consider the form of the sentence, we realize that it is a rewriting of a line from one of Verlaine's *Poèmes saturniens*: 'Souvenir, Souvenir, que me veux-tu?' ('Memory, Memory, what do you want of me?').[5] This sentence, therefore, combines syntax borrowed from Verlaine with a content implicitly taken from Descartes. And this system of embedding one intertext within another is sustained throughout the passage. 'Manger du fruit de' seems to be a syntactical borrowing from the passage in Genesis where Adam and Eve eat the fruit of the tree of the knowledge of good and evil. 'Impératif Catégorique' clearly gestures towards the whole of Kantian philosophy, but the expression is immediately transformed into 'Impératif Climatérique', which brings Darwinian ideas to mind.[6] Such a profusion of intertexts and transformations justifies the use of the term 'bricolage intertextuel' ('intertextual bricolage').[7] Yet beyond the heterogeneity of the various hypotexts, Hamlet's statement retains its peculiar unity. The hero assumes the role of one who announces the coming of a new philosophy. Rejecting lock, stock and barrel the old systems of Descartes and Kant (in which Reason dominates), Laforgue's Hamlet becomes the prophet of a New Law, which is provided by Hartmann's system, associated with Darwinianism.[8] Thus Laforgue renders Hamlet the true disciple of the German philosopher.

However, the question of how seriously the author, or at least the narrator, takes the (here) somewhat anachronistic figure of the Prince of Denmark is a difficult one to answer. Clearly, there is a comic effect in this joyous medley of borrowed ideas and syntactical forms, which is untrammelled by any concern with dates or the justifiability of the bringing-together of such elements. Moreover, the narrator adopts an ironic tone when he introduces Hamlet's speech by the verb *divaguer* ('to ramble'), and goes on to comment: 'Le prince Hamlet en a comme ça long sur le cœur, plus long qu'il n'en tient en cinq actes, plus long que notre philosophie n'en surveille entre ciel et terre' ('Prince Hamlet has more of all this on his mind, more than five acts can hold, more than our philosophy can encompass between heaven and earth').[9] Nevertheless, the intertextual references provide a new, effective frame through which to read and interpret Hamlet's inability to act – this characteristic being shared by Shakespeare's and Laforgue's respective Hamlets. 'L'Inconscience' ('the Unconscious') is a superior force that dominates him and prevents him from being the hero he wants to be.[10] Thus the presence of irony and comic effect do not in themselves make the intertextual references gratuitous.

Let us now examine the last trace of such philosophical influence in the speeches delivered by Laforgue's Hamlet. During the latter's argument with Laertes, Ophelia's brother challenges him to justify himself:

> – Si vous n'étiez un pauvre dément, irresponsable selon les derniers progrès de la science, vous paieriez à l'instant la mort de mon honorable père et celle de ma sœur, cette jeune fille accomplie, là, sur leurs tombes!
>
> – Ô Laërtes, tout m'est égal. Mais soyez sûr que je prendrai votre point de vue en considération...

('If you weren't a poor demented creature who is irresponsible according to the newest scientific discoveries, you would pay with your head right now for the death of my honorable father, and that accomplished young lady, my sister. There, on their tombs!'

'O Laertes, it's all one to me. But you can be sure that I will take your point of view into consideration...')[11]

The expression 'tout m'est égal' ('it's all one to me'), spoken by Hamlet, can be interpreted as a claim on his part that he has reached that state of supreme indifference advocated by Schopenhauer:

> Lorsqu[e l'homme] a nié son corps par l'ascétisme, et jeté hors de lui tout désir; alors se produit 'l'euthanasie de la volonté', cet état de parfaite indifférence où sujet et objet disparaissent, où il n'y a plus ni volonté, ni représentation, ni monde.
>
> (When man has denied his body through ascetism and expelled all desire from it, there arises 'the euthanasia of Will', that state of perfect indifference, where subject and object disappear, where there is no longer will, nor representation, nor world.)[12]

Here a simple formula retranscribes, in new terms, a philosophical idea in its entirety. This is Laforgue's most characteristic manner of rewriting. Reading the expression intertextually is worthwhile, because this approach throws light on the different concepts of responsibility that are defended by the two characters. According to Laertes, Hamlet bears no responsibility for his own actions because he is mad. Hamlet's suspected insanity is taken directly from Shakespeare's play.[13] Nevertheless, in Laforgue's version, Hamlet no longer uses insanity as a strategy, but proposes instead ideas to be found in Hartmann and Schopenhauer. Thus Laforgue adapts certain motifs of the original play, and at the same time requires us to read them through the interpretive framework that he attaches to the text. His Hamlet, who had announced himself to be a prophet of the New Law at the beginning of the novella, seems at least in the course of the story to have applied that law to himself.

Most of the philosophical rewritings contained in the novella are present in the words spoken by Hamlet. However, there are also three instances where the narrator himself performs a similar move. Here I will cite only the last of these, which coincides with Hamlet's death:

> Il parvient à articuler:
> – Ah! Ah! *Qualis... artifex... pereo!*
> Et rend son âme hamlétique à la nature inamovible.

(He manages somehow to utter:
'Ah, ah, *Qualis...artifex...pereo!*'
And then he renders to everlasting nature his Hamletic soul.)[14]

The idea that nature is 'inamovible' and that its life force continues beyond the death of individuals is frequently expressed by Hartmann and Schopenhauer.[15] The narrator's participation in philosophical intertextuality creates an effect of completion or closure, given that (as stated above) this is the third and final use of the device, the previous two having occurred before Hamlet first speaks.[16] This framing effect suggests that the narrator ultimately shares the references used by Hamlet as a disciple of Hartmann and Schopenhauer, and that he agrees with his hero's stated position, even if he cast doubt on this during the course of the tale.

Now let us turn to the other protagonist whom Laforgue casts as the perfect disciple of the two philosophers: Salome. I will focus on the passage that contains the most striking philosophical intertext: the *vocéro* ('the wailing speech') spoken by the eponymous heroine during the feast given by the Tetrarch, which replaces the seduction dance of the original legend. Because of its whimsical tone, the extravagance of the images and its setting (the stage of Alcazar), this passage has often been considered as a purely verbal game, in which the vocabulary of Hartmann and Schopenhauer is used in an approximative fashion.[17] However, a detailed study of the passages concerned will reveal the argumentative and logical nature of Laforgue's text, as well as the traces of the philosophical texts that serve to structure it – in spite of the radical reformulation they undergo.

Salome sets the tone with her opening words. She will celebrate the void, which is the goal that can be gained through the liberation of humanity, according to both philosophers: 'Que le Néant, c'est-à-dire la Vie latente qui verra le jour après-demain au plus tôt, est estimable, absolvant, coexistant à l'Infini, limpide comme tout!' ('How estimable the Void is! The Void, that is to say, the Latent Life that will flower the day after tomorrow at the earliest – how estimable, how absolving, co-existing with Infinity, just as limpid as it can be!').[18] This opening has the ring of a credo. The words 'Que le Néant [...] est estimable!' may well be a reformulation of a passage in *Pensées et fragments*: 'A considérer la vie sous sa valeur objective, il est au moins douteux qu'elle soit préférable au néant; et je dirais même que si l'expérience et la réflexion pouvaient se faire entendre, c'est en faveur du néant qu'elles élèveraient la voix' ('Considering life objectively, it is at least doubtful that it is preferable to the void; and I would even say that if experience and reflection could be heard, they would speak in favour of the void').[19] The equivalence created between the Void and life by 'c'est-à-dire' may seem bizarre on first reading, but becomes comprehensible when we consider the context of the story: the Void is Nirvana, or the state of life beyond individuality to which not only Buddhists but also followers of Schopenhauer aspire. Besides this equivalence, the first sentence is remarkable for a clash of register, as the unusual, technical phrase 'coexistant à l'Infini' jars with the more casual, familiar syntax of 'limpide comme tout'. This jarring effect will be sustained throughout the *vocéro*, making it difficult for the reader to decide if he or she is reading a serious philosophical discourse or an extended hoax.

A little further on, Salome addresses her audience, to whom she offers copious advice:

> L'Essentiel actif s'aime (suivez-moi bien), s'aime dynamiquement, plus ou moins à son gré: c'est une belle âme qui se joue du biniou à jamais, ça la regarde. Soyez, vous, les passifs naturels; entrez automatiques comme Tout, dans les Ordres de l'Harmonie Bien-Veillante! Et vous m'en direz des nouvelles.
>
> (The active essential loves itself – now follow me carefully – loves itself dynamically, more or less according to its own inclination: it's a lovely soul that plays indefinitely on its own bagpipe – let it play. Now, all of you, be naturally passive: as automatic as Everything, enter into the Orders of Well-intentioned Harmony. And let me know how you make out.)[20]

As in the passage examined above, Laforgue uses obscure formulations, and the capitalized nouns do not clearly and explicitly allude to identifiable thinkers, since (apart from the word 'Tout') they are not used in specifically philosophical contexts.[21] Nevertheless, the philosophical intertext makes its presence felt in the opposition between 'actif' and 'passifs'. This opposition can be found in Hartmann, who applies it to his two great concepts, the Idea and the Will. According to him, in order to be realized,

> la Volonté attire à elle et saisit l'Idée; et également de son côté l'Idée se livre à la Volonté. Cet abandon que l'Idée fait d'elle-même est purement passif, n'exige aucune activité positive de sa part; et suppose seulement qu'elle n'oppose à la volonté aucune action négative, aucune résistance. On voit clairement ici que la Volonté

et l'Idée sont vis-à-vis l'une de l'autre dans le rapport du principe
masculin au principe féminin.

(The Will attracts and seizes the Idea, whereas the Idea surrenders
to the Will. This self-abandonment on the part of the Idea is purely
passive, and requires no positive activity from it; and only supposes
that it should not act against or put up a resistance to the Will. We
can clearly see that the relationship of the Will to the Idea parallels
that of the masculine to the feminine principle.)[22]

In the light of this, 'L'Essentiel actif' corresponds to the Will, as the
principle that is sustained by the love between the sexes. The verb
'aimer' is, then, to be understood in a physical sense, as emphasized by
the expression 'jouer du biniou', which has erotic connotations. As for
individuals, they should imitate the Idea in surrendering to the active
power that is the Will, which also implies surrendering to the Will's
primary mode of expression: the instinct to reproduce.

However, the playfulness introduced by the mixture of registers raises
the question: How seriously should we take this bravura set piece and
the intertextual references that it brings into play? Our other examples
suggest that Laforgue was not merely interested in verbal games, but
wanted to effect a true rewriting, making use of his sources without
parodying them. Yet the author's precise attitude is a complex matter,
for when this speech is placed in its immediate context, and indeed in a
wider context, ambiguity results. Salome's fictional audience seems not to
appreciate the *vocéro* at all.[23] However, they are characterized as extremely
literal-minded individuals, who are incapable of understanding any
philosophical profundity that Salome may have mustered. As for Salome
herself, while she does not seem to 'se pren[dre] au sérieux' ('take herself
seriously')[24] at the beginning of her speech, towards the end she reveals
that, to achieve her ends, she has offered her audience, 'encore que
coupé d'eau [...] l'élixir distillé dans l'angoisse de cent nuits' ('although
cut with water [...] the elixir distilled from the anxiety of a hundred
nights').[25] Her *vocéro* therefore contained the quintessence of her esoteric
meditations.

So what is Laforgue's aim in placing an intertextual speech in his
heroine's mouth? Is it, as Michele Hannoosh suggests, to parody himself
in Salome, that delirious little disciple of Hartmann and Schopenhauer?[26]
I would suggest not. Admittedly, the ridiculous death of the character
seems to convey a message, made explicit by the narrator: 'Ainsi connut
le trépas, Salomé [...]; moins victime des hasards illettrés que d'avoir

voulu vivre dans le factice et non à la bonne franquette, à l'instar de chacun de nous' ('So that was how Salome met her death [...] less a victim of illiterate chance than of the desire to live in a world of artifice and not in a simple, wholesome one like the rest of us.').[27] But how can we identify a serious authorial message in the suggestion that all should adopt '[la vie] à la bonne franquette' ('living in a simple, wholesome way') as a standard by which to live? Laforgue lives an artist's life, and so shares his character's social marginality as well as her philosophical intertext. We must conclude that, beneath its surface composed of verbal games and seemingly cobbled-together references, Salome's *vocéro* respects the integrity of the intertextual sources on which it draws.

By way of conclusion, I will examine a third novella from the collection, 'Lohengrin, fils de Parsifal', which rewrites Wagner's opera. Once again, Laforgue exploits a philosophical intertext, but this time the intertextual sources serve to shape the fiction, rather than being expressed in characters' speeches. Thus, at the outset, Laforgue modifies the story of the accusation levelled against Elsa. In Wagner, she is accused of having killed her brother, and only afterwards of having a lover.[28] However, Laforgue only carries forward the second accusation, and increases the gravity of the crime by making Elsa a vestal virgin. At first sight, this seems to be a case of coarsening the tone of Wagner's original, but in fact it is the first stage of a rewriting that consists in the refocusing of the narrative entirely on the relation between the sexes, viewed according to Schopenhauer's ideas.

Only at the end of the novella are we given the key to the philosophical intertext, in the words 'the Metaphysics of Love', which are the title of an essay by Schopenhauer. The fact that Laforgue provides this key is exceptional; it is the only time in the collection that he actually cites the title of the work from which he exploits. And the allusion is extremely precise: it is the name of Schopenhauer's own essay, from which Laforgue borrows philosophical expressions and ideas. Nevertheless, the expression 'the Metaphysics of Love' is not offered as the title of a heterogeneous text to which the author refers but as a physical place, playing its role in the framing of the narrative. It is, in fact, the place to which Lohengrin flees to escape from Elsa, from his relation to Elsa that was, according to Schopenhauerian ideas, necessarily disappointing:

> Et voici que l'oreiller, changé en cygne, éploya ses ailes impérieuses et, chevauché du jeune Lohengrin, s'enleva [...] vers les altitudes de la Métaphysique de l'Amour, aux glaciers miroirs que nulle haleine

de jeune fille ne saurait ternir de buée pour y tracer du doigt son nom avec la date!

(And the pillow, transformed into a swan, spread its imperial wings, and rose, bearing young Lohengrin on its back [...] toward the altitudes of [the Metaphysics of Love], toward the glacial mirrors on which no young lady will ever breathe and trace with her finger on the frosted glass her name and the date!)[29]

Oddly enough, the narrator presents 'la Métaphysique de l'Amour' as the symbolic locus where Lohengrin will at last be able to experience the ideal love that Elsa could not offer him. However, it is the very teaching contained in 'la Métaphysique de l'Amour' that the author adopts and integrates into his story when he characterizes Elsa as a young woman entirely preoccupied with seeking to consummate the marriage, and when he turns the relationship between the two characters into a dialogue of the deaf. Schopenhauer's 'metaphysics of love' is not to be found at the end of the text, in the ideal realm to which Lohengrin flies, but in all that precedes, which is to say all that Lohengrin flees from. Nevertheless, the distancing of the intertext produced by this manipulation of the expression 'la Métaphysique de l'Amour' does not prevent the interpretive key from having its full effect. Thus, the reader understands that the love relationship between the characters was doomed to failure, not because the young woman was going to doubt her fiancé as in Wagner's version, but for the simple reason that, according to the Schopenhauerian philosophy of love, relayed in Hartmann, any such relation promises only suffering, or, at best, an illusory happiness.[30]

In 'Lohengrin, fils de Parsifal', it is not the dialogue but the narrative itself that serves to develop intertextual reference. This time, Laforgue shapes his fiction using Schopenhauer's and Hartmann's theories on love. Laforgue re-reads the lovers' separation, which is central to Wagner's original and can hardly be set aside, as a consequence of the fundamental incomprehension that arises between men and women, and so as illustrating the impossibility of replacing love relations by platonic and fraternal ones – an ideal represented by the utopia that Laforgue contrasts with Schopenhauer and Hartmann's inferences.

Laforgue transforms the original legends he uses, but not the philosophical intertext, which provides, instead, a method of reading those legends, and becomes an instrument with which to transform them. This second-level rewriting is manifested in two ways, which may occur separately or together: first, the transformation of a character into a disciple of Schopenhauer and Hartmann – this happens with Hamlet, Salome and also Lohengrin; second, the shaping of the fiction, via the fate of individual characters, by those philosophers' theories – the case, as we have seen, for Lohengrin and Elsa. In the process, Laforgue treats his intertextual sources very freely. He combines them with texts with which they have no obvious link: even his chosen legends offer no ready-made connections. He joyfully indulges in anachronism, making of a Renaissance prince or a young woman who lived in the time of the last Christian prophet disciples of two philosophers solidly anchored in the nineteenth century. Nevertheless, he almost never distorts his sources; no destructive tendency enters into his use of them.

Laforgue employs philosophical references that were relatively well known in his time. The true originality of his intertextual procedure consists in the fact that he introduces a philosophical discourse into fictions that seem at first to have no metaphysical dimension to them. The question then arises of what becomes of the philosophy in such an unfamiliar context. In fact, it remains intact when certain characters speak as its disciples or use it as an intertextual foundation for their own ideology. However, Laforgue uses it more strikingly still to shape not only individual characters but the novella as a whole. The double intertext originating in Schopenhauer and Hartmann thus becomes a reading method; we might also call it the prism through which Jules Laforgue passes the original legends to offer a rewriting and a reinterpretation that are, in the other sense of the word, truly 'original'.

Notes

1. See, for instance: P. Challemel-Lacour, 'Un bouddhiste contemporain en Allemagne. Arthur Schopenhauer', *Revue des Deux Mondes*, 86 (1870), 296–332; Théodule Ribot, *La Philosophie de Schopenhauer* (Paris: Germer Baillière, 1874); Arthur Schopenhauer, *Pensées et fragments*, trans. by J. Bourdeau (Paris: Germer Baillière, 1881).
2. Eduard von Hartmann, *Philosophie de l'inconscient*, trans. by D. Nolen, 2 vols (Paris: Germer Baillière, 1877).
3. Jules Laforgue, 'Letter to Gustave Kahn' (12 or 29 December 1880), in *Œuvres complètes*, 3 vols (Lausanne: L'Age d'homme, 1986), I, p. 687. Unless otherwise indicated, translations are my own.
4. Jules Laforgue, *Moralités légendaires*, ed. by Daniel Grojnowski and Henri Scepi (Paris: GF-Flammarion, 2000), pp. 61–2; trans. by William J. Smith as *Moral Tales* (New York: New Directions, 1985), p. 10.

5. These words open Verlaine's poem 'Nevermore'.
6. The editors of the GF-Flammarion edition of *Moralités légendaires* write: 'Hamlet substitue au principe métaphysique de la morale kantienne (l'Impératif catégorique), les données naturalistes de la loi du milieu, telles que Darwin a pu les exposer notamment au chapitre III [...] et au chapitre V [...] de *L'Origine des espèces*' ('Hamlet substitutes natural selection, outlined by Darwin in chapters III and V of *The Origin of Species*, for the metaphysical principle of Kant's morals [the Categorical Imperative]') (p. 222).
7. See Tiphaine Samoyault, *L'Intertextualité: mémoire de la littérature* (Paris: Nathan, 2001), p. 49.
8. Hartmann himself makes the link between his own thought and that of Darwin (see *Philosophie de l'inconscient*, II, pp. 291–3).
9. *Moralités légendaires*, p. 62; *Moral Tales*, pp. 9–10.
10. 'Ah! que je fusse seulement poussé à m'en donner la peine!' ('Ah, if I could just be forced to take the trouble!') (ibid., p. 61; p. 9).
11. Ibid., p. 87; p. 40.
12. Ribot, *La Philosophie de Schopenhauer*, pp. 148–9.
13. 'As I, perchance, hereafter shall think meet / To put an antick disposition on' ('Il se peut bien qu'à l'avenir je croie utile / De me couvrir du masque d'un bouffon') (William Shakespeare, *Hamlet*, bilingual edition, with French translations by François Maguin [Paris: GF-Flammarion, 1995], p. 129).
14. *Moralités légendaires*, p. 88; *Moral Tales*, p. 40.
15. See, for instance, Schopenhauer, *Pensées et fragments*, p. 74.
16. The earlier occurrences are two uses of the adjective *inconscient*, in the expressions 'floraisons inconscientes' ('the unconscious blossom'), and 'l'heureux panorama inconscient' ('the happy, unconscious panorama') respectively. See *Moralités légendaires*, pp. 60, 61; *Moral Tales*, pp. 8, 9.
17. See Michele Hannoosh, *Parody and Decadence: Laforgue's 'Moralités légendaires'* (Colombus: Ohio State University Press, 1989), p. 164.
18. *Moralités légendaires*, p. 148; *Moral Tales*, p. 103.
19. Schopenhauer, *Pensées et fragments*, p. 77.
20. *Moralités légendaires*, p. 148; *Moral Tales*, p. 104.
21. A central concept in Hartmann is 'l'Un-Tout' ('the All-one Being'), which designates the Unconscious as that which encompasses all being(s).
22. Hartmann, *Philosophie de l'inconscient*, II, p. 535.
23. This is shown by the following extract: 'L'assistance intoxiquée s'essuyait les tempes par contenance. [...] Les princes du Nord n'osaient tirer leur montre, encore moins demander: "A quelle heure la couche-t-on?"' ('The intoxicated auditors, to cover their embarrassment, wiped their brows [...]. The Princes of the North dared not take out their watches, much less ask, "When is her bedtime?"') (*Moralités légendaires*, p. 150; *Moral Tales*, p. 106).

24. Ibid., p. 148; p. 103.
25. Ibid., p. 152; p. 108.
26. See Hannoosh, *Parody and Decadence*, p. 150.
27. *Moralités légendaires*, p. 153; *Moral Tales*, p. 109.
28. Richard Wagner, *Quatre poèmes d'opéra traduits en prose française, précédés d'une lettre sur la musique* (Paris: A. Bourdilliat, 1861), pp. 179–80.
29. *Moralités légendaires*, p. 129; *Moral Tales*, p. 83. We have slightly modified Smith's translation here in order to keep the intertextual reference intact.
30. See Schopenhauer, *Pensées et fragments*, p. 96.

5
Text, Image and Music: Paul Valéry's Melodrama *Sémiramis* and the Influence of the Ballets Russes

Natasha Grigorian

Paul Valéry, famous as a poet, essayist and political figure, certainly occupies a special place in French and European culture. He was remarkable as a literary phenomenon linking the nineteenth and twentieth centuries, with their disparate artistic movements, such as Parnassianism, Symbolism and Surrealism, among others. He was also exceptional as a polymath who was equally interested in the arts and the sciences. Not surprisingly, one of his intellectual role models was Leonardo da Vinci; painting itself was among his pastimes. Given the extraordinary range of Valéry's interests and impact both within and beyond the arts, it is particularly revealing to examine the influence of different art forms and media on his literary work. In this context, influence will be considered as a constructive force that stands at the very core of artistic originality, yielding a distinctive creative gain through the imaginative transformation of elements that may have been inspired by an artist's predecessors. As Harold Bloom has famously remarked in *The Anxiety of Influence*, 'Weaker talents idealize; figures of capable imagination appropriate for themselves.'[1] It is especially rewarding to focus on the creative impulses that Valéry found in Symbolist poetry and painting in France, in the music dramas of Richard Wagner, and in the performances of Sergei Diaghilev's famous ballet company, the Ballets Russes (active in Paris from 1909 to 1929). A complex international network of inter-art connections emerges as a result of Valéry's engagement with these diverse artistic phenomena. A close comparative analysis of such links provides illuminating insights not only into Valéry's work, but also into the origins of intermedial art forms in European culture around the turn of the century.

It is well known that Valéry was initiated into poetic writing by his friend and mentor Stéphane Mallarmé, who was arguably the leader of French literary Symbolism. It was also through Mallarmé and the wider Symbolist circles that Valéry came to admire Wagner's music dramas and to appreciate them in depth. Mallarmé's devotion to Wagner was expressed many times in his writing: 'Singulier défi qu'aux poètes dont il usurpe le devoir avec la plus candide et splendide bravoure, inflige Richard Wagner!' ('What a singular challenge Richard Wagner inflicts on poets, whose duty he usurps with a most candid and splendid bravery!').[2] Indeed, Valéry first heard the prelude to *Lohengrin* in 1887, while still a teenager, and was greatly impressed by it.[3] He attended performances of Wagner's operas in Paris in the 1890s, experiencing *Die Walküre* in 1893 with his brother, for example.[4] Valéry would later write in his personal notes: 'Rien ne m'a plus influencé que l'œuvre de ce Wagner, ou du moins certains caractères de cette œuvre' ('Nothing has had a greater influence on me than the work of this Wagner, or at least certain features of this work').[5] Significantly, as late as 1934, a month before the première of his melodrama *Sémiramis*, Valéry still recalled Wagner with great admiration and in terms that suggest the poet's particular interest in the composite nature of an opera constructed according to the principles of a 'Gesamtkunstwerk': 'l'homme que j'ai envié, c'est Wagner. Et non pour autre chose que pour le plaisir qu'il a dû avoir à construire, combiner, composer ses grandes machines musicales' ('the man I have always envied is Wagner. And not for any other reason than the pleasure he must have had in constructing, combining and composing his great musical machines').[6]

Valéry's melodrama *Sémiramis* was first performed at the Opéra de Paris in 1934 to the music of Arthur Honegger. The melodrama is a remarkable work in which both different senses and diverse art forms are closely intertwined. In many ways, it is a 'spectacle total' ('Gesamtkunstwerk'), in the Wagnerian sense, which combines the declamation of a poetic text, music, choreography, dramatic action and spectacular stage and costume design. Taking into account this Wagnerian dimension, the present essay will consider anew the artistic links between *Sémiramis* and the ballet *Schéhérazade*, which was originally produced by Diaghilev in 1910 for one of the first Paris seasons of the Ballets Russes. The choreography was by Mikhail Fokine (also known as Michel Fokine) and Ida Rubinstein danced the main role. Indeed, Valéry personally attended performances of the Ballets Russes in Paris, especially in 1910, and preserved a lifelong admiration for the ballets and their creators. Moreover, both the producer and the choreographer of *Sémiramis* in

1934 were major stars from the Diaghilev team: Ida Rubinstein (who also performed the title role) and Mikhail Fokine respectively. Overall, the influence of the Ballets Russes can therefore be traced in *Sémiramis* on at least two levels: both in its creation as a literary work and in its production on stage. On close inspection, such connections significantly enhance our critical interpretation of Valéry's melodrama. I shall argue that such parallels shed light on the interrelation between the verbal, the visual and the aural in *Sémiramis*.

Schéhérazade is a colourful, exotic ballet in oriental style danced to music by Nikolai Rimsky-Korsakov. Inspired by the *Arabian Nights*, this is the story of Sultan Shahryar, who decides to test the loyalty of his favourite wife, Zobeide. Together with his younger brother, Shah Zaman, the Sultan pretends to leave on a hunting expedition. When the two men return shortly afterwards, they find the women of the harem involved in a whirling orgy together with the male slaves. Zobeide is no exception, as she is courted by the Golden Slave. The Sultan has everyone put to death except for Zobeide. He is about to forgive her, but his brother reminds him of her infidelity with the Golden Slave. Zobeide snatches a dagger from a nearby guard and kills herself at the Sultan's feet.[7] These dramatic events stand at the very origin of the tale that frames the *Arabian Nights*: Zobeide's betrayal will prompt Shahryar to marry and then execute a new wife every day until he weds Scheherazade. We can see that the ballet story is structured by patriarchal despotism: for all her status as the sultan's wife, Zobeide is little more than her husband's slave, and can only escape from this subjugation when she commits suicide.

Let us now compare this to the story of Valéry's *Sémiramis*. Semiramis is portrayed in classical Greek and Roman historical writings as a legendary queen of ancient Babylon, famous for her military conquests and for allegedly constructing the Hanging Gardens of Babylon, one of the original Seven Wonders of the World. There follows a slightly abridged version of the summary of Valéry's melodrama by Harry Halbreich that accompanies the 1992 Timpani recording of Honegger's music:

> In spite of her oriental, burning sensuousness, the Babylonian queen is totally inhuman in her overwhelming pride, a fact reflected in the music's barbaric glare. [...] True to the dramatic subject-matter, the music is mostly harsh, austere and dissonant, which in no way precludes Honegger's powerful and expressive lyricism.
>
> In Act One (*Le Char*, the Chariot), the most animated of the three, soldiers and servants brutally push the prisoners into the large hall

of the palace, where they collapse in front of the throne. The brief and violent introduction features the first of the proud queen's three main themes, a jagged, stepwise ascending profile. Semiramis appears on her chariot pulled by eight captive kings to the sounds of her second main theme, a hard and glittering brass polyphony in dissonant E-Major, symbolizing her royal majesty. She walks to the throne over the bodies of the now unharnessed kings. Her dressing takes place to the contrasting sounds of a graceful processional [...]. Then she has the idols of the conquered smashed to pieces [...], when suddenly one of them rises. Semiramis, overwhelmed by his beauty (her third theme is a love theme full of yearning sung by the Ondes Martenot), has him untied and sinks to his feet, subjugated. The prisoner, first dumbfounded, gently caresses her hair, and the curtain drops [...].

The second Act (*Le Lit*, the Bed) is a love scene taking place in Semiramis' celebrated hanging gardens. *Like a slave she attends to her prisoner*, but when he becomes rash to the point of raising his hand against her, she suddenly recovers herself, calls for the help of her amazons and pierces the body of her ephemeral lover with her own javelin. [...]

A gradual release of tension leads to the third Act (*La Tour*, the Tower). The breathless Semiramis reaches the terrace on top of the tower. *She knows her fate: having loved a man, she must die.* When the sun rises, she offers her body to its consuming rays, and from the blazing light of the now empty altar, a dove soars towards the sky...[8]

A number of remarkable reciprocities as well as asymmetries on the level of plot confirm the artistic continuity between *Schéhérazade* and *Sémiramis*. At first sight, the role of Semiramis seems to correspond directly to that of Sultan Shahryar, in a striking replacement of the patriarchal order with a similarly tyrannical matriarchal rule. Just as Zobeide is subjugated to the sultan, the handsome foreigner is a prisoner of the Babylonian queen; and finally, the slave's disobedience is punished by death in both works, the only difference being that Zobeide kills herself, while the handsome prisoner is killed by Semiramis. At the same time, it is possible to draw another set of parallels, now, paradoxically, between Semiramis and Zobeide: the enamoured Semiramis attends to her lover like a slave,[9] and once she has consummated her love for a man, she must die – from her own hand, like Zobeide. We can see that in contrast to the ballet, which clearly demonstrates Zobeide's self-liberation in death, Valéry's melodrama is deeply ambivalent: is Semiramis a despot or a slave? Does the Babylonian queen enforce tyranny by killing her lover, or does she secure freedom by committing suicide?

Indeed, the divergences between the two plots are so clearly contrastive that they validate the deeper artistic connection between *Schéhérazade* and *Sémiramis*, just as the similarities do. This connection is not only conditioned by Valéry's direct links to the Ballets Russes and collaboration with Ida Rubinstein, but also by the cultural roots shared by the two works. In a wider context, both the ballet and the melodrama draw on the *fin-de-siècle* topos of the *femme fatale* that goes back to the Symbolist movement in France and Europe. This topos embraces a wide range of possibilities, from a passionate beloved to an imperious queen to a fatal enchantress with magic powers. Particularly relevant are works by Gustave Moreau, Stéphane Mallarmé and Oscar Wilde, resulting in a fascinating network of influences. In 1876, the French painter Gustave Moreau (1826–1898) created a sensation by exhibiting two works at the Salon in Paris: the oil painting *Salomé dansant devant Hérode* (*Salome Dancing before Herod*)[10] and the companion watercolour *L'Apparition* (*The Apparition*),[11] both dealing with the biblical myth of Salome and St John the Baptist.[12] On the one hand, it is more than likely that Mallarmé's famous *Hérodiade* (1864–1898) was written in a two-way creative dialogue with Moreau's Salome representations.[13] On the other hand, Moreau's visual work inspired many other literary texts, including Oscar Wilde's drama *Salome* (1891), originally written in Paris in French. At the same time, the Diaghilev group in St Petersburg, which included the painters and stage designers Léon Bakst and Alexandre Benois, showed particular admiration for Moreau in the 1890s. Indeed, in 1899, Diaghilev organized an international art exhibition in St Petersburg, which included paintings by the Parisian artist.[14] The flamboyant and exotic style of stage and costume designs by Bakst and Benois gives every reason to think that Moreau's similarly exotic mythological subject matter and jewel-like pictorial surfaces did leave their mark on the two Russian artists. All these different branches of the influence network unexpectedly came together when the young and then unknown Ida Rubinstein staged and performed in the title role in Wilde's *Salome* in 1908 (still in St Petersburg), with Léon Bakst as her set and costume designer and Mikhail Fokine as choreographer. Indeed, images of Rubinstein as Salome in Wilde's drama (1908) and as Zobeide in the ballet *Schéhérazade* (1910), with both productions featuring designs by Bakst, strangely (or perhaps understandably) remind us of Moreau's Salome representations.

The Diaghilev team, complete with Bakst, Benois and Rubinstein, took Paris by storm, starting with the debut of the Ballets Russes in the

French capital in 1909. Valéry's *Sémiramis* is the ultimate culmination of the successive stages of influence examined here, and the poet shows sensitivity to them all. Being both a favourite disciple of Mallarmé and a critical observer of Moreau's work, Valéry was familiar both with the metaphysical pitfalls of Mallarmé's *Hérodiade* and with the bejewelled splendour of the more sensual *fin-de-siècle* fatal enchantresses, as portrayed and inspired by Moreau. Indeed, Valéry's earliest treatment of the Semiramis legend, the poem 'Air de Sémiramis', dates back to the 1890s, when both Mallarmé and Moreau were still artistically very active (both died in 1898).[15] Valéry saw Ida Rubinstein on stage as Zobeide in 1910. And finally, in 1934, all these strands came together when Valéry and Rubinstein set out to create Semiramis as a character on stage.

Originally from St Petersburg, Ida Rubinstein was a dancer, dramatic actress, and eventually an impresario. Her career was launched in the 1900s thanks to Diaghilev and his close artistic collaborators Mikhail Fokine, Léon Bakst and Alexandre Benois. Rubinstein danced for the Ballets Russes during their 1909 and 1910 seasons. Based in Paris, she later became independent in her artistic projects. Thanks to her substantial private fortune, she was able to commission and produce a wide range of works for the stage, which were to include masterpieces by such composers as Debussy and Ravel, Stravinsky and Honegger, and such writers as D'Annunzio, Gide and, of course, Valéry. Alexandre Benois described her as 'a real, fatal enchantress' in 1909, referring to her performance in the title role of *Cléopâtre*.[16] This fits in well with everything we know about Rubinstein from her other contemporaries, as summarized by Elaine Brody:

> An intense, domineering woman with inimitable panache, Ida Rubinstein created a sensation whenever and wherever she appeared in public, usually on the arm of a distinguished gentleman such as the British beer magnate Guinness, the Parisian Baron de Montesquiou or the Italian poet d'Annunzio. Her taste in clothes was faultless; when she wore black, she decorated her ensemble with white pearls, and when she donned white, she sported black ones. She spoke several languages, had a child's laugh, and the carriage of a goddess. Several contemporaries report that she lived on biscuits and champagne. Occasionally, she disappeared for a few weeks or months on jaunts to distant, exotic lands. She also hunted wild game. Among her eccentricities was a penchant for harboring what some considered wild beasts – for example, a leopard cub and a panther as household

pets. The panther proved too much for Diaghilev. Once when he entered her suite at the Meurice in Paris, the panther snarled at his frock coat, which the animal evidently disliked. Diaghilev jumped on a table, frightening the panther who proceeded to snort and howl while he crouched in a corner. Rubinstein thought the whole affair hilarious. Not so Diaghilev, who arranged for the police to remove the animal as a threat to human safety.[17]

Thus, it was highly appropriate that this real-life fatal enchantress should perform the character of Semiramis, as conceived by the favourite pupil of Stéphane Mallarmé. So what light does our knowledge of *Schéhérazade* and its cultural background throw on our understanding of *Sémiramis*? I shall give a very selective analysis here, focusing on the visual and verbal media, as well as briefly touching on dance and music.

Dance is central to both works and combines sight, movement, sound and rhythm. In *Schéhérazade*, dance is the very essence of the dramatic action: it expresses the Sultan's power via the splendid exuberance of the *corps de ballet*, but also the passion of Zobeide and the Golden Slave in their *pas de deux*. Similarly, in *Sémiramis*, dance serves to highlight the splendour of the queen's power in Act 1, as described by the choreographer himself, Mikhail Fokine, in a contemporary interview:

> Vous y verrez la danse des lions, taureaux et griffons dominés par un seul homme, Vilzac, le beau danseur et vedette masculine de la troupe, l'entrée des Amazones tirant par leur langue percée d'un anneau les princes prisonniers enchaînés au char de Sémiramis victorieuse qui, pour atteindre son trône éclairé par des cierges, tel un autel, marchera sur les dos courbés de ses victimes.
>
> (There, you will see the dance of lions, bulls and griffins dominated by one man, Vilzac, the handsome dancer and male star of the company; the entrance of Amazons pulling by their tongue pierced with a ring the captive princes chained to the chariot of victorious Semiramis who, in order to reach her candlelit throne, reminiscent of an altar, will walk on the bent backs of her victims.)[18]

At the same time, the voluptuous dance movements of Semiramis in Act 3 evoke, in one last echo, the sensuality of the love scene in Act 2. Dance is arguably one of the markers that clearly assign Valéry's melodrama to the same realm of elevated artistic fantasy as *Schéhérazade*, and this choreographic influence no doubt attenuates the violence of the action, even if the dance movements of *Sémiramis* are not constrained by the strict symmetries of classical ballet.

Amid the vast range of visual elements in *Sémiramis*, from which its choreography is inseparable, it is worth focusing on the queen's costume in particular. In Act 2, she is wearing only jewels and is thus closest to the ballet: 'Sémiramis n'est vêtue que de pierreries' ('Semiramis is dressed only in jewels').[19] We can link this to the oriental costume of Zobeide (as danced by Rubinstein and others), as well as to Moreau's Salome in *L'Apparition* and Rubinstein's Salome role of 1908: all of these heroines sport semi-transparent garments largely made up of jewels. The jewelled attire of Semiramis thus represents the sensuality of a *femme fatale*. The other two acts diverge significantly from the ballet. In Act 1, the Babylonian queen is wearing only armour: 'Elle est en armure noire écaillée' ('She is in black armour, of overlapping scales').[20] This costume is quite similar to that of Rubinstein as Cleopatra in 1920 (in a production of Shakespeare's play translated by André Gide). Indeed, Cleopatra is a favourite theme with Gustave Moreau, too, and can be seen in his pastel of 1887.[21] Although slightly untypical, the costume of Semiramis in Act 1 is therefore still within the *femme fatale* topos and evokes the power of an Amazon. In contrast, Act 3 is very unusual, leaving behind any immediate influence of *Schéhérazade* and Symbolism. At the end of Act 2 and during Act 3, Semiramis is wrapped in a long black mantle, one corner of which covers her head like a hood: 'Sémiramis haletante surgit, drapée dans sa très longue et très souple mante noire, dont un pan lui couvre la tête' ('Semiramis rises panting, draped in her very long and soft black mantle, her head covered by a fold of it').[22] Does this costume link her to Wagner's Wotan in the disguise of a Wanderer perhaps, as he appears in *The Ring of the Nibelung* (*Siegfried*)?[23] It is highly unorthodox to portray a female character in the guise of a male king of the gods: Semiramis is aspiring to an official divine status here.

Music is what makes *Sémiramis* dramatically different from *Schéhérazade*, at least on the surface. The music by Rimsky-Korsakov used in *Schéhérazade* is classical in its style and oriental in its character, with a decorative, appeasing quality; this music is primarily conditioned by harmony and is often melodious. Indeed, in some of the passages, it seems as if the music is recounting a fairy tale. In contrast, Honegger's music in *Sémiramis* is atmospheric rather than classical; harmony is replaced by dissonance and the imitation of real-life sounds. Thus, in Act 1, Scene 2 ('Entrée des captifs' ['The Entry of the Captives']), for example, one distinctly hears the clanking chains of the captive kings. This music is expressive rather than appeasing. As we compare the two different kinds of music, the following questions arise: In making the transition from the ballet to the melodrama, do we move from a vision of woman as a decorative object of desire to the representation of a fully rounded female character? Or does Valéry replace the genuinely passionate woman of *Schéhérazade* with an inhuman despot? The ambivalence on Valéry's part is deliberate: Is Semiramis a woman or an abstraction? We are never quite sure, and the music certainly enhances the heroine's almost supernatural aura. Honegger's score is therefore one of the chief elements that allows *Sémiramis* to go beyond the influence of *Schéhérazade* and other classical ballets and to assert its largely dissonant and polysemic originality.

Another such element is, of course, Valéry's poetic text. Although the verbal medium is absent from the ballet, it is essential to Valéry's melodrama; language pulls together all the other media. Indeed, since there is very little text in Acts 1 and 2, the spectator must necessarily pay special attention to the monologue of Semiramis that takes up most of Act 3 (a mixture of free verse and poetic prose). Some of the key themes of this monologue are as follows. First, Semiramis is an absolute embodiment of a *femme fatale*: 'Je trouble qui je veux. Mon cœur change et surprend, / Et mon corps est un piège, et les délices qu'il dispense / Sont fatales...' ('I trouble whom I please. My heart changes and surprises, / And my body ensnares, and the delights it lavishes / Are deathly...').[24] At the same time, she claims to be unaffected by love: 'Et je ne serai plus par l'amour / Pareille à toutes les femmes...' ('And shall not be again, for love, / As others, as all women are...').[25] Moreover, she is beyond life and death, thus rejecting both womanhood and the human condition: 'je ne veux ni de la vie ni de la mort!...' ('I have no wish for life and none for death!...').[26] After all, she is a ruler with absolute power:

> J'ai fait briser, souiller
> Les Autels étrangers;
> J'ai fait rompre leurs dieux,
> Foulé de mes pieds implacables
> La chair palpitante des Rois!...
>
> (I have had the Altars of the foreign peoples
> Broken and bemired;
> I have ordered their gods shattered, and
> Trampled under my feet, implacable,
> The quivering flesh of Kings!...)[27]

And finally, she portrays herself as the epitome of the realm of the spirit and its masculinity:

> Ivre de volupté, aussitôt l'Amant se crut maître [...]
> Mais plus mâle est Sémiramis!
> La Colombe l'offre aux vautours...
>
> (Drunk with voluptuousness, the Lover soon thought himself master [...]
> But Semiramis is more a man than he!
> The Dove gives him to the vultures...)[28]

All in all, Semiramis is 'une créature de l'esprit' ('a creation of the spirit'): '*Incroyable*, – et par là, *divine*...' ('*Unthinkable* – and thus *divine*...').[29]

Ultimately, Valéry's heroine embodies the triumph of art over life: the striking unconventionality of her matriarchal power symbolizes the supremacy of intellectual creation over the material reality perceived by the senses. Paradoxically, this supremacy is expressed through a 'spectacle total', or 'Gesamtkunstwerk', that appeals to most human senses, as well as to the mind.[30] The intellect may be superior to the senses, but can ultimately only exist through them and thanks to them. Regarding the role of influence within such a work of total art, it seems that at least three different responses to the original source(s), such as *Schéhérazade*, can be detected in the case of *Sémiramis*: first, a creative borrowing of specific structural features (dance is one example); second, fruitful transformation and/or distortion (as epitomized by the queen's costumes); and third, complete negation and/or deliberate contrast (which is what happens with music, certain aspects of the plot and the insertion of poetic text). Because a range of media are involved, each of these response types can become more complex thanks to intermedial transpositions: for example, the visual allure of Zobeide as a *femme fatale* is transposed not only into costume, but also into language in *Sémiramis*, while the oriental music of *Schéhérazade* arguably finds its antithesis in Honegger's score and its counterpart in the exotic stage design of Valéry's melodrama. This key idea of intermediality creates a number of exciting critical challenges that will provide a wealth of material for future research.[31] As for the artistic legacy of *Sémiramis*, Honegger's music for this work was performed again and recorded in 1992, after a long pause; indeed, this was its first noteworthy performance since 1936. This leaves hope that Valéry's melodrama has the potential to be similarly resuscitated: after all, some of its key features have paved the way for the multimedia trends that are symptomatic of the performing arts today.

Notes

1. Harold Bloom, *The Anxiety of Influence: A Theory of Poetry*, 2nd edn (New York and Oxford: Oxford University Press, 1997), p. 5.
2. Stéphane Mallarmé, 'Richard Wagner. Rêverie d'un poète français', in *Igitur. Divagations. Un coup de dés* (Paris: Gallimard, 1976), pp. 168–76 (p. 169). Unless otherwise indicated, translations are my own.
3. See Paul Valéry, *Œuvres*, ed. by Jean Hytier, 2 vols (Paris: Gallimard, 1957–1960), I, p. 16.
4. See ibid., p. 20.
5. Ibid., p. 14.
6. Ibid., p. 60.
7. The basis for this summary is a 1997 Kirov Ballet programme. Originally created by Diaghilev's team, *Schéhérazade* is still being performed by major ballet companies today. The Kirov Ballet production was restaged by Mikhail Fokine's granddaughter, Isabelle Fokine.
8. Harry Halbreich, 'From Semiramis… to Blues', article in booklet accompanying 1992 Timpani recording of Arthur Honegger, *Sémiramis et autres inédits d'orchestre*, Orchestre symphonique de RTL, cond. by Leopold Hager, November 1992 (France: Timpani, 1993 [Audio CD]), pp. 10–13 (pp. 11–12). Emphasis added.
9. Valéry provides the following stage direction in his *Sémiramis*: 'Elle le sert en esclave' ('She serves him, she is his slave'); see Paul Valéry, *Sémiramis*, in *Poésies* (Paris: Gallimard, 1958), pp. 139–60 (p. 149). Valéry's work is available in English as *Semiramis*, in Paul Valéry, *Plays*, trans. by David Paul and Robert Fitzgerald (London: Routledge and Kegan Paul, 1960), pp. 271–309. All further page references are to this translation.
10. Gustave Moreau, *Salomé dansant devant Hérode*, 1876. Oil on canvas. Los Angeles, The Armand Hammer Museum of Art and Cultural Center (The Armand Hammer Collection, Gift of the Armand Hammer Foundation).
11. Gustave Moreau, *L'Apparition*, 1876. Watercolour. Paris, Musée du Louvre, Département des Arts graphiques (fonds Orsay), RF2130.
12. On Moreau's role as the founder of pictorial Symbolism in France and on his wide-ranging influence on Symbolist poetry and prose, see Natasha Grigorian, *European Symbolism: In Search of Myth (1860–1910)* (Oxford: Peter Lang, 2009).
13. For a detailed discussion, see Sylviane Huot, *Le Mythe d'Hérodiade chez Mallarmé: genèse et évolution* (Paris: Nizet, 1977).

14. See Avril Pyman, *A History of Russian Symbolism* (Cambridge: Cambridge University Press, 1994), pp. 95, 113. *Mir Iskusstva*, the journal of the Diaghilev circle, also published a detailed article on Moreau in 1899, which discussed some of his major mythological paintings: see Richard Muther, 'Gustave Moreau', *Mir Iskusstva*, 1899 (Issue 4), 12–16. In the same journal, the following works by Moreau were reproduced in 1899 and 1901: *La Source* (*Mir Iskusstva*, 1899 [Issue 3], 53); *Europe*, *Hercule*, and *Le Poète et la sirène* (*Mir Iskusstva*, 1901 [Issue 7], 31–2). The titles are given in Russian with very few further details. There were also other Moreau reproductions in major Russian artistic (Symbolist) journals between 1890 and 1910.
15. For some of Valéry's critical references to Moreau's art, see Paul Valéry, *Degas Danse Dessin* (Paris: Gallimard, 1983), pp. 49–50.
16. Elaine Brody, 'The Legacy of Ida Rubinstein: Mata Hari of the *Ballets Russes*', *The Journal of Musicology*, 4.4 (Autumn 1985–Autumn 1986), 491–506 (p. 493).
17. Ibid., pp. 502–3.
18. Quoted in Huguette Laurenti, *Paul Valéry et le théâtre* (Paris: Gallimard, 1973), p. 467. Indeed, most of Act 1 in *Sémiramis* is dominated by Fokine's sumptuous and expressive choreography.
19. Valéry, *Sémiramis*, p. 147; *Semiramis*, p. 285.
20. Ibid., p. 143; p. 277.
21. Gustave Moreau, *Cléopâtre*, ca. 1887. Black ink, pastel and oil. Paris, Musée du Louvre, Département des Arts graphiques (fonds Orsay), RF27900.
22. See Valéry's stage directions: *Sémiramis*, p. 153; *Semiramis*, p. 295.
23. *Der Ring des Nibelungen* is a cycle of four epic operas, or music dramas, composed by Richard Wagner from 1848 to 1874. *Siegfried* is the third drama in the cycle.
24. *Sémiramis*, p. 155; *Semiramis*, p. 301.
25. Ibid., p. 154; p. 297.
26. Ibid., p. 158; p. 305.
27. Ibid., p. 154; p. 299.
28. Ibid., p. 156; p. 301.
29. Ibid., p. 159; p. 309. Emphasis in original.
30. Quite strikingly, while perfume is absent from the ballet *Schéhérazade*, *Sémiramis* introduces the olfactory medium to the stage: 'Un énorme candélabre brûle-parfum' ('An enormous candelabrum of incense burners') enhances the sensuality of the love scene in Act 2 (ibid., p. 147; p. 285). These instructions were meticulously followed in Rubinstein's 1934 production. Significantly, Symbolist paintings representing *femme fatale* figures sometimes feature burning incense: Moreau's *Salomé dansant devant Hérode* is one example.

31. As Irina Rajewsky puts it, 'intermediality may serve foremost as a generic term for all those phenomena that (as indicated by the prefix *inter*) in some way take place *between* media. "Intermedial" therefore designates those configurations which have to do with a crossing of borders between media'; Irina O. Rajewsky, 'Intermediality, Intertextuality, and Remediation: A Literary Perspective on Intermediality', *Intermédialités*, 6 (Spring 2006), 43–64 (pp. 45–6), available at cri.histart.umontreal.ca/cri/fr/intermedialites/interface/numeros.html.../ p6_rajewsky_text.pdf (accessed 25 June 2013). Emphasis in original. For a detailed examination of intermediality as a critical and theoretical concept, see Irina O. Rajewsky, *Intermedialität* (Tübingen: A. Francke, 2002).

6
Influence as Appropriation of the Creative Gesture: Henri Matisse's *Poèmes de Charles d'Orléans*

Kathryn Brown

This chapter examines the theme of influence by analysing the combined acts of illustrating and transcribing the output of another artist for the purposes of producing a new, original artwork. The example on which I shall focus is Henri Matisse's *livre d'artiste* ('artist's book') based on the poetry of fifteenth-century poet and duke Charles d'Orléans. Conceived between 1941 and 1943, reworked in 1947, but not published until 1950, this was the last artist's book that Matisse published during his lifetime.[1] Presented in large, loose-leaf format, the book comprises 40 *chansons*, *rondeaux* and *ballades* composed by Charles d'Orléans, each poem written by Matisse in manuscript and accompanied by brilliantly coloured crayon drawings, borders and variations on the fleur-de-lis motif.

This chapter is divided into three sections. In the first, I shall examine analogies between Matisse's creation of this *livre d'artiste* and the circumstances under which Charles composed a significant part of his poetic output. Having regard to the painter's life in Nice under the Occupation and the poet's incarceration and exile in England following French defeat in the battle of Azincourt, I shall argue that Matisse invokes the imprisonment of a historical figure for the purposes of asserting a French cultural tradition during a period when the nation's future appeared uncertain. The second section examines Matisse's transposition of late medieval poetry to the modernist art world of the twentieth century. I shall discuss the relationship between word and image in Matisse's book and will focus, in particular, on ways in which Matisse formulated the imaginative collaboration between painter and poet in the genre of the *livre d'artiste*. The final section explores the painter's act of retracing Charles's poetry in the context of other modernist artworks that employ the theme of copying. I shall contrast the act of transcription in Matisse's *Poèmes de Charles d'Orléans* (*Poems of Charles of Orléans*) with works by Rainer Maria Rilke and Jorge Luis Borges that involve 're-originating' the handwork of a predecessor in a new historical context. I shall argue that, in contrast to both Rilke and Borges, the model of influence found in Matisse's work consists in eliminating difference between two artistic gestures for the purposes of isolating and manifesting the painter's own original style of mark-making.

Imprisonment

Biographical evidence makes clear that the idea of creating a *livre d'artiste* based on handwritten versions of Charles's poetry arose from discussions between Matisse and his close friend André Rouveyre.[2] Throughout the extensive correspondence conducted between the two artists during the early 1940s, Rouveyre became accustomed to receiving beautifully decorated letters and envelopes from Matisse. On occasion, Matisse would simply send an ornamented transcription of one of Charles's poems, a sharing of literary enthusiasm that consisted in the act of displaying a poem to his friend in a new and highly personal way.

This exchange prompted a detailed discussion about the poet and his works between Matisse and Rouveyre. In a letter dated 3 February 1943, Rouveyre raised the idea of an artist's book comprising Charles's poems, but written solely in Matisse's hand. He suggested the creation of

> une suite où *tout* serait de ta main sans le moindre apport d'imprimerie de caractères typographiques. Ce qui découle de cette sorte de jaillissement spontané que sont tes enveloppes c'est un mariage étroit, et délicieux entre la lettre et le dessin qui ne font qu'un [...] Le dessin est lettre, la lettre est dessin [...] tu es porté non seulement à lire, à déguster ces poèmes mais aussi à les écrire [...] Or, maintenant tu es porté à dessiner ton écriture, à faire passer dans ton écriture la sève qui est dans tes dessins.

> (a suite in which *everything* would be by your hand without the slightest trace of printing or typeface. What flows from this sort of spontaneous outpouring of [the work on] your envelopes is an intimate and delicious marriage between lettering and drawing that

become one [...] The drawing is lettering, the lettering is drawing [...] you are driven not just to read, to sample these poems, but also to write them [...] And now you are driven to draw your own writing, to allow the sap contained in your drawings to soak into your writing.)[3]

Rouveyre's characterization of the act of transcription supports an idea of the painter's originality in two ways. The first element is based on exclusion: there is to be no interference of the printer's typeface in the final work of art. Instead, this *livre d'artiste* is to be visually sealed, composed of words and images produced solely by the painter.

The second element concerns the object of representation. By writing out Charles's works, Matisse would transform poems into visual objects intended to be appreciated as images in addition to being read as texts. Supporting this view, Rouveyre posits not the poems, but Matisse's own handwriting as the aesthetic object of the final work. The original poems become a means of facilitating a display of the painter's 'écrit dessiné' ('drawn writing').[4]

Rouveyre repeatedly invokes the image of dripping 'sap' ('la sève') to describe Matisse's working method. This organic metaphor captures, first, the gestural extension from drawing to writing that unites the different forms of mark-making on the page. Secondly, it conveys the relationship between the creative acts of the two artists. When reading the poems in Matisse's handwriting, Rouveyre notes his awareness of 'ta sève en mouvement sur le cher d'Orléans' ('your sap flowing over dear Orléans').[5] In this vivid account, Matisse's painterly gestures seep over the poet's words, making the former both author and object of the finished work.

That the style of this *livre d'artiste* has its origins in Matisse's correspondence with Rouveyre complements the epistolary character of many of the poems themselves. It is known that much of the poetry written by Charles during his 25-year imprisonment in England took the form of communications that were carried by various secretaries to friends and allies in France. Critics have drawn attention to the *ballades*, in particular, as works that fulfilled both practical and literary functions.[6] Making a connection that will be important for the argument of this chapter, David Fein has analysed repeated references to physical acts of writing that occur throughout the early *ballades*.[7] Whether an expression of intimacy to an absent lover or an instruction to those managing his estates and political affairs, the writerly gesture assumes a vital communicative and thematic significance in Charles's poetic world.

The epistolary character of both the poems and Matisse's subsequent reworking of them underpins a more significant analogy between the personal circumstances of painter and poet during the creation of their respective works. While Charles produced much of his poetry in the context of exile and incarceration, Matisse worked on his *livre d'artiste* during a period of recovery from major surgery and subsequent isolation in southern France during the Occupation.[8] The experience of imprisonment thus unites two acts of artistic creation that took place in otherwise radically different historical periods.

For Louis Aragon, whose *Henri Matisse, roman* (*Henri Matisse: A Novel*) appeared in 1971, the image of the prisoner was a central, though unspoken background figure in this artist's book.[9] More than an expression of artistic influence, Aragon interprets Matisse's attraction to Charles's poetry and, in particular, the painter's insistence on the symbol of the fleur-de-lis in this and other works produced during this period, as a political gesture that constituted a personal act of resistance to the Occupation: 'c'est à mes yeux une sorte de protestation solaire au nom de notre pays' ('it is, in my view, a brilliant protest in the name of our country').[10] Aragon posits a connection between Matisse's work and his own attraction to 'imitation' in the form of variations on French medieval and classical versification that he had advanced during the 1940s.[11] Just as poetry's implicit reflection on literary history could constitute 'une arme [...] pour l'homme désarmé' ('a weapon [...] for the unarmed man'), so too Matisse's immersion in French medieval tradition expressed, in Aragon's eyes, a small tribute to 'la splendeur française' ('French splendour') at a time when national identity was threatened and France was in need of hope.[12]

The placement of Matisse's *Poèmes de Charles d'Orléans* in a longer history of French poetry was also enunciated by Rouveyre at the time of the work's production. In his letters to the painter, he notes that the originality of this artist's book depended on striking a careful balance between the respective contributions of artist and poet. In addition to advising Matisse on the eradication of typeface from the finished piece, Rouveyre counselled against the inclusion of any language (including titles and comments) that did not form part of the poet's original works. The reasons underlying Matisse's selection of poems and his attraction to the poet's writing should, in his view, be apparent solely from the structure of the finished work.[13] For Rouveyre, such a pared-down expression of the relationship between poet and painter would manifest a unique form of reciprocal influence:

> Si nous savons que ton choix est guidé parce que justement tu trouves que dans cette pièce il traduit fort bien ton sentiment vis-à-vis de lui,

poète, on peut très bien imaginer que lui-même, Charles, pourrait écrire cette poésie en te considérant toi et tes dessins auprès de lui.

(If we know that your choice is guided simply because you find that a certain piece properly translates your thoughts about him, the poet, one could well imagine that he, Charles, could have written this poetry while thinking of you and your drawings beside him.)[14]

On its face, Rouveyre's comment playfully reverses a typical conception of influence: rather than positing Charles's poetry as a source of inspiration for Matisse, the poet is supposed to have imagined the works of the later artist as he writes. However, Rouveyre's comment goes beyond the paradox of historical inversion by implicating both poet and painter in the self-conscious maintenance of an artistic tradition. As Svetlana Alpers has argued in a different context, the relationship between artists from different historical periods is not necessarily 'a matter of development or progress [...] so much as it is a matter of persistence, of continuity'.[15] An earlier artist can thus 'resemble' a later artist because of an assumed 'continuity of interests' that functions as both a 'resource and constraint'.[16] Importantly for the purposes of the present discussion, I would add that the notion of reciprocal influence suggests that an artist may conceive of his or her output not as a finished product, but as the opening up of a space of creative possibility within which later artists may express their own ideas.

Matisse's imaginative occupation of the creative spaces offered by existing works of literature and painting has a broader resonance within his oeuvre as a whole. Alastair Wright has examined tensions between Matisse and his early critics regarding the artist's apparent indebtedness to the stylistic influence of the Neo-Impressionists and the Nabis.[17] Matisse's experimentation with familiar styles in the first decades of the twentieth century contributed to what Wright describes as an 'uncertainty of the index' and generated a critical questioning of what, if anything, could serve as guarantor of the painter's originality.[18] John Elderfield's discussion of Matisse's large-scale, early canvases, *Luxe, calme et volupté* (*Luxury, Calm and Pleasure*, 1904) and *Le Bonheur de vivre* (*The Joy of Life*, 1905–6) places the theme of influence in a more optimistic light, suggesting that the artist interfaced with pictorial tradition for the purpose of countering the sense of rupture that modernist art perceived in relation to its own history.[19] In Elderfield's account, Matisse's early works incorporate into their composition the symbolic vision of an ideal, but unfamiliar past for the purposes of communicating harmony between the present and the authority of pictorial antecedents.[20] In contrast to the idea that modernist art celebrated a rift with traditions of Western beauty and iconography, Elderfield's argument shows a way in which Matisse's early compositions sought to reconnect modernist painting 'to the loftiest products of the Western tradition'.[21]

The *livres d'artiste* that Matisse produced throughout his career serve as a more direct self-placement in relation to artistic tradition. Choosing not only works by his contemporaries, but also poetry that, by the 1940s, formed part of the canon of French literature (Ronsard, Charles d'Orléans, Baudelaire, Mallarmé), Matisse located his own mature style in the context of a lengthy literary history. In the final section of this chapter, I shall analyse how Matisse uses this historical tradition for the purposes of isolating and expressing his own originality. At this point, however, I want to turn to the way in which Matisse conceived of his own relationship to Charles d'Orléans and the impact this had on the interface between word and image in his completed *livre d'artiste*.

From Illustration to Illumination

While Matisse's contemporaries were keen to explore connections between the output of painter and poet, there was also considerable critical interest in articulating the stylistic confrontation between the two artistic gestures that comprise this artist's book: one component having been produced in the context of late medieval court poetry, the other in the modernist art world of the twentieth century. Discussing Matisse's *livre d'artiste* based on the poems of Ronsard (a work executed during the same period as the *Poèmes de Charles d'Orléans*), Aragon noted his impression that a distinctively twentieth-century aesthetic came to the fore in the book.[22]

Aragon's intuition captures an aspect of Matisse's own modernizing attitude to the fifteenth- and sixteenth-century texts that formed the basis of his artist's books of the 1940s. Discussing his reading and illustration of Ronsard in a letter to Rouveyre of 1941, Matisse notes: 'Ronsard est toujours près de moi. Il chante sa chanson sur tous les tons et il faut que j'en fasse quelque chose. Je crois que je ferai simplement du Matisse' (Ronsard is always with me. He sings his verse in all keys and I must do something with them I think I'll just make a Matisse.)[23]

The idea of producing a 'Matisse' from the work of another artist raises questions about both artistic collaboration and the relationship between word and image in the genre of the *livre d'artiste*. In his writings on this subject, Matisse insisted that illustrating a text was by no means an attempt to 'complete' a poem. If a poet's work required this, the poet's efforts would, according to Matisse, have been deficient. Instead, Matisse thought that painter and poet could work in parallel (even if they did not strictly work 'together'), the picture being a 'plastic equivalent' of the poem.[24] But this 'plasticity' is by no means understood to be the visual realization of a particular theme or motif contained in a text. Instead, Matisse argues that the important factor is the 'enrichment' of the painter's own means of expression through contact with the output of the poet. Supporting the argument that the work of one artist can serve as a space of creative possibility for the imaginative work of another, Matisse argues that the visual artist must not adhere too strictly to the written text and should, instead, work freely in order to express his own sensibility.[25] In an essay on his artist's books published in 1946, Matisse went on to characterize the relationship between image and text as a form of musical transposition rather than a literal rendering of textual meaning.[26]

Matisse's attempts to capture the relationship between word and image, painter and poet in the *livre d'artiste* exemplify a tension that runs throughout this genre: because texts are typically the point of origin for an artist's book, are the accompanying images implicitly derivative and, hence, subordinate to textual meaning? Anne Mœglin-Delcroix has analysed different ways in which twentieth-century and contemporary artists have approached this problem, rejecting the supporting role played by illustration in *éditions de luxe* and reconceiving of the book format as an imaginative space shared equally by painter and writer.[27] She notes, in particular, that the reference to 'illustration' evokes an ancillary role for the visual artist by suggesting the signifying primacy and generative potential of the accompanying text.[28]

The difficulty of expressing the relationship between Charles's poetry and Matisse's drawing, writing and ornamentation was a recurrent theme in letters exchanged between Matisse and Rouveyre throughout the work's production. During a search for a way in which to describe the creative endeavour of the painter in a note to appear at the end of the book, various options were rehearsed and discarded. Anticipating Mœglin-Delcroix's point, description of the poems as having been 'illustrated' by Matisse (a formulation proposed by the painter himself) prompted a strong response from Rouveyre:

> *Illustrées* ne me paraît guère possible, tant c'est vulgarisé; et le mot est assez peu défini: qu'est-ce que ça veut dire en vérité? [...] Mais c'est surtout la vulgarisation de l'emploi qui paraît gênante, employée *pour*

toi [...] pour désigner quelque chose de toi. On ne peut admettre que tu fais là œuvre *d'illustrateur.*

(*Illustrated* hardly seems possible to me, it has been so vulgarized; and the word itself is so ill defined: what could it really mean? [...] But it is mainly the debased use of the word that is problematic when applied *to you* [...] to describe something produced by you. One would not want to suggest that you had done the work of an *illustrator.*)[29]

A compromise was eventually reached. While the term 'illustrated' appeared on the title page, the description at the end of the work characterized the painter's act in more specific detail: 'Ce livre manuscrit a été entièrement composé par Henri Matisse. L'artiste a écrit à la main et enluminé les "Poèmes de Charles d'Orléans"' ('This handwritten book has been entirely composed by Henri Matisse. The artist has written by hand and illuminated the 'Poems of Charles d'Orléans').[30] The choice of terms for this statement is important for a broader interpretation of the relationship between painter and poet.

First, the reference to 'illumination' places the work on a specific footing within book history by invoking the style of medieval illuminated manuscripts. Once again, Matisse draws attention to the longer literary and artistic tradition in which his *livre d'artiste* is to be understood and read. The term 'illumination' also has a broader meaning in this context. Developing the idea of 'reciprocal influence' discussed in the previous section, Matisse's 'rewriting' of the poems expresses a way in which new meaning can accrue to cultural texts and artefacts. As letters 're-sent' by the painter for his own purposes and as an assertion of French cultural identity during the Occupation, the poems are imbued with additional significance by their 're-enactment' and publication in a new context.

Secondly, references to 'handwriting' emphasize the gestural work of the painter in connection with the production of the texts themselves. Reinforcing Rouveyre's point that the aesthetic object of the finished book is Matisse's 'écrit dessiné', attention is drawn to coincidences between the physical handwork of poet and painter. This emphasis on manuscript constitutes a powerful assertion of Matisse's own authorial status: the work has been composed *entirely* by the hand of the painter. Accordingly, it sets the tone for the relationship between Matisse and the creator of the poems. In contrast to the 'uncertainty of the index' that Wright identifies in the reception of the artist's early paintings, the work of transcription has become an expression of Matisse's own originality rather than that of the poet.

Although Matisse's concluding statement emphasizes the originality of the hand-drawn ornaments and poems, this is not to suggest that Charles d'Orléans is overlooked or expunged from the finished work. On the contrary, Matisse acknowledges the poet on the frontispiece by including a freely drawn portrait of him – an image that was inspired by depictions of the poet's family that the artist had found in various histories of France and reproductions of medieval paintings. The 'portrait' is, therefore, a composite, being composed from a variety of sources from which Matisse claimed to have taken the 'essential features'.[31] Just as Matisse expresses his own creativity by inhabiting the gestural acts of the poet, so too the poet is brought vividly to life for the reader/viewer in the medium of the painter.

While Matisse provides a visual confirmation of the work's underlying textual authorship in this introductory image, he accords a different value and function to the poems themselves. It is within language, rather than imagery, that Matisse claims to have identified the true character of Charles d'Orléans and to have most deeply associated himself with the poet: 'J'étais dans sa poésie; j'étais avec lui. Chez les personnages de sa famille, je ne recherchais que l'extérieur, les traits. Mais l'esprit, la vie, vient de sa poésie même' ('I inhabited his poetry; I was with him. For the individuals in his family, I only sought the exterior, the physical traits. But the spirit, the life comes from the poetry itself').[32]

This sharing of the same textual space exceeds the mere act of reading. Echoing Aragon's comment that Matisse 's'était laissé emporter par Charles d'Orléans' ('allowed himself to be carried away by Charles d'Orléans'), the act of retracting the gestural production of the poet's words becomes the cornerstone of both artistic identification and original expression.[33] Transcription of the poet's work is an attempt neither to obliterate the author nor to become him. Claudine Grammont has argued that the act of copying out the poems enabled Matisse physically to experience the creativity of another artist.[34] I agree with Grammont that this is one aspect of the work's production and that it forms part of Matisse's ideal of authorial identification. However, emphasis on imaginative identification overlooks the way in which an act of gestural appropriation makes this work uniquely 'matissien'. My argument is that Matisse temporarily inhabits the actions made by another artist's hand for the purposes of isolating and displaying the distinctive nature of his own originality. It is to an elaboration of how the poet's writing becomes the trigger for such new performative possibilities that I shall now turn.

Gesture

The manuscript rendering of poems in their entirety distinguishes this *livre d'artiste* from Matisse's other works in this genre. Matisse did, however, repeatedly experiment with the incorporation of handwriting into his artist's books. In his (1947) rendering of Baudelaire's *Les Fleurs du mal* (*The Flowers of Evil*), the first letter of each poem is written by hand.[35] Similarly, his (1946) treatment of the *Lettres portugaises* (*Portuguese Letters*), allegedly written by Marianna Alcoforado, includes handwritten sections of the printed letters beneath 'portraits' of the author of the texts.[36]

There are, however, important differences between the functions of handwriting in these works. In Matisse's presentation of Baudelaire's poetry, manuscript serves a primarily decorative effect, creating a visual transition between drawings, ornaments and typeface. In the *Lettres portugaises*, handwritten additions both accentuate parts of the accompanying prose and recreate the act of letter writing: the reader holds a book, but imaginatively steps into the role of recipient of the original letters. In a postscript to the *Lettres portugaises*, Matisse states that his book has 'done justice' to an author whose name was absent from the work's first publication and whose ownership of the texts had, for over 200 years, been the subject of debate.[37] Through the interface between text, image and handwriting in this *livre d'artiste*, Matisse conjures up the voice, face and writerly gestures of a contested author.

The act of retracing the words of another artist produces a different effect in the *Poèmes de Charles d'Orléans*. Going beyond Grammont's discussion of imaginative identification, my argument is that Matisse's appropriation of the poet's creative gesture can be understood as part of a broader experiment with 're-originating' works of art as part of modernist artistic practice. In order to understand the effect of this in Matisse's work, I want to locate this *livre d'artiste* in the context of two related examples that specifically invoke the theme of transcribing another artist's works by hand.

The first is Rilke's direct and unattributed 'quotation' of the final paragraph of Baudelaire's prose poem, *A une heure du matin*, in *Die Aufzeichnungen des Malte Laurids Brigge* (*The Notebooks of Malte Laurids Brigge*), published in 1910. The quotation immediately follows the narrator's famous articulation of an ideal form of writing (one in which author is written by text) and a time when the hand of the poet will produce words independently and unbidden. The importance of the narrator's quest, and the apparent impossibility of its achievement, is expressed by the combination of hope and despair in Baudelaire's prose poem that follows this description:

> Da liegt es vor mir in meiner eigenen Schrift, was ich gebetet habe, Abend für Abend. Ich habe es mir aus den Büchern, in denen ich es fand, abgeschrieben, damit es mir ganz nahe wäre und aus meiner Hand entsprungen wie Eigenes. Und ich will es jetzt noch einmal schreiben, hier vor meinem Tisch kniend will ich es schreiben; denn so habe ich es länger, als wenn ich es lese, und jedes Wort dauert an und hat Zeit zu verhallen.
> 'Mécontent de tous et mécontent de moi, je voudrais bien me racheter et m'enorgueillir un peu dans le silence et la solitude de la nuit [...].'
>
> (There it is before me, in my own handwriting, that which I've prayed for every night. I copied it out of books that I found so that it could be near to me, as if it had sprung from my own hand. And I'll write it out once more, here kneeling before my desk; that way I'll possess it for longer than if I read it, and every word will linger and have time to resound.
> 'Mécontent de tous et mécontent de moi, je voudrais bien me racheter et m'enorgueillir un peu dans le silence et la solitude de la nuit [...].')[38]

The transcription of Baudelaire's text reinforces the narrator's image of ideal 'unselfing' in the act of poetic creation: the independence of the narrator's hand is symbolized by the tracing of another poet's words. In the context of the narrative, even Baudelaire's poem itself is presented as almost authorless, a text that has simply been taken from 'found books'. Developing the theme of artistic self-effacement that runs throughout Rilke's novel, this re-enactment of another artist's creative gesture becomes a physical and symbolic means of abstracting self from word.

At the opposite end of Rilke's image of selfless poetic writing is the combination of invention and influence that underlies Borges's short story *Pierre Menard: Author of the Quixote* (1941). By no means the mere 'copying' or even transcription of a famous novel, the narrator explains that Pierre Menard's *Don Quixote* is a planned 'coincidence', an act of writing that does not repeat but 'reveals' an existing novel while establishing new, even richer meaning owing to its production in a different context.[39] Rejecting definition of this artistic endeavour as Menard's 'identification' with, or mere updating of, Cervantes, the narrator concludes that Menard produces an authentic work of original expression. This gestural appropriation differs from the act of self-effacement in Rilke's novel as it constitutes a positive assertion of authorial control by Menard himself. However, this act ultimately culminates in a form of universalism that in itself undermines individual distinctiveness in the creative enterprise: 'Every man should be capable of all ideas' is the conclusion.[40]

The question arises as to where Matisse's *Poèmes de Charles d'Orléans* stands in relation to the models of gestural re-enactment in these two modernist works. Each one depicts the appropriation of another person's physical act of handwriting: each artist shows how an existing work can be brought forwards by re-originating a prior creative gesture in a new context. Yet the new works are not counterfeits, pastiches or reinterpretations of the originals. Indeed, Borges's story culminates with an image of 'reciprocal influence' of the type that I discussed above. Suggesting that one might 'read the *Odyssey* as though it came after the *Æneid*', Borges's narrator develops the idea that texts are spaces of atemporal, creative possibility by locating interpretive freedom at the level of reader rather than that of writer or painter.[41]

Of the three works, Matisse's asserts most strongly the creative hand of the 'new' artist, a point confirmed by the statement that the book has been 'entièrement composé par Henri Matisse' ('entirely composed by Henri Matisse'). Unlike the narratives by Rilke and Borges, the work does not simply depict an act of gestural appropriation, but is the product of such an act. Whereas Rilke describes an ideal, but impossible, form of poetic creation through the metaphor of estrangement of hand from body, and Borges emphasizes the role of context in deriving authentic expression from 'coincidence', Matisse retraces the gestures of another person in order to isolate the distinctive nature of his creativity. It is by eliminating difference between his gesture and that of Charles d'Orléans that Matisse isolates and draws attention to his own stylistic originality. As Rouveyre notes: 'J'y voyais la possibilité de mise en fait de l'essence même de ton originalité fondamentale' ('I saw in this the possibility of displaying the very essence of your fundamental originality').[42] The work of art that we, as readers or viewers, are presented with at the end of this action is less an object than the trace of an elaborate performance by the painter.

The influence of Charles's poetry on Matisse's creation of this *livre d'artiste* can thus be understood in the context of a modernist interrogation of the relationship between artistic expression and selfhood, a theme that is explored repeatedly through performances of the creative gesture.

While I have located Matisse's book against the background of two literary examples that invoke the idea of temporarily inhabiting the body of another individual by 're-originating' that person's handwriting, it is equally important to place this attention to gesture in the context of a broader investigation into the physical manifestation of creativity that took place during the 1940s and 1950s: for example, the films made of Picasso's working methods, Cocteau's repeated incorporation of his own handwriting into the mechanical display process of cinema, and the photographs taken of Matisse's self-conscious revision of his own style of artistic production following illness.

In the *Poèmes de Charles d'Orléans*, the texts of the fifteenth-century poet become the script for a new performance by Matisse in the twentieth century. Rather than the product of sympathetic identification with a historical figure, the work is ultimately an investigation into Matisse's own artistic persona. As Rouveyre put it in a letter of 21 January 1943: 'Pour bien des pièces ce pourrait être une recherche à toi en pleine pureté en dehors de toute figure' ('Many of these pieces could serve as a research into your own self in complete purity, beyond the figural').[43] In the model of 'influence' that I have outlined for the purpose of describing this *livre d'artiste*, Matisse inhabits the gestures of the poet for the purpose of staging his own unique 'performance' as a modernist painter.

Notes

1. For details of the genesis of this work, see Hanne Finsen's commentary in Henri Matisse, *Matisse–Rouveyre Correspondance*, ed. by Hanne Finsen (Paris: Flammarion, 2001), pp. 147–8, n. 4. For the purposes of this chapter, I have examined copy number 522 of Matisse's *Poèmes de Charles d'Orléans* (Paris: Tériade, 1950) in the Spencer Collection of the New York Public Library (copy signed by the painter).
2. Matisse, *Matisse–Rouveyre Correspondance*, pp. 147–8, 157, 160–66, 204–5.
3. Ibid., p. 205. Emphasis in original. Unless otherwise indicated, translations are my own.
4. Matisse, *Matisse–Rouveyre Correspondance*, p. 205.
5. Ibid., p. 217.
6. David Fein, *Charles d'Orléans* (Boston: Twayne, 1983), pp. 38–43; Enid McLeod, *Charles of Orleans: Prince and Poet* (London: Chatto & Windus, 1969), pp. 232–9.
7. Fein, *Charles d'Orléans*, p. 38.

8. Matisse, *Matisse–Rouveyre Correspondance*, pp. 20–3. For a discussion of Matisse's confinement following surgery, see Hilary Spurling, *Matisse: The Life* (London: Penguin, 2009), pp. 474–8.
9. Louis Aragon, *Sur Henri Matisse: entretiens avec Jean Ristat* (Paris: Stock, 1999), pp. 75–6.
10. Ibid., pp. 69–70.
11. Louis Aragon, *Œuvres poétiques complètes*, ed. by Olivier Barbarant (Paris: Gallimard, 2007), p. 747.
12. Ibid., p. 757; Louis Aragon, *Henri Matisse, roman* (Paris: Gallimard, 1998), p. 302.
13. Matisse, *Matisse–Rouveyre Correspondance*, p. 227.
14. Ibid.
15. Svetlana Alpers, *The Vexations of Art: Velázquez and Others* (New Haven, CT: Yale University Press, 2005), p. 237.
16. Ibid.
17. Alastair Wright, *Matisse and the Subject of Modernism* (Princeton, NJ and Oxford: Princeton University Press, 2004), pp. 19–30.
18. Ibid., pp. 18 and 48.
19. John Elderfield, *The Drawings of Henri Matisse* (London: Arts Council of Great Britain and Thames & Hudson, 1984), p. 54.
20. Ibid.
21. Ibid., p. 55. There is a stark contrast between Elderfield's position and Arthur Danto's views on modernism's break with tradition in *The Abuse of Beauty: Aesthetics and the Concept of Art* (Chicago and La Salle, IL: Open Court, 2004), pp. 46–9.
22. Aragon, *Henri Matisse*, p. 616; Henri Matisse, *Florilège des amours de Ronsard* (Paris: Skira, 1948).
23. Henri Matisse, *Écrits et propos sur l'art*, ed. by Dominique Fourcade (Paris: Hermann, 2005), p. 218.
24. Ibid., p. 215.
25. Ibid., p. 214.
26. Ibid., p. 213.
27. Anne Mœglin-Delcroix, *Sur le livre d'artiste: articles et écrits de circonstance (1981–2005)* (Marseille: Le Mot et le reste, 2005), pp. 105–9.
28. Ibid., p. 540.
29. Matisse, *Matisse–Rouveyre Correspondance*, p. 225. Emphasis in original.
30. Matisse, *Poèmes de Charles d'Orléans*, 'Postscript'.
31. Matisse, *Écrits et propos*, p. 229.
32. Ibid.
33. Aragon, *Henri Matisse*, p. 300.

34. Claudine Grammont, 'Recreations', in *Matisse: A Second Life*, ed. by Hanne Finsen (Paris: Hazan, 2005), pp. 55–65 (p. 61).
35. Henri Matisse, *Charles Baudelaire, Les Fleurs du mal* (Paris: La Bibliothèque française, 1947).
36. Henri Matisse, *Marianna Alcoforado, Lettres portugaises* (Paris: Tériade, 1946).
37. Ibid., 'Postscript'.
38. Rainer Maria Rilke, *Sämtliche Werke*, ed. by the Rilke Archive, Ruth Sieber-Rilke and Ernst Zinn, 6 vols (Frankfurt a.M.: Insel, 1966), VI, 756–7.
39. Jorge Luis Borges, *Collected Fictions*, trans. by Andrew Hurley (New York: Penguin, 1998), p. 91.
40. Ibid., p. 95.
41. Ibid.
42. Matisse, *Matisse–Rouveyre Correspondance*, p. 166.
43. Ibid., p. 164.

7
Samuel Beckett's Funerary Sculpture

Claire Lozier

In February 1937, Samuel Beckett visited Würzburg cathedral and was particularly struck by the funerary statues he saw there. A number of these statues were made by a sculptor known as the 'Wolfskehlmeister'. In his diary, Beckett describes this fourteenth-century German sculptor as a 'Master of the senile and [the] collapsed', as 'Another man for me', and writes: 'Remember: WOLFSKEHLMEISTER'.[1] In an article published in 2008, James Knowlson suggests that Beckett's enthusiasm for these sculptures can be explained by the 'affinities' between their universe and Beckett's: 'More clearly than anywhere else in the German diaries, his comments on the statues sculpted by the man known as the "Wolfskehlmeister", so named because he had carved the stone statue of Bishop Otto von Wolfskehl, revealed how he recognized in the work of others certain key affinities with his *own* world.'[2] He also argues that, subsequent to his discovery of the Wolfskehlmeister's statues, 'figures of "the senile and the collapsed" were to become even more regular denizens of Beckett's world'.[3] Knowlson concludes his article by affirming that these statues are 'a source of inspiration worthy of the attention of Beckett scholars',[4] thereby identifying a hitherto unexplored area of research on Beckett that I shall try to survey in this essay. The terms employed by Knowlson in the passages cited above – most notably 'affinities', 'regular denizens' and 'source of inspiration' – are bound up intimately with questions of influence.

The congruities between the Wolfskehlmeister's sculptures of the dead and a number of Beckett's narrators are indeed striking. Consider, for example, the narrators of *Malone Dies* and *First Love*, who spend all or much of their time lying down, or those of *Molloy* and *How It Is*, who crawl around and whose bodies are in a state of advanced decrepitude. These creeping creatures remind us, perhaps, of the Wolfskehlmeister's 'collapsed and hopelessly humble' characters.[5] Moreover, Beckett's narrators cling to the notebooks in which they relate the sufferings of their nearly extinguished lives in the first person: we are reminded here of the holy texts clutched by the German sculptor's funerary figures.[6]

There are, in fact, deathly features in Beckett's work that predate his discovery of the Wolfskehlmeister's statues, however, and they are to be found in another of Beckett's narrative works, *Murphy*, written between August 1935 and June 1936.[7] Beckett thus recognizes himself in the work of the Wolfskehlmeister as much as he is inspired by it. In the passage already quoted, Knowlson implies (but without insisting on the distinction) that there are 'certain key affinities' between the Wolfskehlmeister's statues and Beckett's '*own* world', and that those statues are a 'source of inspiration worthy of the attention of Beckett scholars'. We must, however, bear the distinction between self-recognition and 'inspiration' in mind if we are to understand fully the significance of the encounter between Beckett and the Wolfskehlmeister's statues. A separate and important distinction should also be considered: the statues admired by Beckett are represented as upright, whereas the narrators in question spend most of their time lying down. We must also take the implications of this difference in posture into account if we are to appreciate fully the influence of the Wolfskehlmeister's sculptures on Beckett's narrators.

The first part of this essay identifies affinities between the Wolfskehlmeister's works in stone and the narrators of a number of Beckett's narrative works written before and after Beckett's discovery of the statues in 1937. Subsequently, I focus on the difference of posture between the Wolfskehlmeister's statues and Beckett's narrators in an attempt to illuminate the inflections wrought by Beckett's works, through a process of secularization, on the genre of funerary sculpture.

Between Affinity and Inspiration

The protagonists of *Murphy*, *Malone Dies*, *First Love*, *Molloy* and *How It Is* all possess prominent features that link them to the Wolfskehlmeister's 'hopelessly humble', 'senile' and 'collapsed' figures. While *Murphy* anticipates them, the narrators of the remaining texts can be understood as their echo. The narrators are related to the stone statues by virtue of their identifying themselves as dead, their physical degradation and their immobility to the point of petrification.

While we may suppose them alive, the protagonists of Beckett's texts composed after 1937 are nevertheless presented as essentially defunct.

Even though Malone writes, he is not sure that he is alive. His body is now nothing more than a 'carcass' that he has already left behind, and he refuses to sleep because 'Coma is for the living'.[8] Malone is not sure whether he is moribund (but still alive) or dead ('The truth is, if I did not feel myself dying, I could well believe myself dead'):[9] the boundaries between the living and the dead are blurred, leaving us without certainty as to Malone's actual state. Macmann, a character in the stories recounted by Malone to pass the time, is similarly afflicted: his age is 'of a nature to carry him off on the spot'.[10] He suffers from the same hesitation as Malone: while he is still alive, he no longer belongs to the world of the living but to the world of the dying – the waiting room of the world of the dead. The narrator of *First Love*, 'whose corpse was not yet quite up to scratch', belongs to the same world, but hesitation has now been replaced by simultaneity: 'But I did not yet know, at that time, how tender the earth can be for those who have only her and how many graves in her giving, for the living'.[11] Molloy and Moran, the two narrators of *Molloy*, belong in part to the world of the dead. At the beginning of the text, Molloy says that he has attended his own funeral.[12] Moran's grave has already been dug and he claims to be 'faring below the dead' in a place where he has his 'plot in perpetuity'.[13] In *How It Is*, the narrative voice calls itself 'a dumb limp lump flat for ever in the mud'[14] and describes one of its acolytes as 'already a true corpse'.[15]

Malone, Molloy, Moran, the narrator of *First Love* and the crawling creatures in *How It Is* are in their various ways 'dead' or close to death either explicitly or ambiguously. Murphy is not 'dead'. Nevertheless, from the beginning of the novel, he is presented as naked and strapped to his rocking chair with seven scarves that prevent him from moving.[16] Beckett's enumeration of Murphy's bound body parts – shins, thighs, breast, belly and wrists – reduces his character to an inert body whose nudity serves only to accentuate its resemblance to a corpse. Moreover, he possesses some of the qualities of a cadaver, even if he has not fully become one. The French text reads: 'il avait dû avoir le bonheur pendant quelque temps d'être mort apparemment aux choses sensibles' ('he had to have had the good fortune for some time to appear to be dead to perceptible objects').[17] In his search for non-being, Murphy takes offence at sounds that remind him of living things: 'These were sights and sounds that he did not like. They detained him in the world to which they belonged, but not he, as he fondly hoped'.[18] His time in his dwelling place is thus described as a 'superb arrangement' that enables him 'to consume away at pretty well his own gait'.[19] In wanting to be moribund, Murphy is a corpse in the making.

Beckett's defunct characters are also figures of the 'senile and the collapsed'. Malone is 'impotent', his flesh is 'stupid', he lies on a pallet, his body is 'bony'[20] and he is 'toothless'.[21] The narrator of *First Love* is no more than a 'carcass'.[22] Molloy's appearance is 'hideous',[23] his toes fall off[24] and he has no teeth.[25] His age is described as 'astonishing'.[26] Similarly, Moran's dilapidation is well advanced: he sees himself ageing 'as swiftly as a day-fly'[27] and his body is crumbling.[28] The creatures of *How It Is* are 'rags of life' and 'little old men'.[29]

Murphy is not spared these debilitations. He is 'ashen'[30] and remains for long periods in a bed that is described as 'infect' ('squalid') in the French text.[31] His body deteriorates progressively: 'There seemed little left of this body that was not privy to this mind, and that little was usually tired on its own account'.[32] The process of decay has begun.

These characters at the edges of death are locked in an immobility that verges on petrification: they become veritable statues. Malone has not moved from the bed in which he awoke after a blackout.[33] In Lulu/Anne's flat, the narrator of *First Love* chooses a similar fate: he lies down on a sofa that he never leaves; food is brought to him and his chamber pot is emptied daily. In spite of their endless wandering, the creatures of *How It Is* remain still for long periods (and sometimes for several years). They are motionless: 'end of seventh year of stillness beginning of eighth'.[34] While Molloy and Moran are mobile, they nevertheless fall victim to a progressive rigidification: their legs stiffen gradually. Molloy is forced to move less and less[35] and he lives in fear of not being able to move in the future.[36] Similarly, Moran moves with decreasing frequency[37] and increasing difficulty.[38] Nevertheless, he is delighted by the petrification that overcomes him: 'To be literally incapable of motion at last, that must be something!'[39] As for Macmann, he is compared implicitly to a statue: 'a good half of his existence must have been spent in a motionlessness akin to that of stone, not to say the three quarters, or even the four fifths'.[40]

Murphy displays early signs of petrification. He is attached to his rocking chair and does not move; his breathing is imperceptible and his eyes are as 'cold and unwavering as a gull's'.[41] He is in a near cataleptic state. While he does occasionally move, it is unclear whether he is able to speak: 'Sometimes Murphy would begin to make a point, sometimes he may have even finished making one, it was hard to say'.[42] Naked, cold, inert, silent: Murphy is his own statue.

There are thus demonstrably positive links between Beckett's figures and their stony predecessors, and this is the case both before and after Beckett's visit to Würzburg in 1937. Two points need to be made here.

First, the concept of influence invites reflection on both affinities and inspiration: it embraces past resonances as well as future echoes. The play of influence thus obeys both a proleptic and an analeptic logic. Second, while Beckett's texts transform their narrators and other creations into petrified corpses in the making, the Wolfskehlmeister's statues give the dead an eternal body sculpted in stone. Both representations play on an ambiguity: the living are made dead and the dead retain features of the living. Moreover, while the link between funerary sculpture and Beckett's characters (narrators or otherwise) appears certain, their difference in posture must be taken into account. What is the significance of the shift from an upright to a prostrate or supine position? How are we to interpret this apparent inflection of influence?

From the Upright to the Horizontal: Scriptural Humiliation and Secularization

Those protagonists in Beckett's work whom I have compared to the Wolfskehlmeister's funerary statues live either entirely, partly or momentarily lying down. Malone lies on his bed and does not leave it ('It is on my back, that is to say prostrate, no supine, that I feel best […]. I lie on my back'),[43] whereas the narrator of *First Love* spends his life lying on the sofa at Lulu/Anne's. Macmann moves from a prostrate[44] to a supine position.[45] Fearing that he will soon no longer be able to move,[46] Molloy decides to lie down, both on his front and on his back, and to crawl in a 'black slush of leaves'.[47] As for Moran, he likes to spend his time in bed[48] and, in the course of his long journey in search of Molloy, his body becomes so stiff that he is forced to lie on the ground. In *How It Is*, the narrator crawls around interminably in the mud with his companions. While Murphy is initially content to be tied to the rocking chair in which he sits, he succumbs progressively to the pleasures of lying down: 'To sit down was no longer enough, he must insist now on lying down'; 'His body lay down more and more in a less precarious abeyance than that of sleep'.[49]

None of these beings can resist the temptation to lie on the ground. They move from the vertical to the horizontal and, in so doing, bear a certain resemblance to recumbent funerary statues. Malone lies in his bed; the narrator of *First Love* actualizes the epitaph that appears on the fifth page of Beckett's text:

> Hereunder lies the above who up below
> So hourly died that he lived on till now.[50]

Macmann, Molloy and Moran all lie flat on the ground (Moran dreams of inscribing an official 'here lies' on his tomb).[51] The characters in *How It Is* are described explicitly as such, be it the narrative voice ('where I lay abandoned')[52] or its companions ('no more motion than a slab').[53] This text is also invaded by an army of recumbent figures in an apocalyptic and irony-tinged vision: 'a hundred thousand prone glued two by two together vast stretch of time nothing stirring'.[54] It is only Murphy who, though he succumbs to the temptation to lie down, is not likened to a recumbent statue. While Murphy possesses certain distinctive features that align him with the funerary statues so admired by Beckett, he does not feel their direct influence; he anticipates it. In the cathedral at Würzburg, Beckett sees himself in the work of the Wolfskehlmeister (he views him as 'Another man for me') and the encounter will also influence his works to come. Affinities become inspiration. Murphy is thus a recumbent statue who is unaware that he is one.

Recumbent funerary statues were made for the first time in the eleventh century and are especially prevalent in the sixteenth and seventeenth centuries. As Philippe Ariès has observed, they, too, are often marked by a certain ambiguity. They represent the dead as 'entre la mort et la vie' ('neither dead nor alive'):[55] either as they were at the moment of their passing, or as sleeping. However, according to Ariès, 'contrairement aux apparences, le gisant n'est pas [...] un mort allongé, mais un personnage irréel debout, dont les plis des vêtements tombent verticalement, les yeux souvent ouverts, et qui est ensuite renversé et couché, la tête sur son coussin: il repose' ('Despite appearances, the recumbent figure is not [...] a reclining corpse; rather, it is a stylized standing individual, whose clothing is vertically draped and whose eyes are frequently wide open. He has then been laid on his back, with his head on a cushion. He is in repose').[56] The shift from an upright to a lying position is thus a key aspect of these representations. In order to establish a link between the Wolfskehlmeister's statues and the recumbent figures that Ariès describes, it is important to note that in the case of recumbent statues from fourteenth- and fifteenth-century Germany, 'les dalles qui les soutiennent n'étaient pas toujours horizontalement couchées sur le sol, mais dressées verticalement sur le mur' ('the stones that bear them were not always laid flat on the ground, but instead might be affixed vertically to a wall').[57] In terms of the iconography of death, the Wolfskehlmeister's upright figures belong to the category of recumbent statues. Beckett's figures are lying down, but this does not contradict the model on which they are based. In choosing to lay his figures on the ground, Beckett ties them to a glyptic representation that expresses the ineluctability of death and the inanity of the human condition more forcefully than the Wolfskehlmeister's statues. Nevertheless, these figures also drag themselves around in mud and excrement and thereby deny the moral significance that lies in their repose – in their horizontal position.

Funerary statues are objects of piety, often representing monarchs who governed by divine right or religious dignitaries. They belong, therefore, in churches. As Michel Vovelle suggests, these statues convey a 'discours sur la mort' ('discourse on death')[58] that varies according to their specific features (and these depend on when and where they were carved). Recumbent statues of sleeping figures (who are nevertheless dead) may express the permanence of fleshly plenitude, but they may also appear to be awaiting resurrection, prematurely arrayed in the *corps glorieux* they will soon acquire. Another category of recumbent statues, with emaciated features and more prevalent in the north of Europe (to which the Wolfskehlmeister's figures belong), offers 'une rude leçon de morale' ('a tough moral lesson')[59] that affirms the precepts of *contemptus mundi* and *memento mori*.

While related to these representations of the dead in physical terms, Beckett's creatures are bereft, at first sight, of religious significance. Indeed, the religious dimension of these creatures' lives is meticulously undermined. Beckett's recumbent figures lie either in filthy beds or flat on the ground: Malone and the narrator of *First Love* never get up, never wash, and relieve themselves (in bed) in a vase or a stew-pot; Macmann, Molloy, Moran and the creatures of *How It Is* lie down in the mud, which the latter also call 'shit'.[60] Murphy is no exception to the rule: his bed is similarly dirty and his place of rest is described as 'a dwelling [...] unfit for human habitation'.[61] There are no signs of the church or of compunction here. Nevertheless, these beings are genuinely humble as they return to the *humus*, which is made of both earth and organic waste. We can identify here a literal but nevertheless extreme rendering of the 'hopelessly humble' character of the statues whose features Beckett's inventions share. To be humble is to act with humility. Etymologically, it is to lower oneself to ground level – to the level of the *humus*. If Beckett's characters are humble, they are 'hopelessly' so. In any case, their humility is not of a religious kind: it involves wallowing in mud and shit. Both narrators and characters have 'collapsed' entirely in order to go as low as they can. They are, moreover, wretched outsiders rather than monarchs or religious dignitaries: the social hierarchy implied by the funerary sculpture is thus turned upside down. They are all blasphemous, they utter obscenities and pour scorn on the concept of eternity. In following the Wolfskehlmeister's model to the letter, then, Beckett nevertheless creates its opposite.

The vision of the world and of humankind that is conveyed by Beckett's narrators could not be further removed from Christian eschatology (the resurrection of *corps glorieux*) and morality (*contemptus mundi* and *memento mori*) as they are expressed in funerary sculpture. Beckett's texts inflict a process of humiliation – in the literal sense of the word – and of secularization on the funerary statue. This process is part of a more general process of bathetic deflation wrought systematically by Beckett's work on the great, the noble and the tragic.[62] In addition to the aforementioned elements, this process is also enacted at the level of the narrators' speech and writing.

For the most part, the protagonists of the texts on which we have been focusing are simultaneously narrators and characters. This double identity is accompanied by a playful use of oral and written codes. While the narrators' monologues possess markedly oral features, they are nevertheless identified in the narrative as written productions. These take the form of jottings in notebooks (*Molloy* and *How It Is*), fictional accounts and reports (*Malone Dies*) or 'writings'.[63] Malone, Moran and Molloy describe themselves as being in the act of writing (the other narrators, while they are all writers, do not describe themselves as such). Murphy, their ancestor, does not write. A relation to writing, which may or may not be a sign of the influence of the Wolfskehlmeister's statues (all of which hold religious books), only exists for Murphy's descendants. Nevertheless, each of Beckett's texts, including *Murphy*, are meditations on the aberrations and failures of their characters and narrators and on the death that eventually takes hold of them. In Beckett's work, the bibles, prayer books and other holy texts clutched by the recumbent figures of traditional funerary iconography are replaced by notebooks.

Holy words are replaced by individual, profane and mortal words. These words are represented as in the process of being written, whereas the words of the Scriptures are simply revealed. The Word of God is thus desacralized: words are no longer transcendent but immanent, events in the here and now of the act of writing. While the contents of the recumbent figures' books and of the narrators' notebooks share similarities (a meditation on death and records of deeds), they are not straightforwardly comparable. On the one hand, holy texts preach virtue, charity and the salvation of the soul; on the other hand, the narrators' notebooks, which are scattered with biblical allusions, record the egotism, lewdness and wanderings of their authors. Moreover, these notes are usually taken in mud or in excrement. Humiliation and secularization are thus inscribed, to the point of sacrilege, in flesh and word, in bodies and texts.

Beckett's works thus humiliate and secularize the religious dimension of the objects of piety (funerary statues) with which they share certain features. In doing so, these texts serve as disenchantments of a relation to being, to writing and to death favoured in the late Middle Ages and in early modern thought. If an influence obtains, it has nevertheless been literally inflected – thrown onto the ground without being entirely obliterated.

In conclusion, while a link between funerary sculpture of the early modern period and Beckett's work can be established, its significance is in need of careful consideration. The protagonists of *Malone Dies*, *First Love*, *Molloy* and *How It Is* all present characteristics that allow us to relate them to the Wolfskehlmeister's statues so admired by Beckett in Würzburg. While the composition of *Murphy* took place before Beckett's discovery of the German sculptor's creations, its eponymous hero already possesses some of their features. Beckett's characters identify themselves with the dead. They are physically decrepit and immobile to the point of petrification. Words on paper are thus related to works of stone, both retrospectively and proleptically. The play of influence is rooted in the existence of innate affinities, but is not limited to it. By having his creatures adopt a prostrate or supine position, Beckett makes them into avatars of recumbent figures. This horizontal projection is accompanied by a return to the *humus* – in the form of mud and bodily waste – which can be understood as a display of literal humility taken to the extreme. Influence is thus literally inflected. In taking the play of influence to its extreme, Beckett's texts corrupt the religious dimension of the objects of piety to which their protagonists are related. The role of writing and speech can be understood in similar terms: wallowing in the mire, Beckett's narrators write in notebooks that replace the holy books clutched by funerary statues. Thus, in his various engagements with funerary sculpture of the late Middle Ages, Beckett effects an ontological shift that has significant repercussions for any representation of the act of writing. Words must now be understood as essentially human: writing is immanent and desacralized.

Notes

1. The diary entry (in Beckett's 'German Diaries') is from 25 February 1937 and is cited by James Knowlson in 'Beckett the Tourist: Bamberg and Würzburg', in *Beckett at 100: Revolving it All*, ed. by Linda Ben-Zvi and Angela Moorjani (Oxford: Oxford University Press, 2008), pp. 21–31 (p. 29).

2. Ibid. Emphasis in original.
3. Ibid., pp. 29–30.
4. Ibid., p. 30.
5. Beckett cited by Knowlson in ibid., pp. 29–30.
6. The Wolfskelmeister's statues in Würzburg hold bibles, but it is not uncommon for funerary statues to clutch psalters (the recumbent statue of Eleanor of Aquitaine in Fontevraud Abbey, for example), prayer books or other holy texts (records of deeds to be presented at the Final Judgement, for example). For a detailed examination of this funerary glyptography, see Philippe Ariès's *Essais sur l'histoire de la mort en Occident du Moyen-Age à nos jours* (Paris: Seuil, 1977), p. 34.
7. 'He started work on *Murphy* in August 1935 and completed it in June 1936'; Ronan McDonald, *The Cambridge Introduction to Samuel Beckett* (Cambridge: Cambridge University Press, 2006), p. 12.
8. Samuel Beckett, *Malone Dies*, in *The Grove Centenary Editions of Samuel Beckett*, ed. by Paul Auster, 4 vols (New York: Grove Press, 2006), II, pp. 171–281 (pp. 187, 188).
9. Ibid., II, p. 177.
10. Ibid., II, p. 236.
11. Samuel Beckett, *First Love*, in *The Grove Centenary Editions of Samuel Beckett*, IV, pp. 229–46 (pp. 233, 246).
12. Samuel Beckett, *Molloy*, in *The Grove Centenary Editions of Samuel Beckett*, II, pp. 1–170 (p. 32).
13. Ibid., II, p. 129.
14. Samuel Beckett, *How It Is*, in *The Grove Centenary Editions of Samuel Beckett*, IV, 409–521 (p. 446). The French original reads: 'une carcasse inerte et muette à jamais aplatie dans la boue'; Samuel Beckett, *Comment c'est* (Paris: Minuit, 1961), p. 82.
15. Beckett, *How It Is*, IV, p. 478.
16. Samuel Beckett, *Murphy*, in *The Grove Centenary Editions of Samuel Beckett*, I, pp. 1–168 (p. 3).
17. Samuel Beckett, *Murphy* (Paris: Minuit, 1951), p. 27. My translation. This sentence, which appears in Beckett's 1951 French translation of his own text, does not appear in the English original of 1938. It would appear, therefore, that Murphy's condition deteriorates over time.
18. Beckett, *Murphy* (*Grove Centenary Editions of Samuel Beckett*), I, p. 4.
19. Ibid., I, p. 14.
20. Beckett, *Malone Dies*, II, p. 180.
21. Ibid., II, p. 179.
22. Beckett, *First Love*, IV, p. 234.
23. Beckett, *Molloy*, II, p. 29.

24. Ibid., II, p. 51.
25. Ibid., II, p. 49.
26. Ibid., II, p. 76.
27. Ibid., II, p. 142.
28. Ibid., II, p. 143.
29. Beckett, *How It Is*, IV, pp. 422, 448.
30. Beckett, *Murphy* (*Grove Centenary Editions of Samuel Beckett*), I, p. 22. In the French version, his face is 'couleur de galet' ('pebble-coloured'); Beckett, *Murphy* (French translation), p. 28.
31. Beckett, *Murphy* (French translation), p. 34.
32. Beckett, *Murphy* (*Grove Centenary Editions of Samuel Beckett*), I, p. 69.
33. Beckett, *Malone Dies*, II, p. 177.
34. Beckett, *How It Is*, IV, p. 468.
35. Beckett, *Molloy*, II, pp. 76–7.
36. Ibid., II, p. 82.
37. Ibid., II, p. 134.
38. Ibid., II, p. 141.
39. Ibid., II, p. 134.
40. Beckett, *Malone Dies*, II, p. 236.
41. Beckett, *Murphy* (*Grove Centenary Editions of Samuel Beckett*), I, p. 3.
42. Ibid., I, p. 16.
43. Beckett, *Malone Dies*, II, p. 180.
44. Beckett, *Molloy*, II, p. 232.
45. Ibid., II, p. 234.
46. Ibid., II, p. 82.
47. Ibid., II, p. 83.
48. Ibid., II, pp. 105–6.
49. Beckett, *Murphy* (*Grove Centenary Editions of Samuel Beckett*), I, pp. 50, 69.
50. Beckett, *First Love*, IV, p. 230.
51. Beckett, *Molloy*, II, p. 129.
52. Beckett, *How It Is*, IV, p. 491. The French original reads: 'où je gisais abandonné' (Beckett, *Comment c'est*, p. 170).
53. Beckett, *How It Is*, IV, p. 469. The French original reads: 'ça ne bouge pas plus qu'un gisant' (Beckett, *Comment c'est*, p. 127).
54. Beckett, *How It Is*, IV, p. 493. The French original reads: 'cent mille gisants collés deux par deux un temps énorme rien ne bouge' (Beckett, *Comment c'est*, p. 174).
55. Philippe Ariès, *Images de l'homme devant la mort* (Paris: Seuil, 1983), p. 61; translated by Janet Lloyd as *Images of Man and Death* (Cambridge, MA: Harvard University Press, 1985), p. 56.
56. Ibid., p. 54; p. 48.
57. Ibid., p. 68; p. 62.

58. Michel Vovelle, *La Mort et l'occident de 1300 à nos jours* (Paris: Gallimard, 1983), p. 220.
59. Ibid., p. 221.
60. Beckett, *How It Is*, IV, p. 446.
61. Beckett, *Murphy* (*Grove Centenary Editions of Samuel Beckett*), I, p. 78.
62. Beckett's affirmation in a letter to Roger Blin that 'nothing is more grotesque than the tragic' suggests that this process is an essential aspect of his work; cited by Deirdre Bair in *Samuel Beckett: A Biography* (London: Simon, 1990), p. 428.
63. Beckett, *First Love*, IV, p. 230.

8
'Périmer d'avance': Blanchot, Derrida and Influence

John McKeane

What is the influence of deconstruction? We can begin to answer this question by highlighting this double genitive's second meaning: beyond whatever influence deconstruction might or might not have had on wider narratives of the period, we can interrogate the particular model of influence at work within deconstructive thought. Given the latter's attention to Heidegger's notion of overcoming metaphysics – and the general prevalence of vanguardist rhetoric in the 1960s – we might initially identify the influence of deconstruction as an overturning or rejection of the past and its influence on us. On closer analysis, however, an alternative narrative emerges according to which deconstruction is not an act of destruction, but rather an ongoing process of suspension, ironization and *mise-en-abyme*. This means that the very notion of rejecting influence must itself be rejected (and so on – the circumlocutions and suspensions of Derrida's writing explore this point *ad infinitum*). We can see this when, picking up an episode in Freud bearing striking similarities to the Oedipal model of the relationship to previous models of authority, Jean-Luc Nancy writes:

> Dans *Psychologie des masses et analyse du moi*, Freud met en scène le premier récitant, le premier mythologue qui raconte à sa horde qu'il a tué le père: récit de l'impossible, puisque le père n'advient que par ce meurtre, lequel par conséquent n'aura jamais tué que l'animal prépaternel.
>
> (In *Group Psychology and the Analysis of the Ego*, Freud sets on stage the first storyteller, the first mythologian, who recounts to the horde that he has killed the father: a tale of the impossible, since the father

only comes about through the murder, in which one therefore will only ever have killed the prepaternal animal.)[1]

In other words, the desire to kill the father (that is, to reject influence) itself represents the greatest danger, the moment when one becomes a symbolic father oneself, establishing a hierarchy that performs violence against what was only an 'animal'. It therefore seems that, if we want to do more than flog a dead horse, we must entertain the possibilities that influence as an opening to the other represents.

In what follows, we shall explore how such an influence of deconstruction is played out in the vicinity of Maurice Blanchot. In place of the model used for example by the work *Heidegger's Children*, however, a generation of thinkers from Foucault to Nancy and beyond could be described as *Blanchot's Orphans*, thus allowing us to maintain a role for an influence that, even in being withdrawn and indirect, nonetheless holds open the possibility of receptivity to the other.[2] More specifically, we shall explore the role of influence at play between the writing of Blanchot and Derrida. It can be seen in the Derrida passage from which our title is drawn: 's'il n'y avait là grossière attribution de maîtrise et si *Le Pas au-delà* ne périmait d'avance telle métaphore, je dirais que jamais, autant qu'aujourd'hui, je ne l'ai imaginé si loin devant nous' ('if this were not a crude attribution of mastery and if the *Step Not Beyond* did not make the very metaphor obsolete in advance, I would say that never, as much as today, have I pictured him so far ahead of us').[3] We shall attempt to unpack what is at stake in the claim that anything might 'périmer d'avance', looking at two instances of influence in order to assess whether any new thinking of influence is made available by the interaction between Blanchot and Derrida. My reasons for calling this an 'interaction between' rather than simply an 'influence over' will be set out as we address the criticisms levelled at Blanchot by Derrida's early texts, and the writer's unusual response, namely in the secondary mode of writing he proposes by reworking earlier pieces. Subsequently, we shall move on to see how this mode of secondary, diffuse writing in turn provokes a response in Derrida's work.

In addition to being a writer of narratives, throughout the 1940s and 1950s Blanchot was one of the leading lights of French literary criticism, exploring a modern and experimental canon, from Kafka to his own friend Bataille, from Lautréamont to Mallarmé, from Hölderlin to Artaud. In the late 1950s and early 1960s, however, his work begins to mutate, leaving behind the distinction between criticism and narrative, becoming politicized and fragmented (he would later write in a letter that 'j'ai été frappé par le "fragment" et à partir de là promis à l'épuisement, voire à l'extermination, de même que H[ölderlin] fut frappé par Apollon').[4] While the mode of criticism from which Blanchot moves away at this time does not seek to read literature within the terms of any particular school of criticism, whether phenomenological, Marxist or psychoanalytic, it did risk establishing the impersonal authority of the literary itself via concepts such as the book (*le livre*), worklessness (*le désœuvrement*) and the one we shall be exploring, madness. The recalibration that takes place within this work is perhaps that impersonality takes on a more supple, open form, seeking out events through which it could renew itself, whether in the political or intellectual domain.

Derrida mentions Blanchot in 'La Parole soufflée', his essay on Artaud published in the winter of 1965.[5] He looks at how the figure of the mad artist, in this case Artaud, has been viewed by criticism. One example given is Blanchot's reading, which Derrida ventriloquizes as follows: 'ce dont Artaud n'est que le témoin, c'est une essence universelle de la pensée. L'aventure totale d'Artaud ne serait que l'index d'une structure transcendantale' ('what Artaud is only the witness to is a universal essence of thought. Artaud's total adventure is presented as only indicating a transcendental structure'). Indeed, in the Blanchot article in question, we can read a discussion of an '"impouvoir", selon [le] mot [d'Artaud], qui est comme essentiel à la pensée' ([a] '"powerlessness", to use [Artaud's] expression, which is almost essential to speech').[6] Derrida goes on to examine similar statements apropos of Hölderlin before describing Blanchot's coupling of Artaud and Hölderlin under the sign of the mad writer as a 'schéma essentialiste' ('essentialist schema').[7] Derrida seems to be questioning the ability of Artaud or Hölderlin (or of any writer about whom these claims are made), as an example or a *'cas'* (*'case'*),[8] to represent other poets as the essence, destiny and truth of poetry. The allegation being made against essentialism is that it prevents the critic from accounting for her own historicity, and that it causes her to see the writer's work in an ahistorical, objective positivity that ignores the conditions of possibility that, instead, always already unwork it.

We should immediately add that on Derrida's reading, one cannot necessarily hope for anything better than to be aware that such exemplarity is flawed. In this vein, he writes that 'nous croyons qu'aucun commentaire ne peut échapper à ces défaites, faute de se détruire comme commentaire' ('we do not believe that any commentary can escape being defeated by these problems, on pain of being destroyed as a commentary').[9] The challenge he presents to Blanchot, then, is not an anti-idealist championing of singularity. This becomes evident when we see Claude Lévesque, questioning Derrida on this text in 1979, raising the possibility that 'pas plus donc que Blanchot, Derrida ne peut éviter la loi universelle: elle est même l'une des deux exigences simultanées qui divisent irrémédiablement tout nom propre et toute autobiographie' ('Derrida, just like Blanchot, found that the universal law applied to him: it is even one of two simultaneous demands that irremediably divide all proper names and all autobiographies'). Derrida's response is to state that

> A la fin du texte, je remets en question l'apparente accusation que je lance contre Blanchot en disant que moi-même je me suis livré à la même opération, c'est-à-dire que j'ai fait un exemple à mon tour et que c'est inévitable. Il y a une rotation qui montre à la fin de 'La Parole soufflée' que j'ai fait, j'ai dû faire exactement ce que, au début, je semblais rapprocher à Blanchot [...] de faire. C'est-à-dire que j'ai encore fait un exemple et que ce geste est irréductible.
>
> (At the end of the text, I call into question again the accusation that I appear to make against Blanchot by saying that I myself have carried out the same operation and that it is an inevitable one. There is a rotation that shows that at the end of 'La Parole soufflée' I did, I must have done what initially I seemed to reproach Blanchot [...] for doing. Which is to say that I have made yet another example and there is no getting beyond this gesture.)[10]

This statement seems to downplay the position taken against Blanchot by the 1965 article; let us therefore return to that text and re-read the original charge. In a note towards the end of his article, Derrida states:

> Pensant au refus crispé de l'œuvre, ne peut-on dire avec la même intonation le contraire de ce que dit Blanchot dans *Le Livre à venir*? Non pas 'naturellement, ce n'est pas une œuvre' mais 'naturellement, ce n'est encore qu'une œuvre'? Dans cette mesure, elle autorise l'effraction du commentaire et la violence de l'exemplification, celle-là même que nous n'avons pu éviter, au moment où nous entendions nous en défendre. Mais peut-être comprenons-nous mieux maintenant la nécessité de cette incohérence.
>
> (Recalling the terse refusal of the work, can we not use the same intonation to say the opposite of what Blanchot says in *The Book to Come*? Not 'naturally, this is not a work' but 'naturally, this is still

only a work'? If we can do this, this intonation allows commentary to break in, allows for the violence of commentary, the same violence that we were not able to avoid, even in the moment when we meant to take precautions against it. But perhaps now we understand better the necessity for this incoherence.)[11]

While it might be necessary at some level to perform a violent, essentializing gesture, a divergence from Blanchot nonetheless remains: the latter's exemplification is not justified because he does not take Artaud as the author of a work ('naturellement, ce n'est pas une œuvre'), but rather as the direct representative of a *désœuvrement* that would not be directly available without the intermediary of the work. The first part of Derrida's point is that such *désœuvrement* cannot exist in itself without the repeatability and transferability that the work represents. The second part is that Blanchot had transferred Artaud and Hölderlin's experience to other writers, even as he denied that such an experience could be transferred, and that it could form the basis of a work, perhaps in a similar way to Viktor Shklovsky's famously contradictory description of *Tristram Shandy* as 'the most typical novel in world literature'.[12]

In line with the ongoing change in his work, which Derrida's criticisms helped to accelerate, Blanchot's response did not consist in a critical article where these points were answered in turn, nor in a reworking of 'La Cruelle Raison poétique' ('Cruel Poetic Reason'), one of the three articles Derrida had mentioned, on its inclusion in the collection *L'Entretien infini* (*The Infinite Conversation*). Instead, where before Artaud and Hölderlin's experiences stood as sweepingly essential to thought and poetry, now the space evacuated by such essentiality similarly goes beyond discussions of these figures.[13] In other words, Blanchot's response to Derrida makes its influence felt throughout *L'Entretien infini*: he removes the term 'essence' from essays on authors as different as Bonnefoy, Levinas, Nietzsche and Weil.[14] However, the significance of these changes can best be seen in a text on Foucault. Here we can read:

> Dans ce livre [*Histoire de la folie à l'âge classique*], **je rappelle d'abord quelle idée marginale est venue à l'expression**: non pas tant l'histoire de la folie qu'une esquisse de ce que pourrait être 'une histoire des *limites* – de ces gestes obscurs, nécessairement oubliés dès qu'accomplis, par lesquels une culture rejette quelque chose qui sera pour elle l'Extérieur'.

> (**I recall first of all which marginal idea came into language in this book** [*Madness and Civilization*]: not so much the history of madness as a sketch of what could be represented by 'a history of *limits* – of those gestures, necessarily forgotten as soon as they are carried out whereby a culture rejects something that will be for it the Exterior'.)[15]

The section I have placed in bold replaces what we read in the 1961 version of the article: 'viennent à l'expression quelques idées essentielles' ('some essential ideas come to language').[16] In this first version, the non-essential (what is excluded by society: madness, unreason) is essential. In the 1969 version of the essay, Blanchot has not just inverted this hierarchy, but displaced it altogether: it is no longer acceptable to take anything to be essential to thought, even what is non-essential. The only further thing to do was to follow a route that has extreme consequences for the view of the critical subject: not to speak *of* madness, but to speak madly.

This mode of writing therefore reverses the normal processes of influence, which now flows upstream, from Derrida to Blanchot. This new mode of secondary writing, not consisting in moving cleanly to a new text, but rather in rewriting previous ones tacitly, though extensively and tellingly, also seeps beyond the boundaries of *L'Entretien infini*. A year later in 1970, for instance, Blanchot gives expression to this thought of madness as something that criticism cannot say in a three-page supplement added to the republication of 'La Folie par excellence' ('Madness par excellence'), one of the articles that Derrida had criticized. Here he writes:

> La folie serait ainsi un mot en perpétuelle disconvenance avec lui-même et interrogatif de part en part, tel qu'il mettrait en question sa possibilité et, par lui, la possibilité du langage qui le comporterait, donc l'interrogation, elle aussi, en tant qu'elle appartient au jeu du langage. Dire: Hölderlin est fou, c'est dire: est-il fou? Mais, à partir de là, c'est rendre la folie à ce point étrangère à toute affirmation qu'elle ne saurait trouver un langage où s'affirmer sans mettre celui-ci sous la menace de la folie: le langage, comme tel, déjà devenu fou.

> (Madness would thus be a word in perpetual disagreement with itself, thoroughly interrogatory, and such that it calls its own possibility into question as well as the possibility of the language that carries it, namely interrogation, insofar as the latter is part of language. To

say: Hölderlin is mad, is to say: Is he mad?' From here it follows that madness is rendered so foreign to affirmation that it could not be affirmed in any language without placing that language under the threat of madness: language, as such, as already having gone mad.)[17]

In other words, the utter foreignness of madness means that anyone attempting to speak of madness will instead end up speaking madly. And this means not finally speaking of the word madness on its own terms, but according to a 'perpetual disagreement with itself', less *difference* as the static mode of being of what is different than the deferring movement of *différance*. This is a difference that differs even from itself. One must therefore be attentive to the questioning of 'Is he mad?' already suggested by or reverberating within the affirmation that 'Hölderlin is mad'. While this may seem to take away the urgency of engaging with madness as a phenomenon affecting particular people or writers, it ultimately represents a more ambitious project: that of affirming that 'le langage, comme tel, [est] déjà devenu fou' ('language, as such [has] already gone mad'). This project can be seen in a 1969 version of a text where what he had written in 1961 is expressly deleted: 'A la rigueur, la folie peut devenir objet de raison, mais elle ne peut être sujet, elle ne doit pas parler en première personne' ('Strictly speaking, madness can be the object of reason, but it cannot be the subject, it must not speak in the first person').[18]

Beyond the removal of the word 'essence' from *L'Entretien infini* and the supplement to 'La Folie par excellence', Blanchot's indirect response to Derrida also consists in accelerating the change in his mode of writing from criticism to fragmentation. This can be seen in *Le Pas au-delà* of 1973: one of its fragments consists in the republication of the three-page supplement that had been added to 'La Folie par excellence'; while it is reproduced almost verbatim, the main article has dropped away, making this fragment a pure supplement, a secondariness no longer preceded by anything primary. This seems to be crucial for the author's approach to madness, which was no longer to be monumentalized into an essential experience, but instead approached in its unavailability to rational analysis, or in the words that are added to this fragment: 'Folie: supposons un langage [...] où la recherche effrayée, interdite, de ce seul mot perdu et constamment interrogateur, suffirait, orientant toutes les possibilités de parole, à soumettre le langage au seul mot qui l'aurait déserté' ('Madness: let us imagine a language [...] where the frightened, disconcerted search – a search for this single ever-questioning word that has been lost – would suffice to submit language to the only word that has deserted it, and in this way would give orientation to all possible speech').[19] The aspects of this approach that make it more sensitive and sustainable than movements such as anti-psychiatry or mad pride can be seen when we read:

> Supposons une interruption en quelque sorte absolue et absolument neutre; [...] appelons-la l'ultime, l'hyperbolique. Aurions-nous avec elle atteint la rupture qui nous délivrerait, fût-ce hyperboliquement, non seulement de toute raison (ce serait peu), mais de toute déraison, c'est-à-dire de cette raison qu'est encore la folie?
>
> (Let us imagine an interruption that would be somehow absolute and absolutely neutral; [...] let us call it the ultimate, the hyperbolical interruption. Would it allow us to attain the rupture capable of delivering us, even if hyperbolically, not only from all reason (this would be small beer), but from all unreason, that is from this reason that madness remains?)[20]

Le Pas au-delà allows us to move on to the second key scene in which Blanchot and Derrida interact, in which the older writer's openness to the influence of an emergent one itself comes to influence a thinker who by the mid-1970s was enjoying considerable success. We shall look at Derrida's text 'Pas' of 1976, a title whose polyphony in French (it can be translated as not, step, pace, nots, steps, paces, for example) repeats and rebroadcasts that of *Le Pas au-delà*, meaning both that there is no beyond ([*il n'y a*] *pas* [*d'*]*au-delà*) – and that this realization itself is a step beyond, a *pas au-delà*.[21]

In the introduction to *Parages*, the collection of texts responding to Blanchot, we are told that the dialogue form of 'Pas' presents 'deux voix dont l'une, manifestement masculine, se prend parfois aux pièges de l'autorité enseignante ou magistrale alors que l'autre, plutôt féminine, cite à comparaître la citation qui l'appelle – et dit *viens*' ('two voices, one of which, manifestly masculine, sometimes falls into the trap of being didactic or of lecturing from a position of authority, while the other, which is more feminine, summonses the very citation that is used to call on it – and says *come*').[22] The masculine voice dominates for much of the early part of the text, limiting the feminine voice's interventions to one line, and thus thematizing the French *cours magistral* or lecture, which is striking given that Blanchot, whom it addresses, maintained an unwavering distance from teaching and the university. Despite or due to this, his influence has made Derrida go back to school, which does not prevent the feminine voice's question from suggesting that such institutional authority falls short of intimacy with the author being discussed: '– Oseriez-vous tutoyer Blanchot?' ('– Would you dare to address Blanchot as *tu*?').[23] This didactic scenario becomes clearer when we realize that the feminine voice's intervention 'summonses the very citation that is used to call on it – and says *come*'. The text discusses the triple origin of this *come*, from the Blanchot narratives *L'Arrêt de mort* (*Death Sentence*), *Celui qui ne m'accompagnait pas* (*He Who Did Not Accompany Me*) and *L'Attente l'oubli* (*Awaiting Oblivion*), where in each case it represents a different appeal or opening to a feminine other that at times appears as a woman character, at other times as thought (*la pensée*) or speech (*la parole*). 'Pas' uses the feminine voice's appropriation of this invocation to explore the same questions of singularity and exemplarity, transferability and horizons of expectation that were at play in the debate over Artaud and Hölderlin. This can be seen in the following exchange, in which the feminine voice speaks first:

> – La citation me blesse, éternellement. J'ai toujours le sentiment que vous me parlez de son nom, depuis son nom, en son nom. Si vous dîtes par exemple...
> – Je t'aime.
> – Oui, si vous me le dîtes, que vous m'appelez, sera-ce moi, l'unique?
>
> (– Citation wounds me, eternally. I always feel that you are telling me about its name, beginning with its name, speaking in its name. If you say for instance...
> – I love you.
> – Yes, if you say that to me, if you call out to me, will I be the only one?)[24]

The feminine voice chides the dominant one, addressing Derrida's infamously circuitous and playful writing: '– Vous allez faire ce que [Blanchot] ne fait jamais: jouer d'une insistance indiscrète sur la langue, exhiber une maîtrise économe, vous rendre intraduisible dans le propos même' ('– You are about to do what [Blanchot] never does: use an indiscreet insistency to play on language, exhibit an economy of mastery, and make your very proposition untranslatable').[25] In other words, Blanchot is here being invoked as a writer who resists Derrida's trademark style and provokes a form of self-criticism by the latter. Interestingly for our current investigation into influence, therefore, the response that comes is: 'Le texte qu'il aura signé, sans signer, est l'un des très rares devant lequel mon retrait, ma faiblesse, celle dont tu me parles et qui peut prendre la forme d'une indiscrétion de maîtrise, je les prenne sur moi et m'en réjouisse. Pourquoi pas?' ('The text that he will have signed, without signing, is one of the very few that cause me to assume and celebrate – why not? – my withdrawal and my weakness – the weakness of which you speak to me and which can take the form of a masterful indiscretion').[26] While it would be an elementary error to identify unambiguously this responding, masculine voice as Derrida's, we can say that the text does much to suggest such a link playfully, if only to better place itself beyond the authority of its author (for instance by the tacit quotation of Blanchot's *L'Arrêt de mort*).[27]

Approaching the influence (etymologically: the influx) of another text via the motif of quotation also allows us to study influence as a model informing Derrida's reading of Blanchot. Many of the two interlocutors' interventions consist only of quotations from the *récits* mentioned above or from *Le Pas au-delà*, often running to several pages and with many of the same passages being repeated numerous times, or doubly quoted, throughout 'Pas'. Derrida's text was preceded on its publication in 1976 by the author's response to a letter from the journal's editor, a response consisting in two short Blanchot passages and then the following words: 'En sa version première et inachevée, voici le fragment d'un texte que j'écris "en ce moment". [Il est] [i]ndirect et, autant que possible, fictif' ('In an initial and unfinished version, here is the fragment of a text that I am "currently" writing. [It is] indirect and, as far as possible, fictitious').[28] The inverted commas around 'en ce moment' question the ability of any particular moment, of any particular quotation, to reproduce what 'Pas' calls 'l'imprésentable temps du récit' ('the unpresentable time of the *récit*').[29] Presenting an amalgam of passages in this way refers to a similar practice in Blanchot's work of the 1960s, and thus quotes him, as it were, twice. The movement that took Blanchot out of the domain of essayistic, critical writing did not simply abandon the reflexes of that domain, but rather pushed them to the extreme of their own logic. In other words, the practice of quotation, where notionally the critic refers back impartially to major moments in a text, establishing the discursive corpus before proposing her own reading, in fact already determines one's argument. So far so unsurprising, one might say, but this is pushed to the fore in *L'Entretien infini*, whether in a critical essay on Jena Romanticism,[30] or in a dialogue at moments composed entirely of Beckett quotations (which Blanchot places in italics):

– Mais quelle est cette voix?
– A la fin, il y a une sorte d'hypothèse: c'est peut-être la voix de tous, la parole impersonnelle, errante, continue, simultanée, successive, dans laquelle chacun de nous, sous la fausse identité qu'il s'attribue, découpe ou projette la part qui lui revient, *rumeur transmissible à l'infini dans les deux sens*, procession qui, ne s'arrêtant pas, réserve une certaine possibilité de communication: *le voilà donc ce pas des nôtres nous y voilà enfin qui s'écoute soi-même et en prêtant l'oreille à notre murmure ne fait que la prêter à une histoire de son cru mal inspirée mal dite et chaque fois si ancienne si oubliée que peut lui paraître conforme celle qu'à la boue nous lui murmurons*
– *et cette vie dans le noir dans la boue ses joies et peines voyages intimités et abandons telle que d'une seule voix sans cesse brisée tantôt une moitié d'entre nous tantôt l'autre nous l'exhalons quand ça cesse de haleter celle à peu de choses près qu'il avait formulée*
– *et dont sans se lasser tous les quelque vingt ou quarante ans au dire de certains de ses chiffres il rappelle à nos abandonnés les grandes lignes*

(– But what is this voice?
– At the end, there is a sort of hypothesis: it is perhaps everybody's voice: impersonal, errant, continuous, simultaneous, successive speech, from which each of us selects, onto which each of us projects what is relevant to him and the false identity he adopts, a murmuring that can be transmitted infinitely and endlessly, a procession that, never stopping, reserves a certain possibility of communication: *here he is then this not one of us here we are finally here he is listening to himself and in lending his ear to our murmuring he is only lending it to a story of his ill inspired and ill said devising and each time anew so ancient and so forgotten that it can seem to him to be consistent with mud we murmur to him*
– *and this life in the dark in the mud his sins voyages intimacies and abandonments such as ceaselessly from a single broken voice now one half of us now the other half we exhale it when its panting ceases the one that he had formulated give or take*
– *and of whose main points he reminds those that we have abandoned every twenty or forty years according to some of his figures*)[31]

Derrida's text not only presents the relatively straightforward influence of Blanchot by quoting him, but extends the latter's own thinking – its hyperbolization or ironization – of influence by declaring a fragmentary bundle of quotations to be an original text.

That 'Pas' should be a reading, rewriting, quotation, citation or recitation of Blanchot's early *récits*, of the quotation chains and of *Le Pas au-delà*, is not so idiosyncratic as it might appear, because the 1973 work itself proposes a return to the early fiction. After *L'Entretien infini* had closed with a note presenting its chapters as 'déjà posthumes' ('already posthumous'), Blanchot presents a backwards view over the totality of his writing career: the first line of narrative he ever published, 'Thomas s'assit et regarda la mer' ('Thomas sat down and looked at the sea') from *Thomas l'obscur* (*Thomas the Obscure*) of 1941, is crystallized into the expression 'il – la mer' ('he – the sea') at the beginning of *Le Pas au-delà*. Thus the fragmentary form of this work at once attempts to interrupt the continuity inherent in narrative, and to account for the repetitive compulsion to narrate, this latter giving rise to various narrative threads running through the book (one of them presents a river flooding through a study). The importance of the river and the sea is taken up by Derrida's approach to Blanchot's text as something as formless as water, as a medium in which the various propositions and fragments are dissolved. The text's main characteristic is the repetition of fragments, which could be seen as a lapping of waves. Derrida writes, for instance:

> *Eau:* je prononce ainsi pour nommer à la fois la lettre, la syllabe ou le mot (nom ou élément du nom) et la chose en ce passage où ils coulent les uns dans les autres. Et dans son texte si régulièrement, immensément, démesurément. Nous ne cesserons pas de nous y retrouver, de nous y perdre, de nous y noyer.
>
> (*Eau:* I pronounce it thus in order to name at once the letter, the syllable and the word (the noun or noun-ending) on the one hand, and the thing on the other, in this passage where they flow into one another. And they do so in [Blanchot's] text so regularly, immensely, measurelessly. We will ceaselessly find ourselves back in it, get lost in it, drown in it.)[32]

Here and elsewhere, Derrida's reading is related to the experience of drowning, which is not to say that mentions of baptism and rebirth are absent from 'Pas'. However, perhaps the most significant presence of water lies in the motif of drifting, *dérive*. He writes:

> La dérive, certes, met en garde contre toutes les sécurités de l'ancrage, du rivage, de la propriété, mais elle met en garde, justement, et garde

encore, peut-être, contre ce qui arrive, le pire ou le meilleur, venant d'en face ou de l'abîme, au centre sans fond du centre. 'Dérivant sans rivage' (*Le Pas au-delà*).

(Drifting, of course, warns us against all the certainties of being anchored, of the shore, of property, but precisely it warns us against, cautions us against what happens, for better or worse, coming directly towards us or from the abyss, to the ever more central centre. 'Drifting without shore' (*The Step Not Beyond*).)[33]

One therefore drifts in ignorance of either shore, in an indeterminate middleness. We could say that Derrida's drifting meditations on the term *dérive* in 'Pas', whereby he explores nothing other than the derivative as an aspect of influence, form a response both to the indeterminate movement created between the fragments of *Le Pas au-delà* and to the thinking of madness that Blanchot developed after the criticisms of the mid-1960s, where one must be wary of arriving at a self-identical other shore of 'cette raison qu'est encore la folie'. To finish, then, we have seen two configurations whereby influence can have validity beyond the authority of the writing subject: first with Blanchot responding to a younger writer's criticisms, and secondly in Derrida's thematization of Blanchot's influence, which provokes a questioning of the idiosyncratic writing on which his own burgeoning reputation in the late 1970s was based. These are some of the implications of thinking influence as an influx or rising flood. *Après 'moi', le déluge.*

Notes

1. Jean-Luc Nancy, *L'Adoration (déconstruction du christianisme, 2)* (Paris: Galilée, 2010), p. 146. All translations are my own.
2. Richard Wolin, *Heidegger's Children: Hannah Arendt, Karl Löwith, Hans Jonas and Herbert Marcuse* (Princeton, NJ: Princeton University Press, 2001).
3. Jacques Derrida, 'Pas', in *Parages* (Paris: Galilée, 2003), pp. 17–108 (p. 51).
4. 'I have been struck by the "fragment" and from this moment on, given over to exhaustion, even extermination, like H[ölderlin] being struck by Apollo'; Maurice Blanchot, *Lettres à Vadim Kozovoï suivi de La Parole ascendante*, ed. by Denis Aucouturier (Houilles: Manucius, 2009), p. 77.
5. In Alan Bass's translation *Writing and Difference* (London: Routledge, 1978), the text's title is not translated, a decision doubtless taken in the light of its ambiguity, given that it means both 'whispered speech' and, calked on *le souffleur* or the prompt in the theatre, 'prompted speech'.

6. Jacques Derrida, *L'Écriture et la différence* (Paris: Seuil, 1967), p. 256; Maurice Blanchot, *Le Livre à venir* (Paris: Gallimard, 1959), p. 53.
7. Derrida, *L'Écriture et la différence*, p. 257.
8. Ibid., p. 255. Emphasis in original.
9. Ibid., p. 260.
10. Claude Lévesque and Jacques Derrida in Eugenio Donato, Jacques Derrida et al., 'Table ronde sur l'autobiographie', in *L'Oreille de l'autre: otobiographies, transferts, traductions. Textes et débats avec Jacques Derrida*, ed. by Claude Lévesque and Christie McDonald (Montréal: VLB, 1982), pp. 57–121 (pp. 103, 106).
11. Derrida, *L'Écriture et la différence*, p. 290.
12. Viktor Shklovsky, quoted in Emily Finer, *Turning into Sterne: Viktor Shklovskii and Literary Reception* (Oxford: Legenda, 2010), p. 2.
13. Michael Holland suggests that a shift in Blanchot's writing had already broadly occurred by the time Derrida's criticisms (in 1965, of texts from the 1950s) were made; see 'The Time of his Life', *Paragraph*, 30.3 (November 2007), 46–66 (p. 54). As Holland points out, as early as 1960 one can find Blanchot writing of a '– Parole différante, qui porte de-ci de-là, et elle-même différant de parler' ('– Differing speech, which carries us here and there, and itself deferring speaking') in *L'Entretien infini* (Paris: Gallimard, 1969), p. 40. However, as we shall see shortly, the change in Blanchot's writing is ongoing, providing impetus to the rewriting of earlier texts in *L'Entretien infini* and beyond.
14. Derrida refers to Blanchot's changes in *Résistances: de la psychanalyse* (Paris: Galilée, 1996), pp. 89–146 (p. 80).
15. Blanchot, *L'Entretien infini*, p. 292. Emphasis in original.
16. Maurice Blanchot, 'Le Grand Renfermement', *Nouvelle Revue Française*, 106 (October 1961), 676–86 (p. 679).
17. Maurice Blanchot, 'La Folie par excellence', in Karl Jaspers and Maurice Blanchot, *Strindberg et Van Gogh, Swedenborg et Hölderlin* (Paris: Minuit, 1970), pp. 9–32 (pp. 30–1). Emphasis in original. The first version of Blanchot's article appeared in *Critique*, 45 (February 1951), 99–118.
18. Blanchot, 'Le Grand Renfermement', p. 683. The passage that had contained these words is reprinted in *L'Entretien infini*, p. 296.
19. Blanchot, *Le Pas au-delà*, p. 65.
20. Blanchot, *L'Entretien infini*, p. 111.
21. Given these difficulties of translation, I have left the title of the text as 'Pas' when I refer to it.
22. Derrida, 'Pas', p. 14. Emphasis in original.
23. Ibid., p. 24.
24. Ibid., p. 103.

25. Ibid., p. 34.
26. Ibid.
27. 'Ce malheur je le prends sur moi et je m'en réjouis sans mesure' ('I take this affliction upon myself and I celebrate it without measure'); Maurice Blanchot, L'Arrêt de mort (Paris: Gallimard, 1948), p. 127.
28. Derrida, 'Pas', p. 18.
29. Ibid., p. 95.
30. See Blanchot, L'Entretien infini, pp. 515–27.
31. Ibid., pp. 483–4.
32. Derrida, 'Pas', p. 37.
33. Ibid., p. 60.

9
Figuring Influence: Some Influential Metaphors in Derrida, Valéry and Freud

Paul Earlie

In the first year of the last decade of his life, Paul Valéry contributed a three-page preface to an unusual collection of essays. The slim brochure, commissioned and published by Source Perrier, aimed to extol the virtues of the famous mineral water, chronicling the history of the spring itself, its therapeutic benefits and the precise rituals that should accompany its consumption.[1] Eschewing such commerciality, and without favouring any particular source or origin, Valéry's 'Louanges de l'eau' ('In Praise of Water') is a celebratory treatise on the wider cultural and metaphorical significance of water. Applauding the 'divine lucidité' ('divine clarity') of this 'merveilleux agent de la vie' ('magnificent agent of life'), his text offers a fascinating account of the mythological status that water has assumed in the Western tradition.[2]

In its fascination with the prevalence of aquatic figures in everyday language, Valéry's preface anticipates a preoccupation with metaphor evident in many of Derrida's earliest texts. It is this anticipation that provides the impetus for Derrida's 1971 lecture, 'Qual Quelle: les sources de Valéry' ('Qual Quelle: Valéry's Sources'), first delivered at Johns Hopkins University in commemoration of the centennial of the writer's birth. Noting the compulsive character of a 'surabondance thématique' ('thematic overabundance') of tropes of water, sources and origins in Valéry's work, Derrida here offers what seems like a psychoanalytic reading of the writer's aversion to two of his most influential precursors: Nietzsche and Freud.[3] Valéry repeats these figures of origin obsessively, or so Derrida argues, in order to stress the purity and creative originality of his own intellectual resources.

If both thinkers agree that there is nothing accidental about a language 'plein des louanges de l'EAU' ('brimming with praise for WATER'),[4] it is only in Derrida's work that this observation is accorded a symptomatic value. The greater part of his essay on Valéry is concerned with uncovering the subterranean channels that link the metaphorization of water and the privilege our culture accords to values of truth, unity, purity and originality. In an apparent paradox, Derrida argues that the literal meaning of the word 'source' derives from its metaphorical value, thus calling into question the possibility of a distinction between what is original and what is derivative. Hence, at the lecture's outset, Derrida advises his audience to begin with 'les tours, allégories, figures, métaphores' ('the turns of speech, the allegories, figures, metaphors') already at work in Valéry's text, rather than with the text's supposedly 'literal' meaning.[5]

Following this example, I propose to analyse two recurring figures of influence in Derrida's own work in order to interrogate what deconstruction can tell us about the nature of one thinker's influence on another. I have chosen these metaphors because they seem to me to exemplify most clearly the dual structure that Derrida identifies at the heart of every relationship of influence. The first metaphor, already mentioned, concerns an apparently irreducible relationship between the question of influence and analogies of streams, rivers, sources and cycles, which I will analyse chiefly in relation to Derrida's essay 'Qual Quelle'. I hope to show in my reading of this text how Derrida's notion of 'espacement' ('spacing') can be seen to complicate, if not compromise, the possibility of the coherent transmission of concepts from one thinker to another. This is because, as I argue, the logic underlying Derrida's notion of spacing posits that a past origin (or source) can only be constituted 'after' an initial and irreducible temporo-spatial difference or delay. This inability to grasp a supposedly authentic origin without the intermediary glaze of the present I examine under the heading 'retrojective influence'.

The second influence-metaphor I have chosen to analyse appears later in Derrida's career. The most significant discussion of this analogy occurs in his 1995 text, *Mal d'archive* (*Archive Fever*), a work that bears the crucial subtitle 'une impression freudienne' ('a Freudian impression').[6] The metaphorical 'impression' used by Derrida to describe the continuing influence of psychoanalysis on our thinking today plays a contrapuntal role in his thinking of influence. I read *Mal d'archive* as a text centrally concerned with the future of Freudian concepts. I analyse this emphasis on the future influence of Freud's work under the heading 'prospective influence'. Since common conceptions of influence tend to emphasize only a single intellectual trajectory or lineage (that is, from past to present), I hope to show how Derrida's unique thinking of temporality can help us to think about influence in a way that does justice to the complex and nuanced issues it raises.

Retrojective Influence

It is perhaps not surprising that Harold Bloom's early work on influence abounds with references to the work of his Yale contemporary of the time, Jacques Derrida.[7] Both theorists rely on something like a Freudian framework in their understanding of anxieties of influence. If for Bloom the anxiety of influence results from a quasi-Oedipal relationship between the poet and his precursor-father, for Derrida anxiety is the inevitable consequence of spacing; that is, the irreducible interval that makes of the past (and therefore of the self) an other.[8] Hence, the critic's anxiety faced with the concept of influence (and its relatively under-theorized status in literary studies today)[9] can be taken as resulting, at least in part, from the anxious suspicion of an ineradicable difference separating the past inscription from its 'present' interpretation (*différance*).[10] When we take into account the handful of studies that have ventured a genuine *theory* of artistic influence (as opposed to exploring a particular example of an influence relationship or a more generalized theory of intertextuality), Bloom's much-maligned work on the antagonistic relationship between the apprentice-poet and his precursor seems all the more audacious and sophisticated.

It is through an encounter between Derrida's notion of spacing and the concept of influence, I argue, that we can shed light on the latter's 'retrojective' character. The verb 'to retroject' signifies the action of 'projecting backwards', an illumination of what lies behind from the vantage point of the present. By extension, to retroject signifies 'to apply or attribute (a concept, state of affairs, etc.) to an earlier time or situation' (*OED*). Precisely what is at stake in a retrojective view of influence can be gleaned from an example cited by the *OED*. The critic John Sutherland writes, in his 'Introduction' to the Trollope novel, that 'the psychopathology of *He Knew He Was Right* is as mid-Victorian as its creator. We gain nothing by retrojecting Freudian or Laingian notions into the narrative as some critics have, thinking Trollope the greater in proportion to his being atypical of his time'.[11] As we shall see, Sutherland's easy confidence in the possibility of reawakening Trollope's mid-Victorian psychology (one that is not contaminated by the influence of psychoanalysis on present-day thinking) would not be shared by Derrida. To assert such a structural possibility is to deny what remains for Derrida an irreducible feature of temporality and the construction of meaning: the retrojective illumination of the past by the present moment.

This latter conclusion is the dominant theoretical thread of Derrida's lecture on Valéry. The concept of influence is here signalled from the outset as problematic, with Derrida careful to note that he will not follow 'ce que les historiens nommeraient peut-être les influences [...] vers "les sources" cachées, les origines proches ou détournées, présumées ou vérifiées d'une "oeuvre" voire d'une "pensée"' ('what historians might name "influences" [...] upstream towards their hidden "sources", the near or distant, presumed or verified, origins of a "work", that is of a "thought"').[12] Rather, he will question the very possibility of an original source of influence. Most of the first half of the essay is concerned with an analysis of the repetition of water images in Valéry's work. We have already seen how this thematic 'surabondance' ('overabundance') was reflected in Valéry's Perrier preface. Valéry's attachment to these figures of influence is important for Derrida because it functions as symptomatic of Valéry's immersion, both conscious and unconscious, in a metaphysical culture stressing the twin values of originarity (and consequently originality) and presence. It is because of the logocentric character of our 'metaphysics of presence' that we continue to insist on the unassailable possibility of reconstructing Valéry's sources and influences (for example from his famous *Cahiers*). The notion of spacing that Derrida elaborates in his lecture on Valéry, however, will come to disrupt such assurance.

In 'Qual Quelle', two versions of the same 'source' metaphor symptomize this metaphysical privileging of origins. The first concerns the possibility of returning to a temporally linear origin through traces (for example written traces), in the same way that one can trace the course of a river back to its source or wellspring. Derrida refers to such a metaphor when he refuses to follow 'ce que les historiens nommeraient peut-être les influences [...] vers "les sources" cachées ('what historians might name influences [...] upstream towards their hidden "sources"'),[13] thus revealing the essential complicity between aquatic metaphors of linearity (the river runs from original source to 'mouth') and the faith we evince in unproblematic notions of lineage and inheritance. The second metaphorical symptom concerns the figure of the circuit; that is, an uninterrupted circle of influence best analogized in the metaphor of the water cycle. In 'Qual Quelle', Derrida refers several times to the value of circuity, for example when speaking of the difference between his own meditation on the question of sources and that of Valéry: 'l'anneau de cette réflexion ne se fermera peut-être' ('perhaps we will not close this reflection in ring form').[14]

As one of the most fundamental notions in the conceptual apparatus of deconstruction, the concept of spacing that Derrida elaborates in 'Qual Quelle' is designed to displace the confidence in originarity that both of these figural analogies support. Derrida argues that a past trace can only be deciphered in the present through, and indeed in spite of, a minimal differential interval separating the past-'present' of inscription from the present-'present' of interpretation. At its most fundamental, the notion of *différance* is an attempt to come to terms with the irreducibility of such an interval.[15]

Derrida broaches the topic of spacing at the beginning of his lecture on Valéry, where he refers to his awareness of a very concrete interval of spacing. Not having returned to Valéry's texts for some years, he admits being struck by their surprising strangeness. This leads him to pose the question of what exactly spacing is and how it affects our relationship to the text: 'A quelles lois obéissent les re-naissances, les re-découvertes, les occultations aussi, l'éloignement ou la réévaluation d'un texte dont on voudrait naïvement croire, sur la foi d'une signature ou d'une institution qu'il reste le même, à soi constamment identique?' ('What laws do these rebirths, rediscoveries, and occultations too, obey, the distancing or re-evaluation of a text that one naively would like to believe, having put one's faith in a signature or an institution, always remains the same, constantly identical to itself?').[16] For Derrida, the concept of spacing aims at understanding why a past origin is always structurally modified by its relationship to the present. What is 'secondary', or derivative, once again constitutes its supposedly 'primary' origin.

Since this inverted primary–secondary structure of spacing is valid for signification in general, the same structure is at work in every relationship of intellectual influence, whether what is at stake is the origin of a particular motif, image or concept. The primary source is conditioned and accessible only through its derivative. Spacing therefore disturbs the established hierarchy of a commonsensical approach to the question of influence, which tends to emphasize only a single trajectory from the past to the present. A retrojective view of influence calls into question this unidirectional theory of temporal inheritance.

As an irreducible and unconditional structure of experience, the notion of spacing leads to an unavoidable difficulty that must be negotiated in every deconstructive reading: given that the past cannot be wholly reawakened in an original form, does it not follow that we can 'say anything' about the textual origin in question? Contrary to the way in which his thinking has been caricatured, Derrida does not deny the value, and necessity, of attempting to reawaken the original intentions of past inscriptions. The past endures in the form of a trace, but it is and was never 'present' as such. If it can be reawakened, it can only be reawakened in a form that *differs*, however minimally, from its 'original' form.[17] What is pivotal, however, is that our awareness of the retrojective influence we exert on the past must call for a conception of responsibility in reading. Such responsibility insists that the greater our awareness of our own retrojection, the more responsible our reading and the closer we arrive at the origin as such, even if a total justice towards the past can only be conceived of asymptotically.

An excellent example of Derrida's emphasis on responsibility in our interpretation of past traces occurs in *La Carte postale* (*The Post Card*), during a passage in which he alights on a (then) recently published French translation of Marx and Engels' *German Ideology*. The translation renders an injustice both to the specificity of Marx and Engels' text and to the specificity of deconstruction precisely through the violence of retrojective influence outlined above. This movement occurs in a translation of the German 'aufgelöst werden können' by the French 'peuvent être déconstruite' ('can be deconstructed').[18] Without the slightest explanation, Derrida points out, the French translation of the German phrase was modified, diverging considerably from previous versions that had translated the term 'aufgelöst' – 'fidèlement' ('faithfully'), Derrida suggests – by 'résolu' ('resolved') and 'dissous' ('dissolved'). The irresponsibility involved in such a translation must not be underestimated because 'l'amalgame une fois accompli, l'appropriation incorporée, on laisse entendre que la "déconstruction" est destinée à rester limitée à la "critique intellectuelle" des superstructures. Et on fait comme si Marx l'avait déjà dit' ('once the amalgamation is accomplished, the appropriation incorporated, it is implied that "deconstruction" is destined to remain limited to the "intellectual critique" of superstructures. And this is put as if Marx had already said it').[19] In this way, the singularity of both Marxism and deconstruction is effaced. This short example bears out Derrida's emphasis on the necessity of a responsible reading, one that is intrinsically linked to an awareness (albeit an irreducibly limited awareness) of the influence that the present moment exerts on our interpretation of the past.

Prospective Influence

The consequences of spacing, however, are not simply negative. If spacing prevents the ideal repetition of past insights, it also opens up the possibility of creative difference, in which old concepts are inscribed within new temporo-spatial contexts. In what follows, I argue that Derrida's *Mal d'archive*, through its lengthy account of archiving, responsibility and the future of Freudian concepts, can be said to take account of this paradox of influential relationships. In doing so, I highlight the central difference between Derrida's earlier text on Valéry (published in 1972) and his later *Mal d'archive* (published in 1995): a metaphorical and theoretical shift in the way influence is conceived. The earlier critique of fluvial tropes of influence is abandoned in favour of a new figure of inheritance, the importance of which is signalled in the book's subtitle: 'une impression freudienne'.

The context of this shift is worth elaborating. *Mal d'archive* was originally delivered as part of a colloquium entitled 'Memory: The Question of Archives' held at the Freud Museum in London in 1995, in the wake of a number of controversies that dogged the Freud Archives during the 1980s and 1990s.[20] These controversies no doubt contributed to a central theme of Derrida's address: the notion of the responsible reading of archival traces. Derrida examines this theme through a reading of a recent contribution to the ongoing interpretation of the Freud archives, Josef Hayim Yerushalmi's *Freud's Moses*.[21] Drawing on newly discovered archival material, Yerushalmi's book argues that Freud's work was indelibly influenced by his Jewish background. For Derrida, however, Yerushalmi's methodological precautions are not enough to allay the suspicion that his reading of Freud's texts has been excessive, if not violent.

We can begin to understand what is at stake in a concept like the 'impression freudienne' by analysing the chief objection that Derrida brings before Yerushalmi's book. Derrida argues that Yerushalmi's text contradicts itself: on the one hand, it insists on the necessity of the historian's objectivity or distance from the object to be studied; on the other hand, it frequently relies on the luxury ('luxe') of psychoanalytic concepts in order to advance its argument. Yerushalmi cites Freud's turn to biblical themes late in life (in *Moses and Monotheism*) as an example of the psychoanalytic concept of 'deferred obedience' to the dead father.[22] This methodological difficulty occurs because Yerushalmi is unwilling to admit that his work has been irrevocably influenced by the psychoanalytic revolution, that it has already been marked in advance by the Freudian impression. In contrast to Yerushalmi, Derrida not only begins by asserting the indelibility of Freud's breakthrough, he also goes one step further: weaving psychoanalytic concepts into its very fabric, the exemplarity of *Mal d'archive* (at least within the Derridean corpus) lies in its willingness to emphasize what Derrida explicitly calls 'un mode qui croise, d'une façon, la déconstruction et la psychanalyse' ('a mode that in a certain sense crosses psychoanalysis with deconstruction').[23]

As in 'Qual Quelle', Derrida begins with a metaphor. The metaphor of 'impression' is chosen because, like the figure of the 'source' before it, it conceals an underlying logocentric bias regarding the notion of influence.[24] As in English, the French 'impression' can indicate the exact moment of imprinting, thus providing Derrida with a means of examining the privilege that the metaphysics of presence accords to the *punctum* of the present moment. The metaphor recurs consistently throughout his career, but returns with particular force in *Mal d'archive*, where Derrida is concerned to dispel the myth of 'l'unicité de l'imprimante-imprimée, de l'impression et de l'empreinte, de la pression et sa trace' ('the uniqueness of the printer-printed, of the impression and the imprint, of the pressure and its trace').[25] This image describes the myth of a world without spacing and *différance*, in which the present moment is always present to itself in a pure moment of self-identical being. Derrida recalls this myth when he speaks of the 'impression *laissée* par Freud, par l'événement qui porte ce nom de famille, l'*impression* quasiment inoubliable et irrécusable, indéniable' ('the impression *left* by Freud, by the event that carries this family name, the nearly unforgettable and incontestable, undeniable *impression*').[26] In order to complicate this understanding of 'impression' as a moment of pure presence, Derrida appeals to a secondary meaning of the word. 'Impression' also signifies, he tells us, a kind of presentiment or intuition, the 'sentiment instable d'une figure mobile' ('the unstable feeling of a shifting figure').[27] Derrida is attracted to such a use of the word 'impression' because it frustrates the apparently stable logical binaries of presence/absence and certainty/doubt. Unlike 'ce qu'un philosophe ou un savant classiques seraient tentés de faire' ('what a classical philosopher or scholar would be tempted to do'), Derrida refuses to view the notion of an 'impression' as a 'sous-concept' ('subconcept'), nor as 'l'infirmité d'un pré-savoir flou et subjectif' ('the feebleness of a blurred and subjective preknowledge'). On the contrary, he affirms that 'l'avenir même du concept' ('the very future of the concept') rests on thinking through the meaning we attach to the word 'impression'.[28]

The originality of *Mal d'archive* in its relationship to the question of influence hinges on the difficulty of thinking this very notion. Within every concept, Derrida maintains, a certain 'poids d'impensé' ('unknowable weight') is irreducible. This unthought element 'inscrit une impression dans la langue et dans le discours' ('inscribes an impression in language and in discourse').[29] Importantly, Derrida insists that this lack does not imprint itself solely as a 'charge négative' ('negative charge'), since what is at stake is 'tout ce qui lie le savoir et la mémoire à la promesse' ('all that ties knowledge and memory to the promise').[30] Derrida offers a concrete example of this structural belatedness at the beginning of *Mal d'archive* when he asks: 'Quel avenir pour la psychanalyse à l'ère du courrier électronique, de la carte téléphonique, des multimédia et du CDrom?' ('What is the future of psychoanalysis in the era of email, telephone cards, multimedia and CD-ROMs?').[31] It is this originary belatedness that opens the possibility of what we might call prospective influence. Prospective influence refers to the incalculable and unknowable influence that a concept may assume in the future. What Derrida calls the 'poids d'impensé' assures that every concept will contain an 'imprécision ouverte' ('open imprecision'),[32] an openness to the alterity of a future-to-come that is, at the time of formulation, strictly inconceivable. As with retrojective influence, prospective influence calls us to a certain responsibility. Just as the spacing that separates us from the past cannot be wholly reckoned with, despite our continued vigilance, the space separating us from the future (*l'avenir*) will always remain unknowable or *à venir* (to come). Nevertheless, our capacity to provide for this unknowability, however minimally, is not entirely lacking: responsibility consists in ensuring that our concepts remain as far from the sutured closure of dogma as possible. In this regard, for Derrida at least, the figure of Freud is exemplary. From the very beginning of his career, Freud's work evinces a kind of nominalism in its manipulation of conceptual hypotheses. The caution that Freud habitually exercises with regard to the future impact of biological and psychological research on psychoanalysis is exemplified in *Beyond the Pleasure Principle*, where his discussion of an originary dualism between Eros and the death drive repeatedly speculates on future scientific findings: 'biology is truly a land of unlimited possibilities [...] we cannot guess what answers it will return in a few dozen years to the questions we have put to it. They may be of a kind which will blow away the whole of our artificial structure of hypotheses'.[33] Freud's awareness of the prospective influence of his concepts, and of the prospective influence of the future on these concepts, results therefore in a conceptual apparatus that is in many ways open to its reinscription in future contexts.

For Derrida, however, two very different types of openness are at stake here. Freud's theoretical reticence exemplifies a *conscious* opening of his own scientific project, one that will always be of a very limited and circumscribed type, since it can only ever gesture towards the unconditional structural opening that undermines and punctures every concept. It is this latter type of opening that plays a more fundamental role in *Mal d'archive*. As I suggested previously, the theoretical proceeding of *Mal d'archive* performs this theory of prospective influence in its reliance on a new mode 'crossing' deconstruction and psychoanalysis. In this regard, the concept of an archive fever (*mal d'archive*) is exemplary, since in its structure it recalls the composition of the psychoanalytic drive. Such a drive would take as its aim the satisfaction of an innate desire for an origin or a 'source' (the Greek *arkhe*, Derrida recalls on the first page of *Mal d'archive*, means both 'commencement' and 'commandment'). Due to the unconditionality of spacing, however, this foundational desire of the metaphysics of presence remains unsatisfiable. Crucially, in his description of our *mal d'archive*, Derrida draws on motifs borrowed from Freud's concept of the compulsion to repeat, calling it 'un désir compulsif, répétitif et nostalgique, un désir irrépressible de retour à l'origine, un mal de pays, une nostalgie du retour au lieu le plus archaïque du commencement absolu' ('a compulsive, repetitive and nostalgic desire for the archive, an irrepressible desire to return to the origin, a homesickness, a nostalgia for the return to the most archaic place of absolute commencement').[34] This ineradicable drive would thus find expression in metaphorical symptoms dispersed throughout language and throughout the writings of a particular thinker, for instance Valéry's obsessive repetition of the theme of sources that Derrida calls an 'obstination compulsive' ('compulsive obstinacy').[35]

In the final section of *Mal d'archive*, Derrida deploys this quasi-psychoanalytic notion of a feverish desire for origins in a remarkable re-reading of Jensen's short story 'Gradiva', which Freud had famously analysed in 1907.[36] The story involves a sequence of hallucinations in which a German archaeologist Norbert Hanold believes he sees the ghost of a Pompeian woman (Gradiva) killed in the eruption that buried the city. Hanold, travelling to the ruins of Pompeii, eventually encounters the woman 'in the flesh' and is surprised to discover, after he begins speaking to her in German, that she is in reality his beloved childhood friend Zoë. In his reading of the story, Freud mobilizes 'toute la machinerie étiologique de la psychanalyse' ('the whole etiological machinery of psychoanalysis')[37] to produce a thorough and convincing explanation of the archaeologist's phantasms that he sees as resulting from Hanold's externalization of internally repressed drives (in this case, his desire for his childhood friend Zoë).

Derrida's reading, which matches Freud's in its theoretical dexterity, goes one step further. In his interpretation of Hanold's *mal d'archive*, his desire to reawaken the Pompeian past of Gradiva by travelling to the city itself, Derrida retains some basic elements of Freud's reading: repression of desire, compulsivity, repetition, phantasm. He adds, however, one crucial element that remains lacking, or 'unthought', in Freud's version. Freud had insisted that, after seeing a bas-relief of Gradiva in Rome, Hanold goes to Pompeii to find the woman herself. Derrida points out that this does not correspond exactly to Jensen's wording in the original text. On the contrary, 'Hanold est venu chercher ces traces au sens littéral (*im wörtlichen Sinne*)' ('Hanold has come to search for these traces in the literal sense').[38] It is these literal traces of Gradiva's footsteps on the Pompeian soil that constitute the true object of Hanold's trip to Italy. Hanold dreams of reliving the singular impression left by Gradiva on the Pompeian soil.[39] His search for her traces is symptomatic of his desire to reawaken the past at the precise moment in which Gradiva's traces are not yet detached from their source, at the moment when spacing has not yet intervened to impede such reawakening. Rather than searching for a woman who lives on, Hanold goes in search of the woman's surviving traces; in other words, for the 'unicité de l'impression et de l'empreinte, de la pression et de sa trace, *à l'instant* unique où elles ne se distinguent pas encore l'une de l'autre, faisant *à l'instant* un seul corps du pas de Gradiva' ('uniqueness of the impression and the imprint, of the pressure and its trace in the unique *instant* where they are not yet distinguished the one from the other, forming in an *instant* a single body of Gradiva's step').[40] As we saw in our account of spacing, however, the satisfaction of this *mal d'archive* will always be frustrated and deferred by *différance*.

The singular traces of Gradiva's footsteps offer us a powerful image of the complexities of temporality, signification and memory with which Derrida confronts the problematic notion of influence. Even if he succeeded in finding these traces, it would be impossible for Hanold not to retroject his own experiences in his reawakening of the horrific moment of Gradiva's demise. The spacing that separates the archaeologist from an everyday experience of Pompeii before its fall is as such insurmountable. Yet, as an archaeologist, Hanold must continue to work under the belief that, in a phrase of Freud's cited by Derrida several times, '*Saxa loquuntur!* [stones speak!]'.[41] In other words, '*l'origine alors parle d'elle-même. L'arkhé paraît à nu, sans archive*' ('*the origin then speaks by itself.* The *arkhe* appears in the nude, without archive').[42] And in deciphering these traces, the archaeologist archives for the future, against an incalculable interval and without knowing in what context his writings will find their ultimate reinscription. By lightening the 'poids d'impensé' in Freud's reading of 'Gradiva', Derrida's account of Jensen's story provides a compelling example of the way in which Freud's influence can continue to be felt long after one or several 'avis de décès' ('death notices') of psychoanalysis have been written.[43] In its theorization of the trace, of the impossibility of seizing a pure moment of self-presence, Derrida's reading also provides us with a powerful means of thinking through the complex temporal issues that continue to haunt our conception of influence.

Notes

1. Jean Hytier, 'Notes', in Paul Valéry, *Œuvres*, ed. by Jean Hytier, 2 vols (Paris: Gallimard, 1957–1960), I, p. 1710. Unless otherwise indicated, translations are my own. My thanks are due to Rachel McGahern for her benign influence on the final version of this article.
2. Valéry, *Œuvres*, I, p. 202. With its examination of images of water and dependent notions of clarity, depth, reflection and purity, Gaston Bachelard's *L'Eau et les rêves, essai sur l'imagination de la matière* (Paris: Corti, 1942) goes some way towards demystifying this tradition. For Derrida's treatment of Bachelard on metaphor (and additional comments on metaphors of growth, irrigation and circulation in Plato, Condillac and Rousseau), see 'La Mythologie blanche: la métaphore dans le texte philosophique', in *Marges – de la philosophie* (Paris: Minuit, 1972), pp. 247–324. It is not accidental, as Harold Bloom notes in *The Anxiety of Influence: A Theory of Poetry*, 2nd edn (New York and Oxford: Oxford University Press, 1997), that our current concept of influence is derived from an image of astral in-flux: 'the flowing from the stars upon our fates and our personalities' (p. xii). Bloom alludes to this etymology when he argues that 'precursors flood us, and our imaginations can die by drowning in them, but no imaginative life is possible if such inundation is wholly evaded' (p. 154).
3. Derrida, *Marges – de la philosophie*, p. 332; translated by Alan Bass as *Margins of Philosophy* (Chicago: University of Chicago Press, 1982), p. 279.
4. Valéry, *Œuvres*, I, p. 204.
5. Derrida, *Marges*, p. 334; *Margins*, p. 280.

6. Jacques Derrida, *Mal d'archive: une impression freudienne* (Paris: Galilée, 1995); translated by Eric Prenowitz as *Archive Fever: A Freudian Impression* (Chicago: University of Chicago Press, 1998).
7. See in particular *A Map of Misreading* (Oxford: Oxford University Press, 1975), pp. 43–50, and the opening pages of his *Poetry and Repression: Revisionism from Blake to Stevens* (New Haven, CT and London: Yale University Press, 1976).
8. Derrida argues for an intrinsic relationship between anxiety ('Angst'/'angoisse') and spacing in his reading of the child's game of fort-da in Freud's *Beyond the Pleasure Principle*; see *La Carte postale: de Socrate à Freud et au-delà* (Paris: Flammarion, 1980), pp. 314–40; translated by Alan Bass as *The Post Card: From Socrates to Freud and Beyond* (Chicago: University of Chicago Press, 1987), pp. 293–320.
9. For a detailed appraisal of the historical development of influence as a concept in literary history, see Jay Clayton and Eric Rothstein's introductory chapter to their collection, *Influence and Intertextuality in Literary History* (Madison: University of Wisconsin Press, 1991).
10. Chris Baldick's *Oxford Concise Dictionary of Literary Terms* (Oxford: Oxford University Press, 2004) furnishes us with a concrete example of this critical anxiety. Although the dictionary, which 'defines over 1,000 literary terms from absurd to zeugma', contains at least 54 instances of the word 'influence', an entry devoted to the term itself is conspicuously absent. This testifies to a Derridean double bind at the heart of every critical treatment of influence relationships: the concept of influence inevitably provokes our suspicion, if not our scepticism, but as critics we remain 'bound to illuminate the relation of writer to writer, and writer to tradition'; Ihab H. Hassan, 'The Problem of Influence in Literary History: Notes towards a Definition', *The Journal of Aesthetics and Art Criticism*, 14.1 (September 1955), 66–76 (p. 66).
11. John Sutherland, 'Introduction', in Anthony Trollope, *He Knew He Was Right* (Oxford: Oxford University Press, 2008), p. xiv.
12. Derrida, *Marges*, p. 327; *Margins*, p. 275.
13. Ibid.
14. Ibid, p. 330; p. 278.
15. My reading of Derrida's notion of spacing owes much to Martin Hagglünd's lucid account of the term throughout his *Radical Atheism: Derrida and the Time of Life* (Stanford, CA: Stanford University Press, 2008), in particular pp. 17–18.
16. Derrida, *Marges*, p. 331; *Margins*, p. 278.
17. If, indeed, the meaning of the text was ever wholly present even to its author, something Derrida calls into question elsewhere in *Marges*: see 'La

Forme et le vouloir-dire', pp. 185–207; translated as 'Form and Meaning' in *Margins*, pp. 155–53.
18. Derrida, *La Carte postale*, p. 285; *Post Card*, p. 267.
19. Ibid., p. 286; p. 267.
20. These controversies are detailed in J. M. Masson's *The Assault on Truth: Freud's Suppression of the Seduction Theory* (Harmondsworth: Penguin, 1985) and Janet Malcolm's *In the Freud Archives* (London: Macmillan, 1997).
21. Yosef Hayim Yerushalmi, *Freud's Moses: Judaism Terminable and Interminable* (New Haven, CT: Yale University Press, 1991).
22. Derrida, *Mal d'archive*, p. 91; *Archive Fever*, p. 59.
23. Ibid., p. 123; p. 77.
24. The *Trésor de la langue française* offers one reading of 'impression' as: 'influence morale, intellectuelle, artistique' ('moral, intellectual, artistic influence').
25. Derrida, *Mal d'archive*, p. 152; *Archive Fever*, p. 99.
26. Ibid., p. 53; p. 30. Emphasis in original.
27. Ibid., p. 51; p. 29.
28. Ibid.
29. Ibid., p. 52; p. 30.
30. Ibid.
31. Ibid., 'Prière d'insérer'.
32. Ibid., p. 51; p. 29.
33. Sigmund Freud, *Beyond the Pleasure Principle*, in *The Standard Edition of the Complete Psychological Works of Sigmund Freud*, translated under the general editorship of James Strachey, 24 vols (London: Hogarth Press, 1991), XVIII, p. 60. Further references to Freud's work are to this edition.
34. Derrida, *Mal d'archive*, p. 142; *Archive Fever*, p. 91.
35. Derrida, *Marges*, p. 332; *Margins*, p. 304 (translation modified).
36. See Sigmund Freud, *Delusions and Dreams in Jensen's Gradiva*, in *The Standard Edition*, IX, pp. 1–95.
37. Derrida, *Mal d'archive*, p. 136; *Archive Fever*, p. 87.
38. Ibid., p. 151; p. 98.
39. Ibid., p. 151; pp. 98–9.
40. Ibid., p. 152; p. 99. Emphasis in original.
41. Freud, 'The Aetiology of Hysteria', in *The Standard Edition*, III, p. 189.
42. Derrida, *Mal d'archive*, p. 144; *Archive Fever*, p. 92. Emphasis in original.
43. Jacques Derrida and Elisabeth Roudinesco, *De quoi demain... Dialogue* (Paris: Flammarion, 2001), p. 285; translated by Jeff Fort as *For What Tomorrow...: A Dialogue* (Stanford, CA: Stanford University Press, 2004), p. 175.

10
Roland Barthes's Ghosts: Photobiographical Influence and Legacies

Fabien Arribert-Narce

Roland Barthes published a number of texts on photography from the 1950s onwards. In *Mythologies* (published between 1954 and 1956),[1] 'Le Message photographique' ('The Photographic Message', 1961), 'Rhétorique de l'image' ('Rhetoric of the Image', 1964) and 'Le Troisième Sens' ('The Third Meaning', 1970), his approach is largely semiological and sociological.[2] In *Roland Barthes par Roland Barthes* (*Roland Barthes by Roland Barthes*), which opens with a short album of family snapshots, and above all in *La Chambre claire* (*Camera Lucida*), an essay on photography whose publication triggered a surge of interest in photography in France and elsewhere, his approach is more personal. These two books (the first published in 1975 and the second in 1980, the year of Barthes's death) initiated what Antoine Compagnon has called 'une mode contemporaine du récit de vie avec photos' ('a contemporary vogue for life writing using photographs').[3] In this respect, Barthes can be viewed as a second trailblazer of the 'photobiographical' genre after André Breton, whose seminal phototexts *Nadja* and *L'Amour fou* ('Mad Love') appeared in 1928 and 1937 respectively. The term 'photobiographie' ('photobiography') was used for the first time in French by Gilles Mora and Claude Nori in their *L'Été dernier: manifeste photobiographique* (*Last Summer: Photobiographical Manifesto*, 1983). *Roland Barthes par Roland Barthes* and *La Chambre claire* correspond to Mora and Nori's definition of photobiography as a biographical or autobiographical genre in which the photographic image plays a crucial role, be it simply mentioned, described or actually reproduced within the text.[4]

My aim in this essay is to examine the photobiographical contours of Barthes's work and to locate it in relation to the genre. In order to do so,

I will consider the influence of Barthes's work on texts published in the 1970s and 1980s by Hervé Guibert and Denis Roche.

Barthes and Photobiography

What are the defining characteristics of Barthes's photobiographical project? Barthes's reflection on photography is often reduced by critics (be they admirers or detractors of his work) to a series of key words and formulas – to clichés that eventually caricature and distort his original insights. One could cite here such expressions as 'un message sans code' ('a message without a code')[5] and 'le noème de la Photographie [...]: "ça-a-été"' ('the *noeme* of Photography [...]: "that-has-been"'),[6] or the distinction that he draws in *La Chambre claire* between 'studium' and 'punctum', which is quoted time and time again in works more or less related to photography, thus confirming the deep penetration of Barthesian discourse into academic and artistic circles. If these well-known formulae are undeniably important in Barthes's intellectual trajectory, the only way to understand their real impact is to situate them in the context of his complete works. In this respect, I would like to emphasize the coherence and continuity that characterize all of Barthes's texts on photography over the course of his career. This emphasis contradicts a view of *La Chambre claire*, prevalent among critics, as a work that marks a major turning point in Barthes's writing on photography – as a work that does away with the more semiological approach of his previous texts on the subject. In *Le Destin des images* (*The Future of the Image*), for example, Jacques Rancière goes so far as to suggest that the last book published by Barthes in his lifetime should be understood as a repentance:

> Il est peu probable que l'auteur des *Mythologies* ait cru à la fantasmagorie para-scientifique, qui fait de la photographie une émanation directe du corps exposé. Il est plus vraisemblable que ce mythe lui a servi à expier le péché du mythologue d'hier: celui d'avoir voulu ôter au monde visible ses prestiges, d'avoir transformé ses spectacles et ses plaisirs en un grand tissu de symptômes et en un louche commerce des signes. Le sémiologue se repent d'avoir passé une bonne partie de sa vie à dire: Attention! Ce que vous prenez pour une évidence visible est en fait un message crypté par lequel une société ou un pouvoir se légitime en se naturalisant, en se fondant dans l'évidence sans phrase du visible. Il tord le bâton dans l'autre sens en valorisant, au titre du *punctum*, l'évidence sans phrase de la photographie pour rejeter dans la platitude du *studium* le déchiffrement des messages.

(It is unlikely that the author of *Mythologies* believed in the para-scientific phantasmagoria which makes photography a direct emanation of the body displayed. It is more plausible that this myth served to expiate the sin of the former mythologist: the sin of having wished to strip the visible world of its glories, of having transformed its spectacles and pleasures into a great web of symptoms and a seedy exchange of signs. The semiologist repents having spent much of his life saying: Look out! What you are taking for visible self-evidence is in fact an encoded message whereby a society or authority legitimates itself by naturalizing itself, by rooting itself in the obviousness of the visible. He bends the stick in the other direction by valorizing, under the title of *punctum*, the utter self-evidence of the photograph, consigning the decoding of messages to the platitude of the *studium*.)[7]

Contra Rancière, I believe that Barthes's reflection on photography follows an evolution, a trajectory, and that he anticipates the highly personal discourse on photos contained in *La Chambre claire* in a number of earlier texts on the subject. His argument in these latter is thus not incompatible with the last book he published in his lifetime, and he does not repent of it in that work. For Barthes, the photograph is a fundamentally paradoxical and ambivalent object, and this is precisely what the expression 'message without a code' suggests: this object is neither (only) a text, a sign to be read and interpreted (this is, for example, what Victor Burgin argues in *Thinking Photography*, in which he overlooks Barthes's take on the photograph in *La Chambre claire* and other texts), nor is it a pure 'émanation du référent' ('emanation of the referent'), a magic object to which we respond emotionally rather than intellectually.[8] From this perspective, it can be argued that Barthes's conceptual couples created in the 1970s – 'sens obvie' ('obvious meaning') and 'sens obtus' ('obtuse meaning') in the article on the 'Third Meaning'; 'plaisir' ('pleasure') and 'jouissance' ('bliss') in *Le Plaisir du texte* (*The Pleasure of the Text*) of 1973 – anticipate the final distinction between *studium* and *punctum*, which confirms the tension between, on the one hand, a message to be deciphered – 'un intérêt humain' ('a human interest')[9] – and, on the other, a more personal and affective interest (a tension between culture and nature, in other words). These poles are in fact more or less explicitly present in all of Barthes's texts on photography. To borrow a term used by Jacques Derrida, they 'composent' ('compose') together more than they are opposed to one another: they are complementary and meaningful only insofar as they are thought together and in relation to one another.[10] Moreover, their individual presence in Barthes's texts is dependent on the context in which he is writing. After the death of his mother in 1977, for example, he comments less frequently on the *studium* interest of photos (this is true of *La Chambre claire* and the *Journal de deuil* [*Mourning Diary*], published posthumously in 2009). Ultimately, then, the Barthesian photobiographical project forms a complex but continuous whole from which certain polarized notions can only be isolated tendentiously.

Barthes emphasizes this continuity in *La Chambre claire*:

> Les réalistes, dont je suis, et dont j'étais déjà lorsque j'affirmais que la Photographie était une image sans code – même si, c'est évident, des codes viennent en infléchir la lecture – ne prennent pas du tout la photo pour une 'copie' du réel – mais pour une émanation du *réel passé*.
>
> (The realists, of whom I am one and of whom I was already one when I asserted that the Photograph was an image without code – even if, obviously, certain codes do inflect our reading of it – the realists do not take the photograph for a 'copy' of reality, but for an emanation of *past reality*.)[11]

Barthes pinpoints here what, arguably, constitutes the most potent legacy of his work on photography: photographic realism (which can be defined as a belief in the referential power of analogue photography). For Barthes, at least in *La Chambre claire*, an analogue photographic image makes the object or subject it represents *present* and proves that it has existed.[12] As such, the photograph is also considered to be a source of emotion and fascination. In fact, there are very few photobiographers – either writers or artists – who are not 'realists' and who do not adopt, at least partially, this photographic *doxa*. However, Barthes's photobiographical project cannot be limited to these aspects. Indeed, for Barthes, photography was a model and a platform of expression in his search for a notational form of life writing (at the end of his life), enabling him to capture reality without interpreting, analysing or even describing it. What he saw in the photographic image was the possibility of achieving an 'exemption' from meaning and of moving closer to a pure *graphy* – or to use his own vocabulary, to '*signifiance*'.[13] The latter is defined in *Le Plaisir du texte* as 'le sens en ce qu'il est produit sensuellement' ('meaning, insofar as it is sensually produced').[14] It does not refer to the signifier or the signified, but rather constitutes an appeal to sensuality – a form of eroticism – and plural meanings. In such circumstances, a 'photographic' form of writing suggested to Barthes the possibility of escaping from the tyranny of meaning – from the clichés that characterize language – and from images of the self and the imaginary.[15] The comparison in *La Préparation du roman I et II* (*The Preparation of the Novel I and II*) – Barthes's final lecture course at the Collège de France between 1978 and 1980 – between the photograph and Japanese haiku also plays a major role in his development of a photobiographical project in the 1970s. The main formal matrix of this project was the *biographeme* (or 'trait signifiant' ['signifying trait']),[16] defined by Barthes in *Sade, Fourier, Loyola* as a detail, a taste or preference, an inflection.[17] The Barthesian *biographeme* can also have a *studium* or *punctum* interest and the photograph can be viewed either as a *biographeme* – a fragment of life writing – or as a potential source of *biographemes*, of conspicuous details.[18]

Barthes's Ghosts and Successors: Hervé Guibert and Denis Roche

We are now in a position to explore the influence of Barthes's photobiographical project – to look for traces of his approach to the photographic image in the work of his contemporaries. In order to do this, I will focus more specifically on Barthes's influence on two authors whose works are representative of the various types of photobiography that have prevailed in the contemporary period, namely Hervé Guibert and Denis Roche.

Guibert's *L'Image fantôme* (*Ghost Image*) was published in 1981, just one year after *La Chambre claire* (Guibert also wrote a review of Barthes's book in *Le Monde* in 1980). Barthes's ghost is present in Guibert's fragmented autobiographical book, especially in the section entitled 'La Photo, au plus près de la mort' ('The Photograph, as Close to Death as Possible'). Indeed, in this text, Guibert – who was a writer and a photographer – explains that he had planned to take a picture of Barthes accompanied by his mother, Henriette, but that Henriette's death prevented this. Beyond this obvious link between the two writers, Guibert also implicitly adopts the Barthesian distinction between *studium* and *punctum* without concealing his preference for photographs of the second type, especially when they represent human beings and faces that stimulate his (photographic) desire:[19] 'comment voulez-vous parler de photographie sans parler de désir? [...] L'image est l'essence du désir, et désexualiser l'image, ce serait la réduire à la théorie' ('How can you speak of photography without speaking of desire? [...] The image is the essence of desire and if you desexualize the image, you reduce it to theory').[20] Later in the book, Guibert adds: 'ne photographie que tes extrêmes familiers, tes parents, tes frères et sœurs, ton amoureuse, l'antécédent affectif emportera la photo' ('only photograph your nearest and dearest, your parents, your brothers and sisters, your sweetheart, the affective antecedent will bring the photo off').[21] Emphasizing here the emotional nature of his relationship to photographs, Guibert also touches on one of Barthes's principal arguments in *La Chambre claire* concerning the spectrality of the photographic image and its special link to death. He narrates an episode during which he tried to take a picture of his mother but failed because the film of the camera was not loaded: 'une fois la photo prise, l'image fixée, le processus du vieillissement pouvait bien reprendre, et cette fois à une vitesse vertigineuse [...]. Ce moment à blanc (cette mort à blanc? puisqu'on peut tirer "à blanc") resta entre ma mère et moi' ('once the picture was taken, the image fixed, the process of aging would continue, and this time at a dizzying speed [...]. That blank moment (that blank death? since one can shoot "blanks") remained between my mother and me').[22] Both Barthes and Guibert thus strive in their respective texts to ward off the spectral properties of the photographic image as they endeavour to rescue the memory of their mothers. In *La Chambre claire*, the Winter Garden photograph is said to represent Barthes's mother at the age of 5 and helps the writer to retrieve her 'identité essentielle' ('essential identity').[23] However, even if all the photos evoked in *L'Image fantôme* are, like the Winter Garden photograph, nothing but pre-texts (as suggested by the title of the book, these pictures are *ghost* images that are only described and not shown to the reader), Guibert does not use the photographic image as a model for a notational form of life writing (or an exemption from meaning).[24] On the contrary, he exploits the narrative and fictional (or rather autofictional) potential of his photographs in many texts. Guibert is less interested than Barthes in the photographic referent. Unlike the author of *La Chambre claire*, Guibert accounts for the various tricks and artifices of photography as aspects of art.[25] With the example of Guibert, we are in fact dealing with a first type of photobiography that, while it does not correspond to Barthes's photobiographical project, was nevertheless inspired by it. It is based on a structure in which the function of one or several absent photographs is to trigger the autobiographical text (the narration of a story).[26]

I would now like to consider another type of photobiography that is much closer to Barthes's project, as it encompasses works in which photographs are effectively reproduced in the text (and in which the text often takes the minimal form of captions). Major French contemporary artists such as Christian Boltanski and Sophie Calle belong to this photobiographical category. In line with Barthes's notational model, these works are concerned with a reflection on the nature of traces (of life) and material archives. In the work of Roche, this notational life writing takes the form of what he calls an 'antéfixe' ('antefix'), a graphic deposit of life (textual or photographic) that is comparable in many ways to Barthes's *biographeme*. Roche's aim as a writer/photographer is in fact to accumulate autobiographical fragments directly extracted from his everyday life, without filtering them or reading them through an interpretive and analytical grid. In this respect, Roche reinforces Barthes's photographic realism – epitomized by the expression 'ça-a-été' ('that-has-been') – but modifies it so that it is anchored within the personal experience of the photographer. Thus, in Roche's work, the 'that-has-been' is transformed into another principle, the 'j'ai-été-là' ('I-have-been-there'). This crucial modification is the main object of Roche's long letter addressed posthumously to Barthes in *La Disparition des lucioles* (*The Extinction of Fireflies*), published in 1982, only two years after Barthes's death:

> Comment peut-on nier à ce point-là que le photographe opère un choix dans ce qu'il regarde, et qu'il imprime à sa composition l'aspect sensuel ou pathétique ou affectif de son regard, des choses qu'il veut y mettre et qu'il veut y capter.
>
> (How is it possible to deny so much that the photographer makes a selection in what s/he is seeing, and that s/he imprints on the picture the sensual, pathetic or affective character of his/her gaze, and things that s/he wants to see and to capture in this picture.)[27]

Roche targets here what is for him – and others – the most dubious aspect of Barthes's photobiographical influence, namely the relative silence of his writing on photography with regard to the photographic act – the act of the 'operator'. Indeed, unlike Guibert and Roche, Barthes presents himself as a mere spectator. His willingness to see the photograph only as an object, as a receptacle of meaning and emotions, also leads him to view photographic images as a kind of painting – as unique and 'auratic'.[28] In doing so, Barthes deliberately ignores the technical seriality that characterizes the photographic process and plays a central role, in a variety of different ways, in the works of Roche, Calle and Boltanski. If these artists are clearly influenced by Barthes's photobiographical project, they do not hesitate to underline its shortcomings, and criticize the author of *La Chambre claire* for not taking his analysis of the specificity of photography to its logical end. It is no doubt because he wrote his last book – as well as several other texts that refer extensively to photography (*La Préparation du roman*, for example) – during a period of mourning that the photographic image could be nothing other than a melancholic object for Barthes – an object attracting a mesmerized, obstinate gaze characterized by a stagnant repetition. This form of immobile repetition can be opposed to the serial repetition that constitutes (at least for Roche and for other photographers and philosophers such as Derrida) the essence of photographic technology.[29] The association between the experience of mourning and photography in the work of Barthes, which explains to a certain extent his obsession with the unique character of the image and the photographic referent, is explored by Antoine Compagnon in the following terms:

> [Dans *La Chambre claire*,] toute l'expérience du deuil [...] est déplacée sur la photographie, à tel point que l'on pourrait appliquer à la photographie ce que le *Journal [de deuil]* dit du deuil: l'un et l'autre apparaissent comme l'envers du récit en ce qu'ils nient toute confiance en la continuité du monde, condition sine qua non du récit [...]. La photographie perpétue le deuil, elle le retient dans un éternel retour du même excluant toute dialectique, et par là même, toute possibilité de catharsis. Elle est anthropologiquement liée à la mort, par son pouvoir d'immobiliser le temps et l'interprétation.
>
> ([In *La Chambre claire*,] the whole mourning experience [...] is shifted towards photography, so much so that we could apply to photography what the [*Mourning*] *Diary* says about mourning: both appear to be the reverse of the narrative insofar as they deny all confidence in the continuity of the world, which is a prerequisite of the narrative [...]. The photograph perpetuates mourning, maintains it in an eternal return of the same that excludes any dialectic, and for this reason, any possibility of catharsis. It is anthropologically linked to death, because of its power to freeze time and interpretation.)[30]

We are confronted here with the question of the relation between narrative and photography in Barthes's work, a question that, as we have seen, initiated a double photobiographical legacy. On the one hand, *La Chambre claire* can be read as the narrative of a quest (with an initiatory, mythical dimension) or as the beginning of a would-be

Proustian novel, which is suggested by the first sentence of the book: 'Un jour, il y a bien longtemps, je tombai sur une photographie du dernier frère de Napoléon, Jérôme' ('One day, quite some time ago, I happened on a photograph of Napoleon's youngest brother, Jérôme').[31] On the other hand, in *La Préparation du roman* and other texts, Barthes deploys his fantasy of an a-narrative and photographic form of (life-) writing whose model is the haiku.

Conclusion

In an interview with Renaud Matignon published in *France-Observateur* in 1964, Barthes claims that he does not believe in influences, arguing that

> à mon sens, ce qui se transmet, ce ne sont pas des 'idées', mais des 'langages', c'est-à-dire des formes que l'on peut remplir différemment; c'est pourquoi la notion de *circulation* me paraît plus juste que celle d'*influence*; les livres sont plutôt des 'monnaies' que des 'forces'.
>
> (to my mind, what is transmitted is not 'ideas' but 'languages', that is to say forms that we can fill up differently; this is why the notion of *circulation* seems to me to be more suitable than *influence*; books are 'currencies' rather than 'forces'.)[32]

In order to examine the question of Barthes's photobiographical legacy in truly Barthesian terms, we must evaluate the marks and traces left by his work rather than simply proclaim the tightness of its hold over the work of his contemporaries. In fact, we are confronted here with several juxtaposed phenomena that partially overlap: Barthes's own practice; the spectral presence of Barthes, whose terminology is to be found in texts written by other photobiographers; the *circulation* of modes and models of writing, which are more or less copied and discussed by contemporaries. The various types of photobiography that have been described in this essay themselves overlap in many ways. In this respect, none of the authors discussed here (neither Guibert nor Roche, neither Calle nor Boltanski) is more faithful to Barthes than the others; what is at stake is rather a question of forms and formulae extracted from Barthes's oeuvre and reappropriated in distinctive ways. What remains of this oeuvre is a particular approach to photography conceived as a mode of survival, an approach that is by nature individual, being based on the personal emotion triggered by an image.³³ Following this approach, and insofar as photography in general is defined in *La Chambre claire* as 'le Particulier absolu' ('the absolute Particular'),³⁴ it only makes sense to talk about one's private relationship with specific photographs. However, this remark is only relevant for the viewer (of images), and this is precisely what constitutes the limit of a Barthesian photobiographical heritage that is in many ways outdated, stranded at the end of the twentieth century. Moreover, despite his rare reflections on the use of photographs in advertising, Barthes examines what is now, for many, the past of photography (analogue technology) rather than its future (digital technology). In such circumstances, it is difficult to identify a direct Barthesian influence on twenty-first-century photobiographers. This would no doubt have pleased Barthes, who invited his reader, a 'créateur virtuel' ('virtual creator'), to consider his work as a 'recueil de matériaux' ('collection of materials'), a polygraphic assemblage made of texts and photographs to be rewritten and recirculated.³⁵ In 'Les Morts de Roland Barthes', composed just months after Barthes's death, Derrida writes of his own experience of reading and looking at Barthes:

> Revenu de l'expérience un peu insulaire au fond de laquelle avec les deux livres [*Le Degré zéro de l'écriture* et *La Chambre claire*] je m'étais retiré, je ne regarde plus aujourd'hui que les photographies, dans d'autres livres (surtout dans *Roland Barthes...*) et dans des journaux, je ne quitte plus les photographies et l'écriture manuscrite. Je ne sais pas ce que je continue à chercher, mais je cherche du côté de son corps, de ce qu'il en montre et de ce qu'il en dit, de ce qu'il en cache peut-être, comme de ce qu'il ne pouvait pas *voir* dans son écriture.

> (Having returned from the somewhat insular experience wherein I had secluded myself with the two books [*Le Degré zéro de l'écriture* and *La Chambre claire*], I look today only at the photographs in other books (especially in *Roland Barthes by Roland Barthes...*) and in newspapers; I cannot tear myself away from the photographs and the handwriting. I do not know what I am still looking for, but I'm looking for it in the direction of his body, in what he shows and says of it, in what he hides of it, perhaps – like something he could not *see* in his writing.)³⁶

Barthes's assemblage of texts and photographs is thus what remains for us to interpret and equally what resists our interpretation, our own attempts to exercise an 'influence' on Barthes's work.

Notes

1. See, in particular, Roland Barthes, 'L'Acteur d'Harcourt' ('The Harcourt Actor') and 'Photos-choc' ('Shock Photos') in *Mythologies*, in *Œuvres complètes*, ed. by Éric Marty, 5 vols (Paris: Seuil, 2002) I, pp. 688–9 and I, pp. 751–3 (all subsequent references to Barthes's work in French are to this edition). These texts are available in *Mythologies*, trans. by Richard Howard and Annette Lavers (New York: Farrar, Straus and Giroux, 2012), pp. 15–18 and pp. 116–18.
2. See Roland Barthes, 'Le Message photographique' ('The Photographic Message'), I, pp. 1120–33; 'Rhétorique de l'image' ('Rhetoric of the Image'), II, pp. 573–91; 'Le Troisième Sens: notes de recherche sur quelques photogrammes de S. M. Eisenstein' ('The Third Meaning: Research Notes on Some Eisenstein Stills'), III, pp. 485–506. These texts are available in Roland Barthes, *Image Music Text*, ed. and trans. by Stephen Heath (London: Fontana Press, 1977), pp. 15–68.
3. Antoine Compagnon, 'Écrire la vie: Montaigne, Stendhal, Proust', in *Cours et travaux du Collège de France: résumés 2008–2009, annuaire 109ème année* (Paris: Collège de France, 2010), pp. 863–85 (p. 870). My translation.
4. Gilles Mora and Claude Nori, *L'Été dernier: manifeste photobiographique* (Paris: Éditions de l'étoile, 1983).
5. Barthes, 'Le Message photographique', I, p. 1123; 'The Photographic Message', p. 19.
6. Barthes, *La Chambre claire*, V, pp. 785–892 (p. 851); translated by Richard Howard as *Camera Lucida* (London: Vintage Books, 2000), p. 76.
7. Jacques Rancière, *Le Destin des images* (Paris: La Fabrique, 2003), pp. 18–19; translated by Gregory Elliott as *The Future of the Image* (London: Verso, 2007), pp. 10–11.
8. Barthes, *La Chambre claire*, V, p. 854; *Camera Lucida*, p. 80. According to Burgin, Barthes equates the photograph with a text that requires decipherment: 'photographs are *texts* inscribed in terms of what we may call "photographic discourse", but this discourse, like any other, engages discourses beyond itself [...] the "photographic text", like any other, is the site of a complex intertextuality'; 'Looking at Photographs', in *Thinking Photography*, ed. by Victor Burgin (London: Macmillan, 1982), pp. 142–53 (p. 144). Emphasis in original. Burgin fails to mention what Barthes says about photography in *La Chambre claire* and earlier texts.
9. Barthes, *La Chambre claire*, V, p. 809; *Camera Lucida*, p. 26.
10. See Jacques Derrida, 'Les Morts de Roland Barthes', *Poétique*, 47 (1981), 269–92 (p. 274); translated by Catherine Porter as 'The Deaths of Roland Barthes', in *Psyche: Inventions of the Other*, ed. by Peggy Kamuf and Elizabeth

G. Rottenberg (Stanford, CA: Stanford University Press, 2007), pp. 264–98 (p. 271).
11. Barthes, *La Chambre claire*, V, p. 861; *Camera Lucida*, p. 88. Emphasis in original.
12. According to Barthes, 'toute photo est un certificat de présence' (ibid., V, p. 859); 'every photograph is a certificate of presence' (*Camera Lucida*, p. 87).
13. See Barthes, 'Le Troisième Sens', III, p. 487; 'The Third Meaning', p. 54. Barthes uses the expression 'exemption de sens' ('exemption from/of meaning') in several texts, including *L'Empire des signes*: 'c'est aussi un vide de parole qui constitue l'écriture; c'est de ce vide que partent les traits dont le Zen, dans l'exemption de tout sens, écrit les jardins, les gestes, les maisons, les bouquets, les visages, la violence' ('it is also an emptiness of language which constitutes writing; it is from this emptiness that derive the features with which Zen, in the exemption from all meaning, writes gardens, gestures, houses, flower arrangements, faces, violence'); III, p. 352; translated by Richard Howard as *Empire of Signs* (New York: Hill and Wang, 1982), p. 4.
14. Barthes, *Le Plaisir du texte*, IV, pp. 217–64 (p. 257); translated by Richard Miller as *The Pleasure of the Text* (New York: Farrar, Straus and Giroux, 1975), p. 62.
15. See ibid., IV, p. 239; p. 33.
16. Barthes, 'Le Troisième Sens', III, p. 487; 'The Third Meaning', p. 53.
17. 'Si j'étais écrivain, et mort, comme j'aimerais que ma vie se réduisît, par les soins d'un biographe amical et désinvolte, à quelques détails, à quelques goûts, à quelques inflexions, disons: des "biographèmes"' ('Were I a writer, and dead, how I would love it if my life, through the pains of some friendly and detached biographer, were to reduce itself to a few details, a few preferences [tastes], a few inflections, let us say: to "biographemes"'); Roland Barthes, *Sade, Fourier, Loyola*, III, pp. 699–765 (pp. 705–6); translated by Richard Miller as *Sade, Fourier, Loyola* (London: Jonathan Cape, 1977), p. 8. Bernard Comment argues that the haiku functions for Barthes 'comme exemple, comme modèle, comme espoir, pour venir marquer et préciser, concrétiser en quelque sorte, l'horizon du fantasme' ('as an example, a model, a hope, in order to signal, clarify, and in a way materialize the horizon of his fantasy') – the fantasy of a photographic writing of the neutral; Bernard Comment, *Roland Barthes, vers le neutre* (Paris: Bourgois, 2002), p. 192; my translation.
18. For a more exhaustive examination of Barthes's search for a form of photographic writing towards the end of his life, see Comment's *Roland Barthes, vers le neutre*.
19. In his article 'Mort à blanc: Guibert et la photographie', in *Le Corps textuel d'Hervé Guibert*, ed. by Ralph Sarkonak (Paris: La Revue des lettres modernes, 1997), pp. 81–95, Pierre Saint-Amand argues that *L'Image fantôme* contains a reflection on a 'tout-punctum' ('all-punctum') form of photography (p. 87; my translation).

20. Hervé Guibert, *L'Image fantôme* (Paris: Minuit, 1981), p. 89; translated by Robert Bononno as *Ghost Image* (Los Angeles, CA: Sun and Moon Press, 1996) p. 83.
21. Ibid., p. 96; p. 100.
22. Ibid., pp. 14–16; pp. 13–15. On several occasions in *La Chambre claire*, Barthes emphasizes the special link between photography and death. For example: 'en déportant [le] réel vers le passé (*"ça a été"*), [la photo] suggère qu'il est déjà mort' ('by shifting this reality to the past [*"this-has-been"*], the photograph suggests that it is already dead') (*La Chambre claire*, V, p. 853; *Camera Lucida*, p. 79). Emphasis in original.
23. Ibid., V, p. 843; p. 66.
24. In the opening chapter of *L'Image fantôme*, Guibert claims that 'le texte est le désespoir de l'image, et pire qu'une image floue ou voilée: une image fantôme' ('the text is the despair of the image, and worse than a blurred or foggy image – a ghost image') (*L'Image fantôme*, p. 17; *Ghost Image*, p. 16).
25. According to Akane Kawakami, 'this "noème" of the photograph, which Barthes never questions, in spite of his awareness that trick photography, for instance, exists, is central to his arguments in *La Chambre claire*. It is a potential weakness in his argument, and one that Guibert will go on ruthlessly to exploit in his own collection of essays on photography'; '"Un coup de foudre photographique": Autobiography and Photography in Hervé Guibert', *Romance Studies*, 25.3 (2007), 211–25 (pp. 214–15).
26. A number of contemporary works fall into this category, including Marguerite Duras's *L'Amant* (*The Lover*). In this text, an autobiographical narrative published in 1984, Duras describes an 'image absolue' ('absolute image') – a photograph of the author in Indochina at the age of 15 that was never in fact taken.
27. Denis Roche, 'Un discours affectif sur l'image', *Le Magazine littéraire*, 314 (1993), 65–7 (p. 67; my translation).
28. Jacques Derrida argues that 'the cultic value that becomes attached to photography always depends on uniqueness, the non-reproducibility at the heart of the reproducible itself in photography'; *Copy, Archive, Signature*, ed. by Gerhard Richter and trans. by Jeff Fort (Stanford, CA: Stanford University Press, 2010), p. 29.
29. In *Copy, Archive, Signature*, Derrida adds that 'the multiplicity is in principle immediate. A drawing, on the contrary, is singular: there is only one, in any case it does not of itself imply a series, as a photograph does, even if in some cases there is only one. The principle of the series is inscribed in the photographic act' (p. 35).
30. Antoine Compagnon, *Cours et travaux du Collège de France*, p. 880. My translation.

31. Barthes, *La Chambre claire*, V, p. 791; *Camera Lucida*, p. 3.
32. Roland Barthes, 'Je ne crois pas aux influences', II, pp. 615–18 (p. 616). Emphasis in original. My translation.
33. In this respect, it should be noted that *La Chambre claire* is characterized by a phenomenological approach to photography.
34. Barthes, *La Chambre claire*, V, p. 792; *Camera Lucida*, p. 4.
35. Barthes, 'Je ne crois pas aux influences', II, p. 616. My translation.
36. Derrida, 'Les Morts de Roland Barthes', p. 289; 'The Deaths of Roland Barthes', p. 293. Emphasis in original.

11
'Le Cycle de Nestor': Patrick Pécherot's Rewriting of Léo Malet
Angela Kimyongür

The history of the *roman noir* in France is, from its beginnings, one of influence. During the German Occupation of 1940–1944 American films and novels were banned. Nevertheless, American hard-boiled detective fiction became extremely popular after the Liberation, and it was not long before French writers began to imitate the genre. While the first works published by Gallimard's crime fiction series – the *Série noire*, established in 1945 by Marcel Duhamel – were translations into French of works originally published in English by British authors,[1] French authors soon began to write novels in the hard-boiled style. Early examples of the genre were imitations, even pastiches, of the American model: authors often adopted US pseudonyms and set their novels in America.[2] Of this generation of writers, Léo Malet is considered a pioneer of an authentically French *roman noir*, 'le père du roman noir français' ('the father of the French *roman noir*').[3] An avant-garde writer associated with the Parisian Surrealists in the 1920s and 1930s, Malet began his crime writing career during World War II under the pseudonym Frank Harding, which appeared on a series of novels featuring American investigative journalist Johnny Metal. However, the publication of his 1943 novel *120 rue de la Gare* marked a new departure, with a setting much closer to home: Paris during the Occupation, and with a central character, private detective Nestor Burma, who was recognizably, not to say emphatically, French. Burma resembled his creator in a number of ways: his association with anarchism and Surrealism, his pipe-smoking, his appreciation of the cityscape of Paris. After writing a number of individual Burma mysteries, Malet undertook an ambitious project to write a series of Burma novels, each one to be located in a different Parisian *arrondissement*. While the novels were influenced by the American hard-boiled school, the series title, *Les Nouveaux Mystères de*

Paris, evinces another influence on Malet, at least in its conceptual basis: Eugène Sue's nineteenth-century *roman feuilleton Les Mystères de Paris*, a series of detective novels published between 1842 and 1843. Malet's series would also demonstrate the influence of his Surrealist allegiance, with dreams and altered states of consciousness, both foregrounding the importance of the unconscious, featuring regularly in the novels.[4] However, the series was never completed but came to a halt in 1959, a time when Malet was increasingly jaundiced by the rapid changes in the Parisian landscape that had served as his inspiration.

Although the active phase of Malet's writing career came to an end at this point, his cultural influence did not. His novels continued to be read and adapted for television into the 1980s and beyond. His influence, in the guise of his iconic character Nestor Burma, was to resurface in the twenty-first century when, between 2001 and 2005, crime writer Patrick Pécherot published a trilogy of *romans noirs* featuring a detective named Nestor Burma: *Les Brouillards de la Butte* (2001), *Belleville-Barcelone* (2003) and *Boulevard des Branques* (2005), novels that Pécherot has acknowledged to be a tribute to Malet, declaring in his introduction to *Les Brouillards de la Butte* that the novel was 'librement inspiré[s] de l'œuvre et la vie de Léo Malet. [...] [Un] modeste hommage au créateur d'un des personnages mythiques du polar' ('freely inspired by the work and life of Léo Malet. [...] A modest homage to the creator of one of the legendary characters of the crime novel').[5] As this comment indicates, Pécherot's decision to recreate Malet's detective was motivated by nostalgic affection for the writer, or at least for the younger Malet. Although he originally associated with anarchists and Surrealists, in later life Malet moved to the right of the political spectrum and became something of a xenophobe. As will be seen later, some of his novels bear traces of this tendency. Pécherot prefers the younger Malet, the Surrealist *flâneur*: 'A force de gouailler sans garde-fou, il a franchi la ligne. Sa France popu n'est pas black-blanc-beur. [...] Ce Léo là, je le laisse. Et je prends l'autre. Le poète du trottoir et des cadavres exquis [...]. Le vrai Léo' ('Through his relentless cocky humour, he overstepped the mark. His version of popular France isn't exactly multicultural. [...] I've no time for that Léo. I prefer the other one. The poet of the streets and of exquisite cadavers. [...] The real Léo').[6]

This preference is not surprising given Pécherot's own political inclinations. While not associated with a particular political party, he is one of a number of French writers of crime fiction to use the genre as a space within which to articulate broadly left-wing socio-political concerns in novels that often have a political or ideological slant. Given this orientation, Pécherot's preference for 'Le vrai Léo', the young avant-garde poet, is a logical one and emerges through his version of Nestor Burma, who markedly resembles the younger Malet. This similarity is particularly evident in *Les Brouillards de la Butte*, which follows the traces of the impecunious young detective, like Malet subsisting through a range of menial and precarious jobs, against the backdrop of anarchist and Surrealist circles in 1920s Paris. In *Belleville-Barcelone*, Burma works for a private detective agency at the time of the *Front Populaire*, with the main storyline focusing on the consequences of political divisions among Republicans during the Spanish Civil War. The final novel of the trilogy, *Boulevard des Branques*, is set in the early days of the German Occupation and offers a number of parallels with Malet's first Burma novel, *120 rue de la Gare*.

This essay will examine some of the ways in which Pécherot has been inspired by Malet, focusing on this influence as both narrative- and character-driven. However, a more interesting aspect of the dynamics of influence in this case lies in the ways in which Pécherot diverges from Malet, reinventing the Burma character and his responses for a twenty-first-century audience. The most obvious distinctions are political, though they often also reflect differences in perspective related to the historical moment of the novels' composition. The following discussion will focus on a select number of Malet novels that relate in either setting or theme to Pécherot's trilogy.

The title of Pécherot's first Burma novel, *Les Brouillards de la Butte*, in its dual evocation of place and the elements, immediately suggests a parallel with Malet's *Les Neiges de Montmartre*, an unfinished one-chapter work, published in 1974. Set in 1926 in the eighteenth *arrondissement* of Paris, this single chapter introduces a young, poverty-stricken anarchist sympathizer, known only by his nickname of Pipette, who bears a striking resemblance to the youthful Malet, freshly arrived in Paris from the South of France. The embryonic storyline features the discovery of a dead body in a safe, with references to the *bande à Bonnot* and to the Sacco and Vanzetti case that galvanized the attention of the French left.[7] Pécherot takes these bare narrative bones and develops them into a full-length crime story in which Pipette solves the mystery of the body in the safe, meanwhile establishing connections with anarchist and Surrealist circles.

While *Belleville-Barcelone* bears no relationship to a specific Malet novel in terms of its plot or setting, numerous narrative similarities pinpoint Malet's first Burma novel, *120 rue de la Gare*, as an obvious intertextual reference for the informed reader of Pécherot's third Burma novel, *Boulevard des Branques*. Both novels are set in wartime Paris;

hence there are plentiful references in each to the shortages of food, fuel and other basic necessities that characterized the Occupation. In both novels, a mysterious stranger acts as the catalyst to the drama, passing on an apparently impenetrable message that the detective must decode. In *120 rue de la Gare*, the mysterious stranger is known as La Globule, an amnesiac whom Burma meets in a German *Stalag*. Just before he dies, La Globule passes on a cryptic message to Burma: 'Dites à Hélène, 120 rue de la Gare' ('Tell Hélène, 120 rue de la Gare').[8] Pécherot adopts a similar narrative strategy in *Boulevard des Branques*. Stranded in Chartres by disruption caused by the exodus from Paris, Burma's secretary Yvette witnesses the arrival of a train carrying patients from a mental asylum. One of them approaches her, but is mute. He drops a piece of paper containing a message that, by extraordinary coincidence, is addressed to Burma by Luka, an old friend asking for his help: 'Mon vieux Nes, si ce mot te parvient, je t'en supplie, sors-moi de là' ('Nes, my old friend, if this message reaches you, get me out of here, I beg you').[9] Both strangers suffer from conditions that can be seen as traumatic responses to wartime experiences: one has lost his memory and so is unable to remember anything before his capture, while the other has lost the power of speech. Both narratives are driven in part by a search for lost treasure: in *120 rue de la Gare*, pearls belonging to jewel thief Jo Tour Eiffel; and in *Boulevard des Branques*, part of a haul of gold lost during the Spanish Civil War.

Pécherot's most obvious borrowing from Malet is the character of Nestor Burma. In both novelists' work, there are significant similarities between the fictional detective and Malet himself. Malet and Burma are from the South of France, both came to Paris as young men, mixed with anarchists and Surrealists and led a hand-to-mouth existence. Both authors present Burma as the pipe-smoking *privé*, who follows a path through a complex series of events, inevitably discovering an unexpected corpse, falling unconscious at crucial moments in the narrative, usually through a blow to the head as he comes too close to the perpetrator, and often becoming romantically entangled with a female character involved in the investigation. In the original novels, Burma is supported by an entourage of friends who have been described as 'a surrogate family'.[10] Inspector Faroux, Burma's opposite number in the police force, has become Inspector Bailly in Pécherot's novels, equally exasperated by, yet sympathetic towards, the maverick Burma. Faroux has been described as the 'father figure of Burma's world [...] a disciplinarian and protector',[11] while the relationship elaborated in Pécherot's novels is more a relationship of equals, though Burma continues to rely on

Bailly's interventions to smooth the path of his investigations. In Malet's novels, Burma is assisted by secretary Hélène Châtelain, with whom he has a flirtatious yet chaste relationship. Only rarely does she participate in an investigation, and usually only when a female disguise is required. In *Les Brouillards de la Butte*, Pipette is not established as a detective and so does not have an assistant as such. However, in *Belleville-Barcelone* and *Boulevard des Branques*, secretary Yvette is transformed from a somewhat put-upon individual whom Burma initially registers only as a nagging background presence to an assistant who plays an active role in his investigations. Like Hélène, she is called on to disguise herself; in *Belleville-Barcelone*, Burma asks her to pose as a prostitute. Yet, where Hélène remained a background presence, Yvette enters fully into the spirit of the operation, showing herself to be a feisty individual and very much a part of the team. This greater equality comes further into play when Pécherot alters the dynamic of their relationship, transforming it from a chastely flirtatious into a sexual one. This enables Yvette to demonstrate greater agency than is allowed to Hélène and, in particular, to challenge Burma's frequently patriarchal attitudes and assert her autonomy. When Burma asks her to change out of a provocative disguise simply to suit his mood, she challenges his assumption that she dresses only for him.[12] Her boss Bohman, the owner of the detective agency, remarks on the change he sees in her as Burma's lover, noting that she now describes herself as Burma's *associée* and that she will no longer be told what to do.[13]

Malet's influence on Pécherot is evident not just in the characters but in the Parisian setting of the trilogy. The cityscape celebrated in Malet's *Les Nouveaux Mystères de Paris* was geographically anchored in a very particular way, with each novel taking place in a specific *arrondissement*. The city remains a constant reference point in Pécherot's novels, though in a less structured way, as Burma pursues his investigations in the capital, often on foot. Paris is important not merely as a physical backdrop, but intellectually and culturally. In *Les Brouillards de la Butte* Pipette meets André Breton and the Surrealists, for whom the cityscape was aesthetically important. This connection remains a significant feature in *Belleville-Barcelone*. The Paris of *Boulevard des Branques* is very different, with a focus on the daily hardships of the Occupation, yet is still an important backdrop for Burma's *flâneries*.

Yet while Pécherot's recreation of Burma draws substantially on Malet's model, closer analysis of the novels reveals significant divergences between the two writers' treatment of Burma the character and the situations he encounters. These divergences are essentially of two types. First, there are differences of political perspective hinted at in

Pécherot's description of Malet's version of France: 'Sa France popu n'est pas black-blanc-beur', as discussed above; second, we notice differences that can be attributed to Pécherot's access to information not available when Malet was writing his novels, notably in his representation of the Occupation. While Malet's political perspective was not always that of a right-wing xenophobe, one of the most obvious differences between the writers is nonetheless their respective treatment of politics or political themes in the stories. These distinctions are less marked in Pécherot's *Les Brouillards de la Butte*, in part because it does not have an obvious equivalent among Malet's published novels – though as we have seen, there are narrative similarities with the unfinished *Les Neiges de Montmartre*. The latter comprises only one isolated chapter, though in it Malet introduces the debate about illegalism[14] within the anarchist movement, particularly in relation to the activities of the *bande à Bonnot* and the trial of Sacco and Vanzetti in the USA; and he does so with some sympathy, reflecting the ideas of the groups with which he was closely associated as a young man. *Brouillard au pont de Tolbiac* (1956) also briefly evokes this period, with one short episode highlighting differences between the proponents of illegalism and other anarchists. In *Les Brouillards de la Butte*, which features Burma's early days in Paris, Pécherot also highlights the debate about illegalism, the activities of the *bande à Bonnot* and the trial of Sacco and Vanzetti.

Despite these parallels in subject matter, Pécherot's outlook in *Les Brouillards de la Butte* is more politicized than that of Malet in *Les Neiges de Montmartre*. One example of this is to be found in the attention paid by Pécherot to the aftermath of World War I, still evident in the Paris of 1927 but not mentioned in Malet's (admittedly short) text. Pipette recalls childhood memories of wounded veterans and the dark shadows still cast by the war: 'Huit ans après, on essayait toujours d'oublier [...]. Rien à faire. Le plus cul-terreux des villages avait son monument aux morts' ('Eight years later, people were still trying to forget [...]. It was futile. Every village, even in the back of beyond, had its war memorial').[15] Pécherot also references the contemporary critique of war through historical characters such as pacifist Louis Lecoin, who highlights the complicity of industrialists in the continuation of the war: 'Plus la guerre était longue, plus les marchands de canons pouvaient se remplir les poches' ('The longer the war lasted, the more the arms dealers could fill their pockets').[16] This is a critique taken up by Pécherot's version of Breton, who expresses not just Surrealist opposition to the war, but personal experience of the trenches: 'Voilà où elle nous a menés la raison, à l'apocalypse. Et ceux à qui elle a profité continuent leurs combines. [...] Breton s'était levé, les traits creusés. Par la fenêtre, il regardait loin de Paris. Vers les Hurlus et le Chemin des Dames' ('Look where reason has led us, to the apocalypse. And those who have profited by it continue their scheming. [...] Breton had stood up, his features gaunt. Through the window he was looking far beyond Paris to Hurlus and the Chemin des Dames').[17]

Political differences are more in evidence in *Belleville-Barcelone* by virtue of its 1930s setting. The only Malet novel set in the 1930s is *L'Homme au sang bleu*, set in Cannes, far from the intense political debates of the 1930s echoed in *Belleville-Barcelone*, which opens with a series of references to the momentous events taking place in Europe and beyond: the end of the Front Populaire and right-wing resurgence in France; the rise of Hitler, Mussolini and Franco in Europe; and Stalinist purges in the USSR. Burma's investigation of the disappearance of communist sympathizer Pietro, and a subplot involving the theft of weapons from the Cagoule and re-routed to Spanish republicans, mean that the Spanish Civil War forms an important backdrop to the novel, with a particular focus on internal divisions between anarchists and communists. Burma discovers that Pietro, disillusioned by what he saw in Spain, left the Party and was murdered by Stalinists because of his subsequent *rapprochement* with anarchists.[18] Burma has direct experience of the rise of French right-wing movements such as Doriot's Parti Populaire Français through the difficulties of his friend Gopian, an Armenian immigrant. Gopian's bistrot is destroyed by an explosion as a parade of *doriotistes* passes by making Nazi salutes and chanting nationalist slogans. This ominous picture of right-wing nationalism is reinforced by Burma's connection with Milou, a Roma gypsy, who has encountered the Croix de Feu with their ambition to 'En finir avec la subversion, les métèques, tout ce qui pourrissait le pays' ('Put an end to subversives, wogs and everything that's corrupting the country').[19]

References to extreme right-wing organizations highlight another divergence, already hinted at, between Malet and Pécherot: the gulf in their attitudes to other races and ethnic groups. Much has been made of Malet's xenophobia in later life, traces of which can already be seen in various novels in allusions to Jews and other minorities. In *Brouillard au pont de Tolbiac* Burma falls in love with a gypsy woman, Bélita. This emotional attachment does not preclude his maintaining stereotypical assumptions about gypsies. When Belita fails to turn up for a meeting with Faroux, Burma attributes her absence to an innate suspicion of the police, typical of 'une race qui décèle le flic à un kilomètre' ('a race that can detect a cop a kilometre away').[20] An altercation with a member of her family triggers a much more offensive statement: 'Quelle bande de cloches, avec leurs histoires de race! Je me demande ce qu'on a reproché à Hitler' ('What a band of tramps with all their fuss about race! I can't see what people had against Hitler').[21] The contrast with Pécherot's Burma, a man at ease in his relationships with other ethnic groups, could not be stronger. In *Belleville-Barcelone* and in *Boulevard des Branques*, his friendships with the Armenian Gopian and Milou the Roma attest to this.

Attitudes to the Jews are another area where we see divergences between the views of Malet's Burma and Pécherot's Burma. Two of Malet's Burma stories deal with the experiences of Jews during the Occupation and, more specifically, with the Jewish deportations. In *Des Kilomètres de linceuls* (1955), Esther Levyberg is a concentration camp survivor who, in order to punish her family for their opposition to her relationship with her lover, betrayed their Jewish identity to the authorities. The betrayal resulted in their deportation, seeming to imply Jewish complicity in the Holocaust. *Du rébecca rue des Rosiers* (1957) promotes a similarly problematic thesis of Jewish betrayal of other Jews. The murder victim, Rachel Blum, has been killed by her cousin, Isass, acting on behalf of Bramovici, a Jewish collaborator and informer. As David Fraser has commented: 'The twin narratives offered by Malet, of Jewish blameworthiness in bringing the Holocaust upon themselves and then of organizing the persecution and killing of their fellow Jews, echo the worst Nazi propaganda'.[22] In *Pas de bavards à la Muette* (1956), jeweller Rosenbaum is presented both as a man of stereotypical Jewish appearance and as extremely ugly, as though the two were inevitably linked: 'il avait le teint plombé, les yeux glauques et embrumés. Il ruisselait de sueur. Ses abondants tifs frisés lui retombaient sur le front, en mèches tirebouchonnées, grasses, poisseuses et humides' ('His complexion was the colour of lead; his shifty eyes were cloudy. He was dripping with sweat. His abundant curly hair hung down on his forehead in greasy, sticky, moist corkscrew locks').[23] While the description is unpleasant enough, the revelation that Rosenbaum is actually dead is worded in a manner that is even less palatable for a post-Holocaust sensibility: 'Victime d'un pogrome à l'échelle individuelle, il était aussi mort que s'il sortait d'un four crématoire' ('The victim of a personal pogrom, he was as dead as if he had just come out of the ovens').[24]

Pécherot's treatment of Jews and other minorities in *Boulevard des Branques* is very different. While Malet makes no mention of the implications of Vichy's agenda for Jews, even though these were becoming clear before the publication of *120 rue de la Gare*, Pécherot's narrative is informed by a retrospective knowledge of the period, shared by his readership, thus enabling a different perspective not available to Malet. Pécherot's Burma witnesses the breaking of the windows of shops believed to belong to Jews. A very visual juxtaposition is made between a shop owner clearing up the debris on the Champs Élysées and the Swastika floating on the Arc de Triomphe behind, precluding any need for authorial comment: 'un gros type en chemise balayait le trottoir. La mine défaite, il s'est arrêté pour contempler l'arc de triomphe où flottait l'oriflamme à croix gammée' ('A big guy in shirtsleeves was sweeping the pavement. His face haggard, he stopped to look at the Arc de Triomphe where the swastika was flying').[25] A passing reference to the anti-Semitic propaganda film *Le Juif Süss* (*Jew Süss*), first shown in Paris in February 1941, is accompanied by a quotation from a review of the film in *Au pilori*. Its aggressively racist language again needs no commentary from the narrator: 'Le Juif n'est pas un homme, c'est une bête puante' ('The Jew is not a man, he is a stinking animal').[26] Pécherot changes the name of the detective agency for which Burma works. In Malet's novels it was called *Fiat Lux*, an optimistic commentary on the agency's ability to cast light on difficult cases. In Pécherot's novels it has become *Agence Bohman*, enabling the author to foreground the vulnerability of its Jewish owner Bohman, and ultimately of the agency itself. We learn that Bohman, whose cousin Samuel was a victim of Kristallnacht in Berlin, has realised the coming dangers and has left Paris: 'Tout est dans *Mein Kampf*, Nestor, tout. Hitler fera ce qu'il a écrit' ('It's all there in *Mein Kampf*, Nestor. Hitler will do exactly what he wrote').[27] His fears are realized in the novel's final scene where Burma returns to the office to see a freshly posted sign on the wall outside, identifying the agency as an 'entreprise juive' ('Jewish business').[28]

The agency has also undergone a change of location. In Malet's novels it is located in the second *arrondissement*, known as a centre for clothing and tailoring, while Pécherot has moved it to Belleville, a cosmopolitan, working-class area. The resultant presence of characters of different nationalities and political persuasions gives Pécherot the opportunity to demonstrate that minority groups other than the Jewish residents of France are being singled out for discriminatory treatment under Vichy. Republicans who sought refuge in France after the Spanish Civil War are no longer welcome. Max Fehcker, the mute who passed Luka's message to Yvette, escaped Hitler's Germany, fought in the Spanish Civil War and fled to France in 1939 after Franco's victory, only to discover that the political climate was no longer welcoming.[29] Interned in a series of different camps, he gradually loses his grip on sanity. Luka himself was resident in France as a German national for 15 years. Observing the changing circumstances, he feigned insanity, preferring the prospect of internment as a patient in an asylum to feared deportation to a camp.[30] His choice is a tragically ironic one since, unable to escape the asylum, he dies there.

Having witnessed the reassessments of the Occupation and of Vichy through historiography, through the trials of Vichy officials and through film and literature, Pécherot naturally had access to information unavailable to Malet in 1943 when he wrote *120 rue de la Gare*, and was able to deploy this knowledge in his novel. *Boulevard des Branques* makes a contribution to the ongoing process of reassessment of the dark years of Occupation through its consideration of the question of eugenics and, specifically, of allegations made in recent years about the unexpectedly high number of deaths in mental institutions during the Occupation, attributed by some to a deliberate attempt by the Vichy regime to dispose of the mentally unfit.[31] Consequently, despite its surface similarities with *120 rue de la Gare*, *Boulevard des Branques* has more in common with a novel like Daeninckx's *Meurtres pour mémoire* in its ideologically driven unearthing of hidden truths about the war.

As the 'père du roman noir français',[32] Léo Malet has been acknowledged as an important influence on the development of French crime fiction. Pécherot's decision to feature Malet's well-loved character Nestor Burma in his trilogy pays tribute to this influential role. However, the parallels between the work of the two authors do not suggest that Pécherot is blindly influenced by his predecessor. While there are obvious similarities of narrative and character, there are, as has been demonstrated, significant differences between the two authors, above all in their political perspective. The term *hommage* has been used of the trilogy by a number of critics and by Pécherot himself.[33] I would contend that Pécherot goes beyond *hommage*, a term that implies an unproblematic admiration, in order to offer a new take on Malet's Nestor Burma. He has acknowledged that the older Malet crossed a line that made him uncomfortable and, rather than try to make excuses for him and argue 'qu'il était d'un autre temps, celui des colonies, [...] de *Tintin au Congo*' ('that he was from another era, that of the colonies, [...] of *Tintin in the Congo*'),[34] he has instead chosen to be inspired by 'le vrai Léo', the younger writer, and has reinvented Malet's iconic character to make of him a hero more acceptable to a twenty-first-century readership.

Notes

1. See Claire Gorrara, 'Cultural Intersections: The American Hard-Boiled Detective Novel and Early French *roman noir*', *Modern Language Review*, 98.3 (2003), 590–601, for a discussion of the influence of the American hard-boiled on the emergent *Série noire*.
2. The first two French authors to be published in the *Série noire* were Serge Arcouët and Jean Meckert, writing as Terry Stewart and John Amila respectively.
3. Michelle Emanuel quotes the Gallimard website that, on the occasion of the author's death, referred to him as 'le père du roman noir français'. See Michelle Emanuel, *From Surrealism to Less-Exquisite Cadavers: Léo Malet and the Evolution of the French Roman Noir* (Amsterdam and New York: Rodopi, 2006), p. 25. All translations are my own.
4. See ibid., pp. 55–80 (Chapter 2).
5. Patrick Pécherot, *Les Brouillards de la Butte* (Paris: Gallimard, 2001), p. 9.
6. Patrick Pécherot, http://www.pecherot.com/rubrique.php3?id_rubrique=1 (accessed 18 April 2012).
7. The *bande à Bonnot* was a criminal anarchist group that operated in France between 1911 and 1912. Sacco and Vanzetti were suspected anarchists and were tried for murder in the USA in 1927. The trial and their subsequent execution generated a highly politicized debate in France and elsewhere over their guilt or innocence.
8. Léo Malet, *Nestor Burma. Premières enquêtes*, ed. by Nadia Dhoukar (Paris: Robert Laffont, 2006), p. 311.
9. Patrick Pécherot, *Boulevard des Branques* (Paris: Gallimard, 2005), p. 41.
10. Emanuel, *From Surrealism*, p. 27.
11. Ibid., p. 112.
12. Patrick Pécherot, *Belleville-Barcelone* (Paris: Gallimard, 2003), p. 164.
13. Ibid., p. 135.
14. Illegalism was a branch of anarchist philosophy according to which illegal acts were committed not in pursuit of an ideal but simply out of personal interest.
15. Pécherot, *Les Brouillards*, p. 51.
16. Ibid., p. 225.
17. Ibid., p. 257.
18. Pécherot, *Belleville-Barcelone*, p. 192.
19. Ibid, p. 36.
20. Léo Malet, *Nestor Burma. Les Nouveaux Mystères de Paris (I)*, ed. by Nadia Dhoukar (Paris: Robert Laffont, 2006), p. 863.
21. Ibid., p. 893.

22. David Fraser, 'Polarcauste: Law, Justice and the Shoah in French Detective Fiction', *International Journal of Law in Context*, 1.3 (2005), 237–60 (p. 250). A more nuanced analysis of these incidents is offered by Claire Gorrara in 'Forgotten Crimes? Representing Jewish Experience of the Second World War in French Crime Fiction', *South Central Review*, 27.1–2 (2010), 3–20 (pp. 8–9).
23. Malet, *Nestor Burma. Les Nouveaux Mystères de Paris (II)*, ed. by Nadia Dhoukar (Paris: Robert Laffont, 2006), p. 210.
24. Ibid.
25. Pécherot, *Boulevard des Branques*, p. 69.
26. Ibid., p. 260.
27. Ibid., p. 15.
28. Ibid., p. 293. The singling-out of Bohman's agency would have been to enable implementation of a German ordinance of October 1940, 'requiring all Jewish enterprises in the Occupied Zone to be placed under trusteeship as a preliminary to "Aryanization"'; see Julian Jackson, *France: The Dark Years, 1940–1944* (Oxford: Oxford University Press, 2001), p. 356.
29. Pécherot, *Boulevard des Branques*, pp. 158–9.
30. Ibid., p. 245. Luka's fears were well founded. According to Julian Jackson, 'At the end of 1940 the internment camp population stood at about 55,000–60,000, consisting largely of foreign Jewish refugees, former members of the International Brigades, and French Communists' (Jackson, *France: The Dark Years*, p. 151).
31. This aspect of the novel is analysed in Angela Kimyongür, 'Patrick Pécherot, Eugenics and the Occupation of France', in *Violence and War in Culture and the Media: Five Disciplinary Lenses*, ed. by A. Karatzogianni (London & New York: Routledge, 2012), pp. 30–45.
32. Emanuel, *From Surrealism*, p. 25.
33. Among other reviews reproduced on www.pecherot.com: 'Le plus bel hommage qu'on pouvait rêver à Léo Malet' (Gérard Meudal, *Le Monde des livres*); 'un formidable et fraternel hommage' (Jean-Louis Porquet, *Le Canard enchaîné*). See Pécherot, *Les Brouillards* (p. 9), for the author's own use of the term.
34. Pécherot, http://www.pecherot.com/rubrique.php3?id_rubrique=1 (accessed 18 April 2012).

12
Jacques Roubaud's Rejection of *Japoniste* Influence: *Tokyo infra-ordinaire*

Lucy O'Meara

In the spring of 1689, the Japanese poet and teacher Matsuo Bashō sold his house. He left his home in the capital city, Edo, and departed with one companion on a long journey into the wild territories of northern Japan. He was to remain on the road for over two and a half years, and the first six months of the journey became the basis of his most famous travel journal, *Oku no hosomichi* (*The Narrow Road to the Deep North*).[1] Many of the remoter places visited by Bashō were, in poetic terms, uncharted. Japanese poetic composition at this time relied heavily on a long-established system of place names: landmarks of cultural or spiritual significance were known as the *utamakura*, or 'poetic pillows'. Medieval *waka* poets preserved the cultural associations of these places by a system of toponymic references.[2] Bashō, by contrast, wanted to create new *utamakura* from previously unused, commonplace rural scenes. However, he was still obliged to pay appropriate homage to those places that had poetic links with his classical predecessors. Thus when he reached the site of the ancient Shirakawa barrier, gateway to the north, a verse was expected:

> At the post station at Sukagawa, I [was asked] 'How did you find the crossing at the Shirakawa Barrier?' I replied, 'My body and spirit were tired from the pain of the long journey; my heart overwhelmed by the landscape. The thoughts of the distant past tore through me, and I couldn't think straight. But feeling it would be a pity to cross the barrier without producing a single verse, I wrote

beginnings of poetry –
rice-planting songs
of the Deep North

This opening verse was followed by a second verse and then a third; before we knew it, three sequences...[3]

This quotation is representative of Bashō's innovative poetics, in that it accords due attention to the poetic potency of the 'distant past', while simultaneously abandoning the standard poetic tropes of the Shirakawa Barrier and the poet's longing for the capital. Instead, it is in the rice-planters' quotidian task that Bashō finds inspiration.

In 1996, the French poet, mathematician and Oulipian, Jacques Roubaud, left Paris to spend six weeks in Japan. He rented a studio in Shinjuku, the commercial and administrative heart of Tokyo. For a month he travelled around the city centre, taking notes for a future work. The text was to be a *haibun*, or a mixture of prose and poetry, wherein the prose sections provide a backdrop and gloss for brief, incisive landscape poems. It was Bashō's *Narrow Road to the Deep North* that crystallized this previously fragmentary genre into a skilful, interactional form that blended Chinese and Japanese forms, and classical and vernacular idioms.[4] Roubaud had, in 1976, worked on a *haibun* based around a series of walks by the Mississippi river.[5] On this occasion in Japan, Roubaud, like Bashō, planned a journey to the interior – the heart of the capital city. He suffered his own lack of *utamakura*, not knowing quite where to start and being, in Tokyo, 'analphabète, linguistiquement quasi muet, linguistiquement à peu près sourd' ('illiterate, pretty much deaf and dumb, linguistically').[6] He decided therefore to provide himself with a series of landmarks: the structure of the poem would be dictated by the stations on the Yamanote train line, which loops around central Tokyo. Structuring the work thus, he could write an extended 'poème de métro', in accordance with the constraint defined by Roubaud's fellow Oulipian, Jacques Jouet.[7] As Jouet explains, to write a metro poem one composes a short poem during the journey between one metro stop and the next, and writes the poem down while the train is at a station. In doing so, Roubaud encounters difficulties: he reflects during the text on the challenges of writing poems in extremely crowded metro carriages, or on rainy streets. Also, Roubaud was uncertain as to whether the cityscapes in the vicinity of the Yamanote line would provide him with material sufficient to write his *haibun*. He was determined, however, that the resulting work, if there were to be one, would treat contemporary, mundane Japan: 'C'est un Japon très particulier, ce n'est pas du tout le Japon ancien, pas du tout le Japon impressionnant, que voient les touristes ou qu'imaginent les hommes d'affaires; c'est le Japon quotidien, ou le Japon infra-ordinaire comme disait mon ami Georges Perec' ('It's a very particular version of Japan. Not the ancient, impressive Japan that tourists see and that businessmen imagine. Rather, it's a quotidian Japan – an "infra-ordinary" Japan, as my friend Georges Perec might say').[8] Like Bashō, Roubaud would concentrate on finding poetic inspiration in places not normally considered as inherently poetic. At the same time, he would, as Bashō did, render his own homage to the classical literary past.

The work that resulted from Roubaud's six weeks in Tokyo was a *haibun* of sorts, was given the Perecian title *Tokyo infra-ordinaire* and was avowedly 'prosaïque' (*T*, p. 33) in essence. Its 91 pages are vividly expansive: the work is printed in nine colours, with endlessly proliferating subsections being carefully numbered. While *Tokyo infra-ordinaire* is multilingual, exuberant, curious, and is larded with references to classical Japanese literature, it is also primarily focused on resolutely banal everyday life. In all of these ways, the work constitutes an implicit rebuke to the smooth, aestheticized tradition of French writing about Japan.

Since the opening of Japan to the West in the mid-nineteenth century, there has been a rich cross-cultural exchange between France and Japan, the earliest and most striking example of this being the profound impact of *ukiyo-e* prints on the French Impressionists from the 1860s onwards. Recent research into representations of Japan in French writing has demonstrated that the aesthetic focus of nineteenth-century *japonisme* was in large part maintained in twentieth-century French Japanophile travel writing and fiction, as evidenced in the work of writers as varied in their approaches and genres as Claudel, Barthes, Yourcenar, Butor and Gérard Macé.[9] In 1998, in a journal issue discussing the impact of Said's *Orientalism*, the Japanese critic Kojin Karatani published an article entitled 'Uses of Aesthetics: After Orientalism'.[10] Karatani argues that continental European intellectual discourse has still not fully absorbed the implications of Said's work. He makes this point with particular regard to Franco-Japanese literary relations, claiming that French writers are always too willing to 'kneel before the beauty' of the Japanese other.[11] In paying homage to Japanese aesthetics, he writes, such writers screen out or 'bracket' the complexity of Japanese history, and practise what amounts to an Orientalist suppression of contemporary reality. There have certainly been troubling and reductive aspects to the French literary relationship with Japanese sources of inspiration. Chris

Reyns-Chikuma argues that French literature about Japan has been, since its inception, 'esthésicentrique' ('aestheticentric') and one-dimensional, flagrantly unconcerned with historical reality.[12] Even recent French writing about Japan tends to be, in his term, 'postjaponiste', that is, exoticist. Reyns-Chikuma's book closes on a positive note, however. He cites the growth of multicultural debate in twenty-first-century France, as well as a growth of academic interest in contemporary Japan. Owing to these among other factors, contemporary French literature about Japan can now, finally, be claimed as '*post*-exotic' and Reyns-Chikuma is optimistic that, henceforth, this literature will be more 'critical, open and dynamic'.[13]

Roubaud's poem seems to bear out Reyns-Chikuma's point. The work was published online in 2005 as part of an electronic journal initiative called *Projet Jet Stream*.[14] The aim of the project was to sketch 'a fragmentary, dynamic portrait' of contemporary Japan. The vast majority of the texts and images on the Jet Stream website focused on aspects of the European traveller's confused first experience of the Japanese metropolis. More or less explicitly, the texts evince a concern to avoid the clichés of French literary *japonisme*. *Japoniste* settings tend to be rarefied, pre-modern and usually non-urban. The *Projet Jet Stream* texts, by contrast, evoke a mundane urban realism, which implicitly rejects the tenets of aestheticentric *japonisme*.

In Roubaud's case, the 'infra-ordinary' subject matter and the structuring device of the commuter rail line indicate a firm desire to eschew *japoniste* clichés in a diaristic, psycho-geographical evocation of everyday Tokyo. This is all decided by Roubaud in advance:

> <u>Ma décision</u>: bien avant de partir, à Paris, regardant ma carte, j'avais pris conscience d'une sorte d'œil formé par la Yamanote Line et englobant le centre même de Tokyo central. Assez abstrait, bien sûr, mais ce n'est pas plus mal.
>
> <u>Le plan</u>: Aller dans toutes les stations par la Yamanote Line; une station par jour; chaque station constituant une <u>station</u> de mon *haibun* futur.
>
> Rayonner à partir de la station du jour, vers l'intérieur surtout. Profiter des parcs pour la méditation – composition des poèmes.
>
> (<u>My decision</u>: long before I left, while looking at my map in Paris, I realized there's a sort of eye, formed by the Yamanote Line, which encircles the centre of central Tokyo. Fairly abstract, of course, but that's just as well.

The plan: Go to all the stations on the Yamanote Line. One station every day, each one constituting a station of my future *haibun*. Radiate out from the given station, mainly towards the interior. Use the parks for meditation – poetic composition.) (*T*, pp. 23–4)

The poem will start at the point where the traveller to Tokyo first arrives: Shinjuku station, the world's busiest rail station. The opening lines are as follows:

La gare de Shinjuku (Tokyo) est grande. Elle accommoderait sans peine une douzaine de gare du Nord (Paris). Les lignes de métro passent en dessous; les lignes ferroviaires dessus. Les deux entrées principales sont la West Entrance et la East Entrance. Il m'a fallu plusieurs tentatives pour arriver à passer de l'une à l'autre sans m'égarer plusieurs fois.

(Tokyo's Shinjuku Station is big. You could easily fit 12 of Paris's Gare du Nord into it. Metro lines run underneath you and train lines above you. The two main entrances are the West and the East Entrances. It took me several attempts before I could go from one to the other without getting lost several times.) (*T*, p. 7)

We are clearly far removed from the cherry blossoms and Madame Chrysanthèmes of the *japoniste* tradition here. However, the flat description of the rail station does mobilize clichés drawn from the field of more recent Francophone responses to the Japanese metropolis. In the first instance, we have the figure of the circle or the void, in this case described by the Yamanote line: Roubaud here seems to be playing on the trope, found in Western and specifically in Parisian responses to Tokyo, of the 'centrelessness' of Tokyo. Roland Barthes, in his 1970 text *L'Empire des signes* (*Empire of Signs*), a text that has been very influential on subsequent French evocations of Japan, names the centre of Tokyo, the 'centre-ville' ('town centre'), the '*centre-vide*' ('empty centre'). At the very heart of the city, where in a western city the key buildings of business, religion, trade and socializing would be gathered, there is instead, writes Barthes, the forbidden, muffled space of the Imperial Palace:

La ville dont je parle (Tokyo) présente ce paradoxe précieux: elle possède bien un centre, mais ce centre est vide.
    Toute la ville tourne autour d'un lieu à la fois interdit et indifférent, demeure masquée sous la verdure, défendue par des fossés d'eau,

habitée par un empereur qu'on ne voit jamais, c'est-à-dire, [...] par on ne sait qui.

(The city of Tokyo presents this precious paradox: it does have a centre, but this centre is empty. The whole city revolves around a space that's both forbidden and indifferent, hidden under foliage, protected by moats, and inhabited by an emperor you never see – in other words, by an unknown person.)[15]

Barthes's Japan is full of symbols of emptiness: the kanji for 'mu', meaning the void, is given a page to itself at the opening of *L'Empire des signes*. Indeed, much of the critical literature on Barthes's alleged 'orientalism' focuses on the 'void' he finds, not just in the Tokyo cityspace, but in aspects of Japanese culture. This fascination can be easily fitted into an Orientalist critique when aligned with traditionally Orientalist figures of the passive, inscrutable Orient. Nonetheless, Barthes's conception of Tokyo as a centreless labyrinth seems to have entered into the imaginary of contemporary French writers' responses to Japan. The contemporary aesthetic theorist, Christine Buci-Glucksmann, has written at length about the nature of Tokyo's urban space. Avowing her debt to Barthes, Buci-Glucksmann discusses the centreless, labyrinthine nature of Tokyo, ascribing the sensation of confusion that the visitor feels to the fact that it is constructed in a spiraloid fashion; that is, according to a 'non-geometric' abstraction.[16]

Roubaud is clearly aware of the Parisian tropes of Tokyo as an empty-centred labyrinth. The construction of his poem around the unending loop of the Yamanote line seems to play on this. Its shape is, as he puts it, like an eye, a circle, 'assez abstrait'. But, in what can be seen as a reaction against French theorists' abstraction of Tokyo, Roubaud playfully debunks the 'centre-ville, centre-vide' ('city centre, empty centre') conception of Tokyo, concertedly filling his circle with teeming reality. From each station on the Yamanote line he enters the centre, recording the abundance of activity he sees there – schoolchildren in a park, traffic, a vegetable market, bank employees scrubbing the pavement outside their building, the enormous crowds pouring out of all the stations on the Yamanote line. The 'centre-vide' of the Imperial Palace, as evoked by Barthes, is, in Roubaud's version, teeming:

Je marche de station en station de la Yamanote Line. Mais je marche aussi autour du palais. [...] Tour du palais impérial en 1h40

– cyclistes, joggeurs, [...]
– équipes de croquets au jardin imperial
– maillots, n^{os} équipes comme basket, base-ball
– vieux messieurs et dames.

(I walk from station to station on the Yamanote Line. But I also walk around the palace. [...] Full circle takes an hour and forty minutes
– cyclists, joggers [...]
– croquet teams in the imperial gardens
– T-shirts with numbers, like basketball or baseball shirts
– elderly gents and ladies.) (*T*, p. 29)

The full, busy, everyday centre of Tokyo, sprawling in many colours over the pages of Roubaud's *haibun*, seems a rebuke to the idealized symbolism of Barthes's and Buci-Glucksmann's descriptions of the city.

The other major trope of post-modern and anti-*japoniste* French literary responses to Japan is that of the European traveller's sensation of being overwhelmed by the size of Tokyo, and specifically by its transport networks. Thus Barthes devotes a section of *L'Empire des signes* to Tokyo rail stations, their size and the variety of commercial and social activities they accommodate.[17] Buci-Glucksmann discusses the manner in which the extreme multiplication of roads, train lines and overhead motorways seems to render any single perspective on Tokyo unstable, especially for the disorientated European. Roubaud uses the trope of the European's amazement at the Tokyo travel network in the same way as he uses the trope of the void: it forms the basis of his poem, while also being debunked. Thus, as we have seen, the poem opens with a wilfully banal description of the bewildering size of Shinjuku station. Roubaud then immediately digresses from this into matters that interest him more, such as the name of the man from whom he's renting his studio – a name shared with the classical Japanese poet Fujiwara Teika – or the mundane sights of the street where the studio is located. This movement from a knowingly hackneyed response to the bigness of Tokyo, to the minutiae of the street and of Roubaud's interest in Japanese poetry, is common throughout the whole text. The effect is one of a pleasing puncturing of the banality of the awestruck response to Tokyo's sheer scale, as we see here in the drily humorous repetition of 'of course':

bonne architecture de reconstruction post-1945 dans la drabness, le terne, le petit;

> il y a aussi les gratte-ciel insensés,
> of course
> le pont qui boucle sur la mer
> le Rainbow Bridge;
> je n'ai pas pu m'empêcher d'y
> aller voir, en dépit du vertige
> préliminaire
> les autoroutes sur des voies
> ferrées, elle-mêmes sur un canal,
> mais tout le monde sait ça
> of course
>
> (Good post-war architecture – drab, dingy, small;
> there are also insane skyscrapers
> of course
> the bridge that loops over the sea
> the Rainbow Bridge;
> I couldn't help going
> to see it, despite the initial
> vertigo
> motorways over trainlines
> which in turn are over a canal,
> but everyone knows that
> of course) (*T*, p. 14)

Roubaud is determined that his poem be genuinely concerned with the 'infra-ordinariness' of its title. This determination involves a ludic manipulation of the stock contemporary responses to the post-modern cityspace of Tokyo.

The focus on the infra-ordinary also extends to a refusal to employ any clichés of Japanese beauty. This is of course linked to both Roubaud's and other contemporary French writers' desire to evade *japoniste* triteness. Thus, in *Tokyo infra-ordinaire*, if cherry blossoms are mentioned, they are the fake cherry trees in the car park, with their 'feuilles-pétales roses-fluo [...] de plastique' ('fluorescent pink plastic leaf-petals') (*T*, pp. 9–10). These lines are framed by quotations from thirteenth- and eighteenth-century poems in praise of the cherry blossom. Similarly, the presence of Mount Fuji, that most iconic of symbols of Japanese beauty, is concertedly absent from Roubaud's poem, except through the intermediary of medieval poetry. Roubaud says that whenever he is on the bullet train between Tokyo and Kyoto, from which one is supposed to have an excellent view of the snow-topped mountain, he never manages to catch a glimpse of it. He transcribes a (perhaps imagined) conversation:

– avez-vous vu le Fuji?
– non, le Fuji n'est jamais visible; le Fuji n'existe pas; c'est une invention des poètes du Manyôshû,[18] avec la complicité de la Japan National Tourist Organization
– avez-vous vu le Fuji?
– non
– quel dommage!

('Have you seen Fuji?'
'No, Fuji is never visible. Fuji doesn't exist – the Manyoshu poets invented it, aided and abetted by the Japan National Tourist Organization'
'Have you seen Fuji?'
'No'
'What a shame!') (T, p. 31)

There follows a sonnet on the non-existence of Fuji: Roubaud muses that Fuji would surely deign to appear 'pour moi, lecteur du *Genji*, / Moi, du Manyôshû, [...] / Il daignerait, dis-je, dévoiler sa face' ('surely it would deign to show its face to me, reader of *The Tale of Genji*, of the *Manyoshu*'). The mountain, shrouded in cloud, makes no such concession, and the sonnet concludes bathetically: 'Aujourd'hui, hélas [...] / je soupçonne que le grand / Fuji n'existe pas, ou plus' ('Today, alas, I suspect that the great Fuji doesn't exist, or has vanished') (T, p. 32).

The point is not that Roubaud refuses to see beauty. There is an aesthetic imperative, but this decidedly does not take the form of responding to landscape clichés, or to such remnants of Hokusai's world as can still be glimpsed in present-day Tokyo. Roubaud is anxious to avoid the aesthetic hierarchy adopted by most travellers to Tokyo and Kyoto, whereby contemporary reality is shunned in favour of the more rarefied, 'naturalized' beauty of the past. Instead of this simplistic abjuring of the contemporary city, Roubaud uses the mundane, commercial sights of the city around him, with its lorries, vending machines and salarymen, as a springboard for a layering of memories, both rural and urban, which are nourished by his extensive knowledge of Japanese poetry. This can be seen clearly in a section wherein Roubaud explains that it is precisely the *absence* of the natural world in central Tokyo that brings to his mind most potently the *tanka* of the Imperial Japanese anthologies. Just as Bashō found the rice-pickers more inspiring than the Shirakawa gate, Roubaud is more interested in urban parks than temples:

> dans les parcs, dans les cimetières, je me répète les *tanka* encore présents à ma mémoire évanouissante; le 'fait' de la présence du monde naturel aussi peu naturel que possible me restitue une présence forte de ces poèmes, [...] beaucoup plus forte en fait que dans les temples où le sentiment du fabriqué, à tort ou à raison, m'est plus sensible, même si je suis attentif à l'émotion, *omoi*, et au charme, *yoen*, de leur beauté

> (in the parks and cemeteries I repeat to myself the *tanka* that I can still remember. The 'fact' of the natural world, here decidedly unnatural, evokes for me a strong sense of the presence of these poems, [...] much stronger, indeed, than what I experience in the temples, where I feel, rightly or wrongly, that the atmosphere is manufactured – even though I appreciate the emotion (*omoi*) and charm (*yoen*) of the temples' beauty) (*T*, pp. 37–8)

Infra-ordinary Tokyo gives Roubaud access to a strong sense of natural beauty that is indexed on the landscape of his own childhood rather than on a *japoniste* approach to Japanese nature. For, as he explains in *La Bibliothèque de Warburg*, an autobiographical work of which *Tokyo infra-ordinaire* was originally supposed to form a part, his original fascination with the Japanese Imperial *tanka* stemmed from their uniquely strong evocation of nature. Reading these poems in Paris in the 1960s, the descriptions of pine trees and mountains evoked memories of the Mediterranean hills of Roubaud's provincial childhood:

> [Lisant ces poèmes,] je voyais, par exemple, je voyais, se superposant à ces mots, en même temps qu'un mont Fuji de carte postale, un pic des Pyrénées, un mont Canigou de souvenir [...], quand le vent 'marin' permet d'en apercevoir, depuis le Minervois, les neiges; je voyais, en même temps qu'un 'pin' de poème japonais, un pin méditerranéen; en lieu et place des 'ume no hana', les fleurs de cerisier omniprésentes dans les *tanka*, les floraisons des amandiers au-dessus du bassin-piscine de la Tuilerie...

> ([Reading these poems], I saw, for example, I *saw*, superimposed over the lines, both a postcard view of Mount Fuji, and a peak in the

Pyrenees, Mount Canigou, whose snows I remember seeing from the Minervois when the wind was from the coast. As well as the pines of the Japanese text, I saw Mediterranean pines. Instead of the 'ume no hana', the *tanka*'s ubiquitous cherry blossom, I saw the almond trees in bloom over the swimming pool at the Tuilerie...)[19]

Subsequently, Roubaud studied the *tanka* in depth in English translation, and found thereafter that they were overlaid by his memories and love for London. Now, the *tanka* is central to his endeavour in *Tokyo infra-ordinaire*, partly because it involves less 'japoniaiserie'[20] than the genre of the *haiku*:

le Japon est très loin; mais le *tanka* est bien plus loin dans le temps que le *haiku* [...] le *tanka*, en France, en anglo-saxonnie, en Europe, je le vois vite, est resté beaucoup mieux caché que le *haiku*. Il s'ensuit qu'il est moins marqué de 'japoniaiserie'.

(Japan is far away, but the *tanka* is even further away in time than the *haiku* [...] In France, in English-speaking countries and in Europe, the *tanka* has remained less well-known than the *haiku*. Therefore, it's less marred by naïve exoticism.)[21]

Roubaud is well placed to make this comment, having been for over 40 years a scholar of Japanese poetry of the Imperial Heian era (eighth to twelfth centuries).[22] The manner in which the poetry of this era renders the naturality of the world is something for which he aims in his own work; hence the invocation of classical Japanese poetry in the context of a poem that seeks to reveal the *this-ness* of 'infra-ordinary' experience of contemporary Tokyo.

The urban frame of the parks and cemeteries in Tokyo is the trigger of Roubaud's memory and inspiration. An example of this is the sonnet 'Meditation on the Koishikawa Korakuen gardens', included at the close of *Tokyo infra-ordinaire*. Roubaud refuses to see these pleasure grounds, originally laid out in the seventeenth century, in isolation from the surrounding city. Thus he evokes their waterlilies and cascades, but also the noise of traffic and the looming presence of the Tokyo Dome (1988). Significantly, it is only from the vantage point of the walkway around the Dome that inspiration can be found:

> La compassion parfaite
> Des pierres, des nénuphars, et l'arôme

Du passé confiné dans un mouchoir
De sentiers, de cascades, de murmure
À l'intérieur du jardin ne conjure
Aucune image-mémoire. Pour voir
Il faut sortir.

(The perfect compassion
Of the stones and waterlilies, and the scent
Of the past furled up in a handkerchief
Of paths and waterfalls and the murmur of
The garden conjures up
No image-memory. In order to see
I must leave.) (*T*, p. 89)

Throughout the work, Roubaud emphasizes the central role that the mundanity of the contemporary city plays in this work. There is also a constant shuttling between references to classical Japanese poetry and Roubaud's compositional musings, as he uses a selection of classical Japanese aesthetic principles to frame the prose sections of the work. Japanese poets and works are frequently referred to by name. Notably, the 'ten styles' of the twelfth-century poet Kamo no Chomei, ranging from the '*shimmyô-tai*, "style bourré de mystère"' ('the full-of-mystery style') to the '*ryohô-tai*, "style du double sens"' ('the double-meaning style'; *T*, pp. 56–7), are deployed to comic effect: Roubaud uses excerpts from the sumptuous Toto toilet catalogue to exemplify Kamo no Chomei's principles.

The effect of this layering of poetic allusion and contemporary reality is one of extraordinary richness. Not confining himself merely to aestheticentrism – the crime of which critics such as Karatani and Reyns-Chikuma find so many French writers guilty – nor to a flat and unhistoricized account of his impressions of Tokyo, Roubaud successfully treads a fine line: his decades of study of Japanese poetry inform his perception of the city he walks around. It is not a case of betraying a mundane reality by transposing it onto a higher, more literary plane. Rather, the mundanity is seen as being precisely *in keeping* with the subject matter of a longstanding tradition, and as proof of the ongoing relevance of that tradition. This is not a *japoniste* aesthetics of nostalgia, but rather the representation of a symbiotic relationship between the urban space and the aesthetic tradition.

Roubaud's interest is in the medieval Japanese poetry that predates the growth of the more vernacular *haikai* forms in the seventeenth century.

Unlike the poets of the Imperial Anthologies, Bashō is never mentioned by name in *Tokyo infra-ordinaire*. However, the work owes its greatest formal debt to the *haibun* as elaborated by Bashō, whose work is situated at the historical mid-point between the Imperial poets and Roubaud. Bashō tends to be regarded as the poet of the pure, pastoral, ephemeral moment of beauty. If we have only this understanding of Bashō's poetics in mind, he seems an unlikely precursor of Roubaud. Yet, as a recent study by Haruo Shirane demonstrates, Bashō needs to be understood not simply as a poet of rarefied natural beauty, but as an experimental writer, practising his craft at a period of major literary upheaval in Japan, and including in his work a huge range of 'different textual and perceptual planes'.[23] As the 'Shirakawa barrier' quotation shows, Bashō's *haibun* is heteroglossic and multivoiced. Bashō included in his *Narrow Road to the Deep North* an unprecedented variety of textual references – Chinese prose genres, Japanese classical stereotypes, and vernacular language and anecdotes. In several striking respects, his approach is thus similar to Roubaud's. Both poets look to classical and medieval poets for their inspiration, but at the same time practise a contemporary travel writing that is 'parodic, oppositional, and immersed in popular culture'.[24] Bashō is the necessary mediator – both historically and aesthetically – between the rarefied *tanka* of the Imperial anthologies and Roubaud's playful, disjointed Oulipian *haibun*. It is by mobilizing not only the classical poets whom he mentions by name throughout *Tokyo infra-ordinaire*, but also the unspoken heteroglossic model of the Bashō-esque *haibun*, that Roubaud arrives at a text that is both grounded and immediate, which accomplishes a far more positive and complex appreciation of Japanese aesthetics than that provided by any of his *japoniste* and post-*japoniste* predecessors.

Notes

1. Matsuo Bashō, *The Narrow Road to the Deep North and Other Travel Sketches*, trans. by Nobuyuki Yuasa (Harmondsworth: Penguin, 1966).
2. *Waka* is a classical Japanese poetic genre. The term is used to refer to several forms, but especially the 31-syllable *tanka*.
3. Translation by Haruo Shirane in *Early Modern Japanese Literature: An Anthology*, ed. by Haruo Shirane (New York: Columbia University Press, 2008), pp. 106–7.
4. See Haruo Shirane, *Traces of Dreams: Landscape, Cultural Memory and the Poetry of Bashō* (Stanford, CA: Stanford University Press, 1998).
5. 'Mississippi haibun' forms the first chapter of Roubaud's *La Bibliothèque de Warburg: version mixte* (Paris: Seuil, 2002), pp. 7–35.

6. Jacques Roubaud, *Tokyo infra-ordinaire* (Paris: Inventaire-Invention, 2005; henceforward *T*), p. 12. Unless otherwise indicated, translations are my own.
7. See Jacques Jouet, *Poèmes de métro* (Paris: P.O.L., 2000). Roubaud lists Jouet's rules in *Tokyo infra-ordinaire* (p. 36).
8. Pascaline Mourier-Casile and Dominique Moncond'Huy, 'Entretien avec Jacques Roubaud', *Revue La Licorne*, 40 (2006), available at http://edel.univ-poitiers.fr/licorne/document3347.php (accessed 18 April 2012).
9. Akane Kawakami, *Travellers' Visions: French Literary Encounters with Japan, 1881–2004* (Liverpool: Liverpool University Press, 2005); Jan Walsh Hokenson, *Japan, France, and East-West Aesthetics: French Literature, 1867–2000* (Madison, NJ: Fairleigh Dickinson University Press).
10. Kojin Karatani and Sabu Kohso (trans), 'Uses of Aesthetics: After Orientalism', *boundary 2*, 25.2 (1998), 145–60.
11. Ibid., p. 152.
12. Chris Reyns-Chikuma, *Images du Japon en France et ailleurs* (Paris: L'Harmattan, 2005).
13. Ibid., pp. 246–7.
14. Online journal *Inventaire-Invention*, 'Projet Jet Stream', http://www.a360.org/article.php3?id_article=99 (accessed 18 April 2012). Authors in the Japan issue include Agnès Disson, Jean-Philippe Toussaint and Philippe Adam. Since the closure of the publishing house Inventaire-Invention in Spring 2009, the texts are no longer accessible online.
15. Roland Barthes, *L'Empire des signes* (Paris: Seuil, 2005), pp. 47–50.
16. Christine Buci-Glucksmann, *L'Esthétique du temps au Japon: du Zen au virtuel* (Paris: Galilée, 2005), p. 25.
17. 'La Gare', *L'Empire des signes*, pp. 56–60.
18. The *Manyoshu* or *Collection of Ten Thousand Leaves* (eighth century) is the oldest existing collection of Japanese poetry.
19. Roubaud, *Bibliothèque de Warburg*, p. 155.
20. 'Japoniaiserie' is a portmanteau word formed of 'japonisme' and 'niaiserie' ('inanity' or 'silliness').
21. Roubaud, *Bibliothèque de Warburg*, p. 155.
22. See Roubaud's *Mono no aware ou le sentiment des choses: cent-quatre poèmes empruntés au japonais* (Paris: Gallimard, 1970), a collection of *tanka* 'borrowings' from the Imperial Japanese anthologies.
23. Shirane, *Traces*, p. 48.
24. Ibid., p. 8.

13
Ghosts of Influence? Spectrality in the Novels of Marie Darrieussecq

Carine Fréville

Marie Darrieussecq states that her work aims to 'questionner le vide' ('question the void'), a process that involves the concomitant exploration of 'l'absence à soi-même' ('absence from oneself'), which is, for her, the condition of writing as such.[1] All of her work is marked by absence – whether from others or oneself – and by loss (in particular regarding the figure of the dead child). This is linked with the author's own family history, which was indelibly marked by the death of an infant brother. But what is the relation, in Darrieussecq's writing, of absence and loss to influence? The author throws light on this question in an essay she wrote in order to defend herself against accusations of plagiarism: *Rapport de police* (*Police Report*).[2] Here, she sets out her view that the writer's task is 'se transformer en chambre d'échos et de métamorphoses' ('to transform oneself into a room of echoes and metamorphoses').[3] And so she connects what others see as plagiarism with the idea that influences, be they explicit or implicit, avowed or denied, are part of any writer's work.[4] She makes numerous references to works that have inspired her own writing. *Le Bébé* (*The Baby*, 2002), which aimed to recreate the author's own world, was punctuated by quotations and by artistic, literary, cinematic and psychoanalytic references that stop short of word-for-word quotation. It is reasonable to argue that the latter type of references allow Darrieussecq to deploy a strategy whereby she adds implicit to explicit quotations, and so creates 'phantom texts'. This double system of explicit versus implicit (or ghostly) references allows us to think of (literary and artistic) influence and haunting in relation to each other.

In order to read Darrieussecq in this perspective, we must pay attention to the importance of psychoanalysis in her life and writing. Having herself become a psychoanalyst in 2006, she states that she is 'très nourrie de réflexions psychanalytiques' ('very influenced by psychoanalytic thinking').[5] She considers her own approach to writing in fictional form in terms of literature and psychoanalysis together. She has described these two domains as 'deux pratiques qui avancent sur le réel et mettent des mots là où il n'y en a pas' ('two practices that go further than reality and put words where there aren't any').[6] Similarly, Darrieussecq explains that her first novel, *Truismes* (1996), stems from a course of psychoanalysis that allowed her to reach a form of detachment through fiction: 'L'analyse a libéré mon imaginaire, qui était englué dans de l'interdit, du secret, du non-dit. Englué dans du *mort*' ('Psychoanalysis has freed my imagination, which was bogged down in prohibition, in secrets, in the unspoken. Bogged down in *death*').[7] Fiction has become for her both a space of encounter with the Other and a space permitting fantasies to be expressed.[8]

Darrieussecq makes the issue of fantasies and the unconscious in her work explicit, for example with regard to her conception of autofiction:

> L'autofiction décalque sur le papier le jeu, ou le trouble, psychique. Dans le fantasme, y compris le fantasme sexuel, le sujet se met en scène dans des situations fictives, qu'il ne souhaite pas nécessairement vivre, mais qu'il expérimente mentalement. Pour moi l'autofiction c'est ça: un fantasme filé sur la page, sous mon nom, dans ma peau, mais une peau de papier, une peau mentale.
>
> (Autofiction allows the psychic game, or psychic disturbance, to be traced on paper. In fantasy, including sexual fantasy, the subject enacts fictitious situations that she/he doesn't necessarily want to live out, but that she/he tries out mentally. For me autofiction is precisely this: a fantasy spun on the page, in my name, in my skin, but a paper skin, a mental skin.)[9]

There is thus no mutual exclusion for Darrieussecq between the fields of fiction and autofiction. For her, the expression of the self is not restricted to the autobiographical genre. Fictional genres do not express something other than reality; rather, they express reality, but metaphorically: 'Je crois à la métaphore qu'est la fiction pour dire mes hantises, heureuses ou malheureuses, tragiques ou drôles. La fiction, pour moi, dit le réel' ('I place my faith in the metaphor that fiction is to say what haunts me, whether it be happy or sad, tragic or funny. Fiction, for me, talks of reality').[10] For Darrieussecq, fictional writing becomes a space to reflect on and displace her own fears and traumas.

The psychoanalytic concept of the ghost, with regard to what remains unspoken in the history of a family and transmits itself from unconscious to unconscious, is central to a proper understanding of loss and mourning in the work of Darrieussecq.[11] The author has explained how she is 'complètement hantée' ('completely haunted') by the absence, in the case of her dead brother, of a grave (and commemorative words), and how she underwent 'une psychanalyse pendant six ans' ('a six-year psychoanalysis').[12] In several interviews, she has referred to the ghost as a lack of representation of a trauma because of a lack of words, and has asserted that she 'aime la métaphore des fantômes qui agitent leurs chaînes lorsqu'une famille cache des secrets' ('likes the metaphor of ghosts who shake their shackles when a family hides secrets').[13] She thus establishes a relationship between ghosts and the unspoken, and the need to write and work on the unspoken:

> Quand le vide est trop insupportable, on le peuple de fantômes. Pour moi les fantômes, c'est une sorte de jointure, quand tout est séparé et quand tout est cerné par le vide, les enfants en particulier, qui sont seuls face à des secrets ou au silence des adultes, peuplent le silence et le vide de fantômes. [...] Quand vous cachez quelque chose à un enfant, il le sait. Il sent qu'il manque quelque chose dans la structure du langage de ses parents. Il y a un creux. Tous les enfants connaissent ça et moi, je l'ai connu dans des proportions vraiment pénibles. [...] Mes parents ne me disaient rien. [...] C'est sans doute une explication rapide, mais le fait d'écrire est lié à ça, certainement. Il faut que ça parle, que quelque chose soit dit, qu'on arrête de se taire.
>
> (When the void is too unbearable, we fill it up with ghosts. For me, ghosts serve as a kind of joint, when all is separated and when all is surrounded by void; children, in particular, when they find themselves alone before secrets or the silence of adults, populate the silence and the void with ghosts. [...] When you hide something from a child, she/he knows it. There is a hole. All children know this and I have experienced this to a truly painful extent. [...] My parents never said anything to me. [...] This explanation probably seems convenient, but the fact of writing is undoubtedly linked to this [syndrome]. 'It' has to find a voice, something must be said, the silence must be broken.)[14]

Because a heavy silence, fully perceived, surrounds this dead child, many of Darrieussecq's works attempt to talk about this brother, to *name* him.

If fiction allows Darrieussecq to establish a distance and to imagine herself in different situations and contexts, to be Other during the time of writing, her writing also opens up to 'another otherness': not only beings, but also non-beings, through the seeking out and representation of other forms of encounter, other realities, that constitute the spectral dimension that is so characteristic of her works. If the latter do not strictly belong in the genre of the fantastic, nor of course in that of science fiction, most of them nonetheless contain an undeniable fantastical dimension with regard to loss and, more precisely, as the author herself has explained, with regard to anguish: 'Oui, [le fantastique] est une part de mon imaginaire. Disons que c'est une forme de l'angoisse. Et l'angoisse peut prendre des tas de formes' ('Yes, fantasy is part of my imaginary world. Let's say it's a form of anguish. And anguish can take many forms').[15]

Faced with loss, Darrieussecq's protagonists experience situations of 'brokenness' (*cassure*), of rupture, which lead to profound interrogations about themselves and the world, as well as to an (often violent) deconstruction of time, space and reality.[16] This situation, in which distinctions between presence and absence are no longer absolute, creates an entry point for ghosts. The fantastic dimension of Darrieussecq's work is thus situated around these diverse instances of loss in respect of the treatment of time and space. Temporal indetermination recurs in her works and this, coupled with the loss of other familiar reference points, is fundamental to the representation of the protagonists' experiences. At the same time, distancing devices are used. Darrieussecq regularly chooses to place her protagonists in remote places – Argentina in *Bref séjour chez les vivants* (*A Brief Stay with the Living*), the South Pole in *White*, or Australia in *Tom est mort* (*Tom Is Dead*) – as though to place the recurrent figure of the dead child as far away from her as possible.[17] Similarly, temporal shifts of one or two decades in given works seem designed to establish a defence against her fears regarding the death of children, allowing a distance to be established that is necessary for her to write of such experiences of loss and mourning.[18]

The state of mind of various characters is conveyed through very precise descriptions regarding the body and sensations. Darrieussecq has indeed explained that 'chez moi, la psychologie s'incarne dans le physique. Les mouvements psychologiques deviennent mouvements de matière' ('for me, psychology is embodied in the physical. Psychological movements become movements of matter').[19] It is therefore in key instances of 'absence à soi-même' ('absence from oneself'), in a particular attention to the void, in the exploration of these 'movements of matter', that Darrieussecq's works are characterized by an atmosphere of immateriality and weightlessness, by a dislocation of time and an implosion of space. The influence of the fantastic thus impregnates the whole of Darrieussecq's work, for the psychological and physical consequences of situations of rupture are expressed in the register of the fantastic.

Studying the use of the fantastic in Darrieussecq's works, Cécile Narjoux argues:

> si une évolution est notable dans l'exploitation du registre fantastique, celui-ci, en tant que registre, n'est pas là au service du genre fantastique. Les récits de Darrieussecq interrogent avant tout une identité et un rapport au monde problématique, et le registre se met au service de cette quête, et non l'inverse.
>
> (whilst an evolution can be noticed in the exploitation of the register of the fantastic, the fact remains that that register exists to serve the fantastic genre. Darrieussecq's narrations above all explore an identity and a relation to the world that are problematic, and her use of the fantastic register serves this exploration, and not the other way round.)[20]

In using elements of the fantastic genre to render identities problematic and uncertain, Darrieussecq is turning to her own purpose those cornerstones of the fantastic as a (theoretical) genre: hesitation and uncertainty, as analysed by Tzvetan Todorov.[21]

Indeed, according to Laurie Laufer, the experiences of loss in Darrieussecq's work can be considered, within this spectral imaginary, as having 'pour fonction de faire se rencontrer le vivant et le mort dans une intimité fantastique qui articule la mémoire, l'image, le regard et la parole' ('the function of making the living and the dead meet in a fantastic intimacy that articles memory, image, the gaze and speech'), where 'le vivant doit retrouver le mort en un point de rencontre de son fantasme. La figure du disparu apparaît là où une forme du fantasme peut apparaître' ('the living must find the dead at a meeting point within its fantasy. The figure of the dead appears [precisely] where a form of the fantasy can appear').[22]

Let us now illustrate these points by reference to specific works. *Naissance des fantômes* (*My Phantom Husband*) is the story of an unnamed woman and the sudden, unexplained disappearance of her husband. Since she defines herself, and her relationship to the world, through her husband, the reference points that serve to ground her identity – including spatial and temporal ones – are profoundly destabilized by this disappearance. This is suggested by the presence in the novel of a framed wedding picture, which seems to have undergone a transformation: 'La photo avait bougé. Elle était devenue floue. Mon mari s'était tourné vers le fond, comme si quelqu'un, au moment où se déclenchait le flash, avait dévié son attention' ('The photo had shifted. It had become blurry. My husband had turned towards the background, as if someone had distracted him just as the flash went off').[23] She thus sees 'sur l'image un mouvement, une fuite en dégradé noir et brun. C'était une très belle photo. C'était la photo de sa disparition' ('a movement on the picture, a flight in a gradation of blacks and browns. It was a beautiful photo. It was the photo of his disappearance').[24] This instant of life ('immortalized', the phrase goes, by the photographer) is not frozen in time. For as stillness yields to motion, we better understand the narrator's experience; she perceives a representation, not of a disappearance having been accomplished, but of one in process.

In *Bref séjour chez les vivants* (2001) and *Le Pays* (*The Country*, 2005), the focus moves to the death of a brother. In each case, a sister attempts to give him substance, so as to be able to represent his death. In *Bref séjour*, the parents seem to wish to erase all trace of the departed brother: 'les photos, les vêtements, la tombe, ils ont pensé à effacer – mais les traits sur la porte du salon, y sont-ils encore [...] maman aura tout fait repeindre' ('the photos, the clothes, the grave, they have thought about erasing them – but the marks on the sitting room door, are they still there [...] mummy will have had everything painted over').[25] The mode of 'erasure' of photographs and clothes, and especially that of the grave, may seem to call for further explanation, but this is not provided. However, it seems entirely reasonable to connect this with events in the author's life – especially given her own stated views on the relation between fiction, autofiction and reality, cited above. Once again, the death of Darrieussecq's brother was marked by no grave – a fact about which the author has rarely spoken. This absence of a memorial is, for Darrieussecq, a double one: it applies to the material grave, but also to the family's failure to produce words (spoken or written) concerning the brother's death. The 'ghost' of the brother is not, strictly speaking, trapped in the realm of the unconscious, but the failure to refer to him 'in so many words' creates an effect similar to repression.[26]

Space does not permit any detailed analysis of *Le Pays* here. Suffice to say that *Bref séjour* and *Le Pays* together show how the figure of the dead child haunts Darrieussecq's works. Faced with the trauma of loss, perpetuated in silence, and with the fear of a repetition of that loss, she dwells on presence-in-absence, on ghostly apparitions that function as so many attempts, not directly to name but to *represent* the dead person as an alternative to (pathogenic) silence. Thus Darrieussecq links repressed secrets with the fantastic: 'la littérature fantastique, c'est la peur du noir remémorée aux adultes. À l'échelle conjugale, familiale, sociale, ce qui est passé sous silence se fait entendre d'une façon ou d'une autre; c'est un des topos de la psychanalyse. Écrire, c'est donner voix aux fantômes' ('fantastic literature is the fear of the dark, as adults are made to remember it. At the level of the couple, the family, or society, what is kept silent makes itself heard in one way or another; this is one of the topoi of psychoanalysis. To write is to give voice to ghosts').[27] For Darrieussecq, to write is truly to work with but also on words, on the clichés of the French language – or truisms – and on what remains hidden, in the realm of the unspeakable.[28]

In *Tom est mort* (2007), a mother refuses to end her 'travail de deuil' ('grieving process'). Instead, she tries to hold on to her dead son through an idea that she finds in fantasy culture: that he might exist at an 'atomic' level.[29] She decides that her son may survive beyond death if those close to him use memory in a particular way:

> Peut-être y a-t-il des unités de mémoire comme il y a des unités du langage. Peut-être le souvenir peut-il se diviser en fragments de plus en plus petits, jusqu'à trouver les noyaux, les atomes. La mémoire n'est pas un grand récit. Les mots y sont des souvenirs de mots, des souvenirs de phrases dites. Les images et les sensations n'y existent qu'à travers nous. Mettre des mots là-dessus, c'est comme essayer de raconter un rêve, et Tom est dans ce bazar-là. Il n'est plus que là-dedans.
>
> (Maybe there are memory units as there are language units. Maybe a memory can divide itself into smaller and smaller fragments until we get down to the nucleus, the atoms. Memory has no grand narrative. The words are memories of words, memories of sentences spoken. Images and feelings only exist there through us. To put this into words is like trying to relate a dream, and Tom is in this mess. It contains him entirely.)[30]

We have examined the theme of ghostly survival in several of Darrieussecq's fictions; in each case, we have seen that given characters strive, in different ways, to allow the dead to survive, or to find traces of such survival. This is a form of 'influence', and it is useful to remember the term's etymology, with its magical/supernatural connotations. Now let us turn to the ghostly presence, within those same texts (and others by Darrieussecq) of other authors and artists. For, as explained in our introduction, Darrieussecq uses implicit references to create a 'haunting' of her writing by the writing and thought of others, and so foregrounds what other authors might keep secret.

Darrieussecq's characterization of writing as involving an 'absence à soi-même' is reminiscent of Marguerite Duras, who asserts: 'on n'est jamais tout à fait présent quand on écrit, on n'est jamais complètement là' ('one is never really completely present when one writes, one is never completely there').[31] To the extent that Darrieussecq's not 'being completely there' provides space for others, we find the presence of Durassian themes in her work, for instance the omnipresence of the sea, an awareness of the void or the constant re-churning of memories.[32] But more precisely, Darrieussecq has spoken of Duras's influence in terms of spectrality: 'Marguerite Duras a une voix très, très forte et c'est aussi quelqu'un que P.O.L., mon éditeur, a bien connu. C'est un peu un fantôme chez P.O.L., elle est très présente. Même les gens qui l'ont connue très bien en font un mythe' ('Marguerite Duras has a very, very strong voice, and she is also someone that P.O.L., my publisher, knew well. She is a bit like a ghost at P.O.L., she is very present. Even those who knew her very well make a myth of her').[33] Thus she recognizes Duras's presence in her writing. At the same time, she insists that Nathalie Sarraute is a far stronger influence:

> Duras m'a beaucoup influencée en termes de voix, elle a une musicalité très forte, mais je crois que, beaucoup plus profondément, Nathalie Sarraute m'a donné la force de ne pas écrire 'Elle se sentait très angoissée'. J'ai essayé de trouver autre chose. Elle, son truc c'était les sous-conversations, ce qui se passait autour, et moi, ce n'est pas exactement cela, ça serait, comment définir ça, ça serait l'absence à soi-même, c'est-à-dire, on n'est pas où l'on croit qu'on est, non plus. J'essaie de décrire ce vide qu'on est et qui est rempli par des tas d'autres choses qui ne sont pas nous mais qui le deviennent, des allers-retours entre la personne humaine et le non-dit, si vous voulez.
>
> (Duras has influenced me a great deal in terms of her voice, it has a very strong musicality to it, but I think that, much more profoundly, Nathalie Sarraute gave me the strength not to write [for instance]:

'She felt very anxious'. I have tried to find another way of writing. Sarraute's thing was 'sub-conversations', what goes on around what is said; my thing isn't exactly that, it's more (how to put this?) an absence from oneself, that is to say, we are not where we think we are, either. I try and describe this void that we are and that is filled with many things that are not us but become us, these toings and froings between the human person and the unspoken, if you like.)[34]

Another such presence, regularly quoted by Darrieussecq, is that of Patrick Modiano, with whom she shares a fascination with disappearance and flight, photography as a trace, voices heard on the radio or telephone, or the diverse ghostly influences that permeate his work.[35] Nor should we forget that Modiano lost his younger brother Rudy, who died from leukemia at the age of 10. Coincidentally, Rudy is also the name of the dead baby in James Joyce's *Ulysses*, a work of great importance for Darrieussecq. She refers to that work as 'un héritage qu'il faut assimiler et surmonter' ('a heritage one must assimilate and overcome'), and has explained that *Ulysses* was a liberating source of inspiration for her in the writing of *Bref séjour*.[36] Darrieussecq has made references to the dead child in *Ulysses* and to Joyce's literary treatment of this spectral absence, a point to which she returns in *Le Bébé*.[37]

Darrieussecq is also open to intermedial influence. She has a deep interest in contemporary art, and in photography in particular. She has published in exhibition catalogues for photographers (Juergen Teller,[38] Roger-Viollet, Dolorès Marat and Bernard Faucon), artists (Louise Bourgeois, Annette Messager and Nicole Tran Ba Vang[39]) and architects (Le Corbusier and Édouard François).[40] According to Darrieussecq: 'J'écris parfois pour des artistes. Je cherche un équivalent-mots de leur travail plastique, qui ne soit ni critique ni illustratif. Comme si l'artiste avait dû utiliser des mots à la place de son matériau' ('I sometimes write for artists. I look for a verbal equivalent of their visual art, which neither criticizes it nor illustrates it. As if the artists had had to use words instead of materials').[41] The expression *équivalent-mots* accurately describes this process of putting artistic work into writing (or ekphrasis). When we examined *Naissance des fantômes*, above, we saw that a key role was allocated to a photograph of the dead husband. This is just one example of the author's sensitivity to the links between photographic art and literature. The experimentation with the void that we find in her writing can be linked to the work of the photographer Francesca Woodman, one of whose images appears on the cover of the paperback edition of *Naissance des fantômes*, as though to invite cross-referenced readings.[42] Another photographer who shares with Woodman an interest in movements of flight and disappearance is Bernard Faucon, and he also inspires Darrieussecq. Moreover, her interest in traces and phantom texts conjures up the *image fantôme* ('ghost image') in the writing, photographs and videos of Hervé Guibert.[43] We also find other photographs that reveal 'surtout, du vide, du vide flou si une telle chose est possible à photographier' ('mostly a void, a blurry void if it is possible to take a picture of such a thing')[44] in *Naissance des fantômes* and *White*; these make one think of the series *Space²* (1975–76) and *House* (1976) by Francesca Woodman, whose themes include movements of flight and instances of absence. One also thinks of the photographs of Bernard Faucon, mentioned above, in particular the series *Chambres en hiver, chambres d'or* (*Bedrooms in Winter, Golden Bedrooms*, 1987–89), which includes pieces with evocative titles such as *Épiphanie* (*Epiphany*), *L'Apparition* (*The Apparition*) or *Le Fantôme* (*The Ghost*).[45]

In a chapter entitled 'Le Temps des spectres', Lionel Ruffel discusses the 'modernité impure' ('impure modernity') of much contemporary prose fiction, an impurity that (he claims) arises through a 'retour de la modernité' ('return of modernity') in the form of its own spectre.[46] Ruffel's statement concerns literary representations of concentration camps but is not limited to these, for it extends to wider issues of subjectivity and mourning. Reflecting on modern times, he declares the 'années zéro' ('the noughties') to be 'frappées du sceau du fantastique' ('marked by the fantastic'). But this is, he insists, a 'fantastique nouveau' ('a new fantastic'), for 'la spectralité dépasse le cadre d'une pensée sur le temps et sur l'histoire pour devenir une réflexion sur les arts, sur leur impureté, et notamment sur la fiction et ses rapports à l'image; cette image survivante qui laisse en nous une empreinte, une trace fantomatique' ('spectrality goes beyond a theoretical framework on time and on history to become a questioning of the arts, of their impurity, and in particular on fiction and its relationship to image; this surviving image that leaves in us a mark, a ghostly trace').[47] Ruffel cites Darrieussecq as an example of this phenomenon.[48] Clearly, her works chime perfectly with this idea of spectrality as a reflection of the arts and contemporary life. The fictions we have examined, plus *Le Pays*, are all structured around loss. It is as though they spring from loss, but generate new beginnings and openings towards other spaces and other temporalities.

Notes

1. Amy Concannon and Kerry Sweeney, interview with Marie Darrieussecq (2004), available at http://darrieussecq.arizona.edu/eng/eninterview.html (accessed 17 October 2012). Unless otherwise indicated, translations are my own.
2. *Rapport de police – Accusations de plagiat et autres modes de surveillance de la fiction* (*Police Report: Accusations of Plagiarism and Other Modes of Fiction Surveillance*) (Paris: P.O.L., 2010), p. 310. For Darrieussecq's own response to the accusation of plagiarism, see her article 'Sorguina – la réponse de l'auteur de *Truismes* et de *Naissance des fantômes* à Marie NDiaye', *Libération* (10 March 1998). See also Antoine de Gaudemar, 'Marie NDiaye polémique avec Darrieussecq', *Libération* (3 March 1998), available at http://www.liberation.fr/culture/0101241197-marie-ndiaye-polemique-avec-marie-darrieussecq (accessed 19 October 2007); Olivier Le Naire, 'Singeries', *L'Express* (19 March 1998), available at http://www.lexpress.fr/informations/singeries_628270.html (accessed 19 October 2007); Camille Laurens, 'Darrieussecq ou le syndrome du coucou', *La Revue littéraire*, 32 (Autumn 2007), 1–14; Colette Sarrey-Strack, *Fictions contemporaines au féminin – Marie Darrieussecq, Marie NDiaye, Marie Nimier, Marie Redonnet* (Paris: L'Harmattan, 2002), pp. 235–41.
3. *Rapport de police*, p. 310.
4. See online chat with Darrieussecq, 'Darrieussecq: "La littérature s'est toujours faite de lectures et d'influences"', *Libération* (12 January 2010), available at http://www.liberation.fr/livres/1201233-dialoguez-avec-marie-darrieussecq (accessed 15 January 2010).
5. Marie Darrieussecq, 'Écrire, qu'est-ce que c'est?' (transcript of a seminar held at the Institut des Hautes Études en Psychanalyse/ENS, 2008). For Darrieussecq's own account of her becoming a psychoanalyst, see her article 'Je suis devenue psychanalyste', *Lire* (November 2006), available at http://www.lire.fr/entretien.asp/idC=50597/idTC=4/idR=201/idG (accessed 22 February 2008).
6. Transcript of a reading and discussion of *Tom est mort* at the American University of Paris (11 October 2007).
7. Marie Darrieussecq, 'Être libéré de soi', *Le Magazine littéraire*, 473 (March 2008), p. 58. Emphasis in original.
8. *Rapport de police*, p. 267.
9. Marie Darrieussecq, 'Je est unE autre', in *Écrire l'histoire d'une vie*, ed. by Annie Olivier (Rome: Edizioni Spartaco, 2007), available at http://darrieussecq.arizona.edu/fr/collautofiction.doc (accessed 21 December 2012).
10. Darrieussecq, 'Être libéré de soi', p. 58.
11. For important theorizations of this phenomenon, see Nicolas Abraham and Maria Török, *L'Écorce et le noyau*, 2nd edn (Paris: Flammarion, 1987),

translated by Nicholas T. Rand as *The Shell and the Kernel: Renewals of Psychoanalysis* (Chicago: Chicago University Press, 1994); Didier Dumas, *L'Ange et le fantôme*. *Introduction à la clinique de l'impensé généalogique* (Paris: Minuit, 1985); Nina Canault, *Comment paye-t-on les fautes de ses ancêtres: l'inconscient transgénérationnel* (Paris: Desclée de Brouwer, 1998).

12. John Lambeth, 'Entretien avec Darrieussecq', *The French Review*, 79.4 (March 2006), 806–18 (pp. 811–12).
13. Pascale Frey, 'Darrieussecq: l'écriture pour toujours', *Lire* (October 2001), available at http://www.lire.fr/portrait.asp/idC=37851/idTC=5/idR=201/idG=3 (accessed 4 March 2009).
14. Lambeth, 'Entretien avec Darrieussecq', p. 812.
15. Jérémi Sauvage, '"Ce qui m'a toujours déçue dans les films ou dans la littérature fantastique, c'est quand on voit le monstre" – Entretien avec Marie Darrieussecq', *Ténèbres*, 8 (October/December 1999), 61–6 (p. 65).
16. The term *cassure* (break) is used by Darrieussecq herself (see Lambeth, 'Entretien avec Darrieussecq', p. 801). The author also uses the term *rupture*; see Jeanette Gaudet, '"Des livres sur la liberté": conversation avec Darrieussecq', *Dalhousie French Studies*, 59 (2002), 108–18 (p. 108).
17. Bernard Lehut and Thierry Grandillot, interview with Darrieussecq on RTL, radio broadcast *Les livres ont la parole* (September 2007).
18. These temporal discrepancies are described by the author as a way of liberating her imagination: 'avancer de dix ou vingt ans en "science fiction" me libère de la vraisemblance attachée au temps et à l'espace présents, et me donne de la liberté pour inventer [...]. Je peux alors laisser vivre mon imaginaire sans contrainte' ('going forward ten or twenty years in "Science fiction" frees me from the need to seem "true to life" that is attached to present time and space, and gives me the freedom to invent [...]. I can then let my imagination run without any constraints'); Concannon and Sweeney, interview with Darrieussecq (2004).
19. Nelly Kaprièlan, 'Voyages en terres inconnues', special issue of *Nouvelles littératures françaises* (2010), 54–6, originally published to mark the publication of *White* in *Les Inrockuptibles*, 405 (3 September 2003).
20. Cécile Narjoux, 'Darrieussecq et "l'entre-deux-mondes" ou le fantastique à l'œuvre', *IRIS*, 24 (Winter 2002–2003), 233–47 (p. 240).
21. Tzvetan Todorov, *Introduction à la littérature fantastique* (Paris: Seuil, 1970); translated by Richard Howard as *The Fantastic: A Structural Approach to a Literary Genre* (Cleveland, OH: Case Western Reserve University Press, 1973).
22. Laurie Laufer, 'Quand le traumatisme de la perte a plastiqué la mémoire', in *La Chose traumatique*, ed. by Franck Chaumon and Véronique Meneghini (Paris: L'Harmattan, 2005), pp. 97–118 (p. 103).

23. Marie Darrieussecq, *Naissance des fantômes* (Paris: Gallimard, 1999), pp. 49–50.
24. Ibid., p. 50.
25. Marie Darrieussecq, *Bref séjour chez les vivants* (Paris: Gallimard, 2002), p. 161.
26. Generally in Darrieussecq's novels the loss of a child is known to its siblings, but in *Bref séjour* this knowledge is withheld from Nore, who is born after her brother's death. Nevertheless, her thoughts betray that the dead child remains within the family as a traumatic trace, transmitted in the form of an unconscious transgenerational phantom.
27. Becky Miller and Martha Holmes, interview with Marie Darrieussecq (2001), available at http://darrieussecq.arizona.edu/eng/eninterview2001.html (accessed 17 October 2012).
28. *Truismes*, *Le Bébé* and *Le Pays* all explore these issues of gender in French. Darrieussecq, for whom *La Princesse de Clèves* is also a key text, announced her intention to produce a 'feminine rewriting' of Mme de Lafayette's novel. See 'Interview: Darrieussecq, pourquoi aimez-vous *La Princesse de Clèves*?' in Madame de Lafayette, *La Princesse de Clèves* (Paris: Flammarion, 2009), p. ix.
29. Marie Darrieussecq, *Tom est mort* (Paris: P.O.L., 2007), pp. 78–9.
30. Ibid., p. 14.
31. Catherine Rodgers, 'Lectures de la sorcière, ensorcellement de l'écriture', in *Marguerite Duras: lectures plurielles*, ed. by Catherine Rodgers and Raynalle Udris (Amsterdam and Atlanta, GA: Rodopi, 1998), pp. 17–34 (p. 21).
32. On the possible comparisons between Darrieussecq and Duras, see Shirley Jordan, 'Saying the Unsayable: Identities in Crisis in the Early Novels of Darrieussecq', in *Women's Writing in Contemporary France: New Writers, New Literatures in the 1990s*, ed. by Gill Rye and Michael Worton (Manchester: Manchester University Press, 2002), pp. 142–53 (p. 147); and Catherine Rodgers, '"Entrevoir l'absence des bords du monde" dans les romans de Darrieussecq', in *Nouvelles écrivaines: nouvelles voix?*, ed. by Nathalie Morello and Catherine Rodgers (Amsterdam and New York: Rodopi, 2002), pp. 83–103 (p. 94).
33. Gaudet, '"Des livres sur la liberté": conversation avec Darrieussecq', p. 116.
34. John Lambeth, 'Entretien avec Darrieussecq', pp. 808–9.
35. On these themes, see Daniel Parrochia, *Ontologie fantôme: essai sur l'œuvre de Patrick Modiano* (Fougère La Versanne: Encre Marine, 1996) and *Patrick Modiano*, ed. by John E. Flower (Amsterdam and New York: Rodopi, 2007).
36. Charlotte Szlovak, interview with Darrieussecq for *Ulysse à Dublin* (documentary), Zeugma Films/Art France, 2004.
37. Marie Darrieussecq, *Le Bébé* (Paris: P.O.L., 2005), pp. 52–3.
38. Darrieussecq's text, entitled *Juergen, gendre ideal*, accompanies the photographs of Juergen Teller in the catalogue for the exhibition 'Do You Know

What I Mean' at the Fondation Cartier in 2006. This text can also be found in Darrieussecq's short story collection *Zoo* (Paris: P.O.L., 2006), pp. 91–109.
39. Darrieussecq's *On ne se brode pas tous les jours les jambes* was written for Nicole Tran Ba Vang's exhibition 'Collection automne/hiver 2003/04' at the Galerie Taché-Lévy, Brussels. It can also be found in Darrieussecq, *Zoo*, pp. 111–20.
40. Marie Darrieussecq, 'Dans la maison de Louise', in *Louise Bourgeois – œuvres récentes*, CAPC Musée d'Art Contemporain de Bordeaux, exhibition of 6 February to 26 April 1998 (Paris: Réunion des Musées nationaux, Diffusion Seuil, 1997); *Il était une fois...la plage* (Paris: Roger-Viollet/Plume, 2000); untitled text in Annette Messager, *Hors-jeu* (Arles: Actes Sud Nantes, Musée des beaux-arts, 2002), pp. 69–71; 'L'Arrière-saison', in Dolorès Marat (ed.), *Illusion* (Trézélan: Centre des arts d'Enghien-les-Bains/Filigranes Éditions, 2003), pp. 5–14; text by Darrieussecq on Le Corbusier in Darrieussecq, Philippe Rahm, Jean-Luc Vilmouth, *Ghostscape* (Paris: École Nationale des beaux-arts/Poissy, Monum, 2004), pp. 6–7; untitled text on Bernard Faucon's work in *Bernard Faucon* (Arles: Actes Sud, 2005), pp. 21–3; Darrieussecq, Alain Declercq, Béatrice Gross et al., *Jeanne Susplugas – Expiry Works – Date 1999/2007* (Paris: Archibooks, 2007); Darrieussecq, Bérénice Geoffroy-Schneiter, Itzhak Goldbert and Emmanuelle Lequeux, *Louise Bourgeois au Centre Pompidou* (Paris: Beaux Arts Éditions, 2008); Darrieussecq, Isabelle Bourgeois, Juliette Guépratte et al., *B2B2SP: Édouard François* (Paris: Éditions Archibooks, 2008).
41. Darrieussecq, *Zoo*, p. 250.
42. A photograph from the *House* series.
43. Hervé Guibert, *L'Image fantôme* (Paris: Minuit, 1981); translated by Robert Bononno as *Ghost Image* (Los Angeles, CA: Sun and Moon Press, 1996).
44. Marie Darrieussecq, *White* (Paris: P.O.L., 2003), pp. 64–5.
45. Épiphanie is also the name Marie Rivière will give to her daughter in *Le Pays*.
46. Lionel Ruffel, 'Le Temps des spectres', in *Le Roman français aujourd'hui: transformations, perceptions, mythologies*, ed. by Bruno Blanckeman and Jean-Christophe Millois (Paris: Prétexte Éditeur, 2004), pp. 95–117 (pp. 109–10).
47. Ibid., pp. 110–12.
48. Ibid.

14
'Now I See Me, Now You Don't': Working with/against Paternal Influence in Marie Nimier's *Photo-Photo*

Ana de Medeiros

In a recent interview, Marie Nimier states that she sees *Photo-Photo* and her previous works as forming parts of a larger fresco.[1] We might say that she views each novel as though it were part of a puzzle that she is both inventing and discovering as an overall picture emerges. And this puzzle is profoundly concerned with influence, or the effects of the 'absent' on the 'present', when each term of that dichotomy bears the trace of its opposite (a situation that justifies the increasingly common term 'presence-in-absence'). Although it would be reductive to read *Photo-Photo* as exclusively concerned with the absence/presence of the father, I will concentrate below on the influence of that figure on the narrator's portrayal of her life and writing.

The one direct reference in *Photo-Photo* to the narrator's father, and by extension that of the author,[2] is contained in the following passage:

> *Le ciel comme un endroit...* Ces mots souvent me reviendront à l'esprit pendant mon séjour à Baden-Baden. Je les avais lus dans la marge d'un cahier retrouvé dans les affaires de mon père. Je savais qu'un jour, j'écrirais quelque chose, un livre, une nouvelle, une chanson qui porterait ce titre en pensant discrètement à lui.
> Et si ce livre était celui-ci?
>
> (*The sky as a place...* These words will keep coming to mind during my trip to Baden-Baden. I had read them in the margins of a notebook that had been found among my father's things. I knew that one day

I would write something – a book, a novella, a song – with this title, and I would be thinking, discreetly, of him.
And what if that book were this book?)³

This passage invites us to see *Photo-Photo* in a double perspective, which seems appropriate for a book with a double title. Of course, at first glance, that perspective seems a logically impossible one: 'this book' cannot both be and not be 'that book'. For instance, if 'that book' has the title *Le Ciel comme un endroit*, 'this book' (*Photo-Photo*) does not. Yet Nimier does not abandon her conceit. In the closing pages, in a final drawing-together of the novel's key themes and motifs, she writes: 'Le ciel comme un endroit, et le monde à l'envers' ('the sky [*or* Heaven] as a place, and the world turned upside down'; p. 210).⁴ By recalling the title so late in her novel, she seems to insist that *Photo-Photo* 'is and is not' the work suggested by her father's marginal note.⁵

However, perhaps this conceit can be seen as logical in its way, for this passage is one of many self-reflexive ones, which permit us to distinguish between two books within the 'one' we are reading. One of these books is supposedly (so the fiction suggests) in the process of being written as we read, and may or may not end up being published as *Photo-Photo*; that is the book in which the unnamed narrator puzzles over which course her book should take at given moments, and is advised in the process by her boyfriend (or ex-boyfriend) Stephen, who lives in Canada. The second book, which is definitively entitled *Photo-Photo*, is the novel that exists in reality. The latter can no longer be revised (rethought, improved, abandoned and so on), because it is the actual book that the real reader holds in her hands, written by the real author Marie Nimier. The distinction is made in one of many self-referential passages where the narrator ponders her writerly dilemmas:

> Je vivais dans un monde aux frontières flottantes. Ce qui tournait dans ma tête n'avait pas moins de réalité que ce qui était couché sur le papier. [...] Stephen avait raison lorsqu'il parlait de la nécessité d'une rupture, mais parlait-il vraiment du roman?
> S'il parlait bien du roman, il suffirait que le livre existe physiquement, qu'il soit traité comme un objet, empaqueté, ouvert, qu'il ait touché et été touché par des inconnus pour que les deux mondes se séparent.

(I lived in a world with indistinct borders. What I was turning around in my head was not less real than what I had consigned to writing. [...] Stephen was right when he talked about the need for a decisive break, but was he really talking about my novel? If he was, then all that would be required for the two worlds to be separated would be for the book to exist physically, that it should be treated as an object, pre-packaged, opened, that it should have touched and been touched by strangers.) (p. 126)

And, precisely, this decisive break would expose the novel to the gaze of various readers – 'vos regards' – creating various 'angles' from which it would be read. But these would converge, in any given case, to create a single 'place to go':

> Parfois je les imagine, ces regards qui balayent les pages, vos regards – ton regard. Je mesure la distance entre les visages et les mains, les lettres imprimées et les yeux des lecteurs. [...] Et tous ces espaces, ces interstices mis bord à bord, formaient une zone protégée. Un ciel. Un refuge. Un endroit où aller.

> (Sometimes I imagine those glances sweeping across the pages, your glances – your glance. I measure the distance between faces and hands, printed letters and readers' eyes. [...] And all those spaces, those cracks, placed end to end, formed a protected zone. A Heaven. A refuge. A place to go.) (p. 126)

Any given book by Marie Nimier would thus become 'un ciel' for the reader and 'un endroit où aller' – and so would deserve the title of the book her father was supposed to write, *Le Ciel comme un endroit*. The father-author has 'disappeared', but lives on through his daughter. He ambiguously haunts her writing; as she assumes 'his' place, she hesitates to pronounce whether she serves to double his existence or efface it. In an interview, Nimier states: 'En fait il y avait deux façons de parler de l'identité, de la représentation et de la représentation de l'écrivain, c'est de parler du dédoublement mais aussi de l'effacement' ('In fact, there were two ways of speaking of identity, of representation and the representation of the writer: to speak of doubling but also of effacement').[6]

In *Photo-Photo*, Nimier dramatizes the issue by introducing a kind of a double (who might also serve as a replacement) for the father.[7] That role is assumed by Karl Lagerfeld, who is depicted as the 'parrain' ('godfather', or patron) of a charity to help children in difficulty, based in Baden-Baden. Yet he is a metaphorical (god)father not just to those children, but to the narrator and her 'sosie' ('double'), Frederika. The novel opens as it will close – with Karl Lagerfeld, 'le Roi de la mode' ('the King of fashion'), taking a photograph of the narrator in her unfashionable lime-green shoes and a green linen coat bought for her by Stephen. Between these two photographs, it is as though Lagerfeld were 'staging' her life and, in doing so, helping her to find an adult identity that allowed her a greater chance of fulfilment and self-determination than before.

The photograph session, which is related with Nimier's characteristic dry humour, has been commissioned by *Paris Match* to celebrate the *rentrée littéraire* ('literary beginning of the new school year') of 2008. 'Karl' is depicted as extremely busy; he will photograph the narrator 'entre deux' ('between other things'; p. 12). And not only the narrator but the journalist from *Paris Match* will need to wait. As Karl is called to the telephone for an urgent call, he explains to the journalist that, if she does not have enough material for her article, 'vous n'avez qu'à inventer' ('all you need to do is make it up'), adding 'il y a une romancière dans la maison, elle se fera un plaisir de vous aider' ('there is a novelist in the building; she'll be delighted to help you with that'; p. 18). Authorized to fabulate, the narrator invents a middle name for Karl:

– Karl a un deuxième prenom, vous le savez? Otto, il s'appelle Karl Otto.
Comment on écrit Otto? Vous me demandez comment ça s'écrit? Eh bien tout simplement, j'imagine, O, 2T, O, comme Otto Preminger, Otto Rank... Otto, photo, c'est drôle, non? Regardez le dessin que ça fait sur le papier. Deux yeux, un nez, comme Toto en somme. Zéro plus zéro égale?
– La tête à Toto!
– La tête à Toto, nous y sommes. Karl Toto, si vous préférez, vous n'avez qu'à mettre Karl Toto.
– Toto, ou Otto?

('Karl has a middle name, you know. Otto: he's called Karl Otto. How to spell Otto? You are asking how it's spelt? Well, I suppose it's straightforward: O, 2 't's, O, as in Otto Preminger, or Otto Rank... Otto, [sounds like] photo, funny, don't you think? Look at how it looks when you write it down. Two eyes and a nose, like Toto in fact. Zero plus zero equals...?'

'Toto's head!'
'Toto's head, that's it. Karl Toto, if you prefer; you can simply put Karl Toto.'
'Toto or Otto?') (p. 19)

Toto's head refers to a traditional visual joke, in which two zeros, joined by a plus sign, are written out above an 'equals' sign and the whole is enclosed in a circle, creating a face. In the passage above, Nimier suggests that we might think of the plus sign as the back-to-back joining of two 't's, which suggests that the first 't' would need to be written as the inversion, or mirror image, of the second.

The journalist at first asks if Karl's middle name is to be recorded as 'Toto' or 'Otto'. This creates an apparently accidental riddle within this brief passage of dialogue. However, Nimier has skilfully planted a seed to enable this riddle to arise. The narrator mentions Otto Rank as the second of her examples of how to spell 'Otto'. Of course, Rank was the author of a weighty tome on the double, approvingly cited by Freud in *The Uncanny*, where the latter recalls his disciple's idea that belief in the double is linked with a 'primitive' desire to survive beyond death.[8] Nimier highlights the strange coincidence that makes Otto Rank's first name, 'Otto', a kind of inverted *double* of 'ot', as though 'ot' were looking in the mirror. But she has also noticed the further coincidence that 'Toto' (that uncannily familiar face) can be arrived at by inverting the 'original' 'ot'. Finally, by pointing to the similarity between 'otto' and 'photo', she invites us to reflect on the difference between two kinds of resemblance: that of the mirror image, in which all is inverted, and that of the photo, in which nothing seems inverted. When the understandably confused journalist asks 'Toto ou Otto?', she effectively hesitates between a photograph and a mirror image.

In her conversation with the journalist, the narrator fleshes Karl's supposed middle name into a fantasized flesh-and-blood double, but (in a macabre twist) one that inhabits his body parasitically: 'quand il était petit, Karl était persuadé qu'il partageait sa vie avec lui. Avec Otto. Ils étaient deux à manger, deux à parler, deux dans un même corps' ('when he was small, Karl was sure that he shared his life with him. With Otto. They ate as a pair, they spoke as a pair, the two of them shared one body'; p. 19). Finally, she imagines that when Lagerfeld famously lost weight, it was 'pour perdre effectivement les kilos de cet être avec qui il cohabitait depuis sa naissance' ('to lose in effect the kilos that made up this being with whom he had cohabited since birth'; p. 20).

This ingenious passage weaves a web of associations around Karl Lagerfeld, Otto Rank and the theme of the double. But (not for the first or last time in *Photo-Photo*) it is followed by a passage that relates it back to the narrator herself. As she is prepared for the photo shoot by an incredibly deft Japanese make-up artist, Lagerfeld explains that he is 'Une perle [...] capable de travailler une heure sur un modèle sans laisser trace de son passage. Ce qu'il ajoute est invisible, comme s'il maquillait la personne de l'intérieur' ('A treasure [...] capable of working for a whole hour on a model without leaving a trace of his presence. What he adds is invisible, as though he were applying the makeup to the person from the inside'; p. 23). Shiro, it seems, brings out an inner face, a double of the person on whom he works. Although the narrator has been warned that this is his art, she is surprised to see that he has rendered her 'la même, même pas en mieux. Juste un peu plus pâle. Comme cirée. Seuls les yeux avaient remonté d'un ton' ('the same, not even an improved version. Just a bit paler. As if [I had been] waxed. Only my eyes had become a shade lighter'; p. 30). We are, once again, confronted with an identity that is not quite complete, that 'is and is not' the same as the original.[9] This passage condenses a major theme of the novel: the comforts and anxieties associated with the quest for a double. On the one hand, 'I' can perhaps found a sense of self in perception of the other that resembles 'me'; on the other, I may feel alienated by seeing what I consider my unique and private self reduplicated as an external object. Yet the passage also stresses the paradoxical interdependence of resemblance and difference.

Photographs are popularly credited with proving the existence of the real.[10] However, the narrator realizes that the published photograph is a professional, photoshopped ensemble of nine authors of the *rentrée littéraire* invited by the magazine. They posed separately, and each image became a piece of a puzzle to be fitted together by electronic means.[11] If the narrator has no expectation that photographs are representative of the truth, she did expect them to provide visible proof that something specific had taken place some time, somewhere, although even that documentary function has been lost: 'Ce n'est même pas un état des lieux, puisque ce moment n'a jamais eu lieu' ('It's not even any kind of inventory, because this moment never happened'; p. 44). The narrator is disoriented when she does not recognize herself in the photograph. Nor can she even distinguish the guiding presence of the photographer, since elements of 'her photograph' taken by Lagerfeld have simply been subsumed within an entirely fabricated image. Using a word that often, in Nimier, connotes death as well as 'mere' disappearance, the narrator asks: 'Comment tout cela a-t-il pu disparaître?' ('How could all that disappear?'; p. 43).

So photographs lie – as the elderly Karl Lagerfeld enthusiast Huguette Malo will later say, of her album: 'Huguette Malo parlait toujours des photos, page après page, ou plutôt de tout ce qui se cachait derrière les photos, car les images elle-mêmes lui inspiraient de la méfiance, comme si elles n'étaient que le témoignage d'une mise en scène destinée à tromper le monde' ('Huguette Malo was still speaking about her photos, page by page, or rather about everything that was hidden behind the photos, for the images themselves made her suspicious, as if they merely bore witness to a set-up designed to deceive'; p. 75). Indeed, at their most sinister they mark the disappearance of the very people whose existence they are supposed to confirm. Immediately after the shoot, in the opening pages of the chapter entitled 'Missing', the narrator passes the wall in the Gare Saint-Lazare where there are photographs of children and others who are 'PORTÉS DISPARUS' ('REPORTED MISSING'; p. 38). The likelihood that most of these people are dead gives a certain substance to the superstitious idea (evoked earlier) that the photographic image 'kills' its subject.[12] Perhaps, then, we should prefer Otto to Toto, or the mirror image to the photograph? Of course, the comfort of its immediate presence may be accompanied by an uneasy sense that it involves a total inversion, but can we not simply invert the inversion, to restore the original? Apparently not, as the narrator will later comment (concerning a film project dreamed up by Édouard Levé): 'l'envers inversé n'est pas l'endroit' ('the reversal of the reversal is not the original'; p. 194).[13]

The phrase 'l'envers inversé n'est pas l'endroit' will become the new slogan of the art club for children run by the narrator's 'double'. This seems entirely appropriate, given the narrator's fascination with doubles that 'are and are not' the same as the original. Certainly, when Nimier's narrator meets her 'double', she is struck as much by their (physical) differences as by any similarities. The process begins bathetically: 'M'attendais-je sincèrement à rencontrer mon double, comme dans les romans de Dostoëvski?' ('Was I sincerely expecting to meet my double, as in Dostoevsky's novels?'). She compares the situation to 'le jeu des sept erreurs' ('the game of seven mistakes'), a variation on 'spot the difference'. However, between herself and Frederika there were not 'sept erreurs' but 'douze, vingt-quatre, des milliers' ('twelve, twenty-four, thousands'; p. 154). The narrator realizes that the identification of a double is a matter of selection, and is driven not by perception, but by desire. We find our doubles where we can, and where we will, according to wishes rather than appearances: 'Pourquoi toujours, comme dans le jeu des sept erreurs, vouloir mettre en lumière ce qui fait défaut? Ce qui sépare?' ('Why do we always, as in the game of 'spot the difference', want to focus on what is missing? On what separates us?'; p. 194). Why not choose the opposite, 'l'évidence' ('the obvious [resemblances]'), as an anchor for identity? Frederika asserts that in the play of difference within identity, the children she works with find release: 'Et c'est dans cet espace-là, affirma-t-elle, dans cet intervalle entre l'envers inversé et l'endroit, que les enfants pourraient s'envoler' ('And it's in that space, she asserted, in that gap between the inverted other side and the upper surface, that the children could take flight'; p. 194). If she does not allow herself to escape joyfully into the play of identity versus difference, the narrator may become 'stuck' in her quest for knowing 'à quoi je ressemble' ('what I am like/what I look like'): 'comment ressembler à quelqu'un qui vous ressemble quand on ne se ressemble pas soi-même?' ('how to resemble someone who resembles us when we don't resemble ourselves?'; p. 170).[14] She speculates that Karl Lagerfeld knew this all along, and chose to 'hypnotize' her and (presumably) Frederika into seeing each other as doubles (p. 175). However, the true wishful identification that haunts her – and we might say, with confidence, that it haunts Marie Nimier, the author – is one with the father, the father-author who might have written *Le Ciel comme un endroit*, had he lived. Yet to embrace this identification, she has to overcome the greatest obstacle of all: that of gender.

When the narrator travels to Baden-Baden, she takes with her a drawing that she has kept since the age of approximately 8. A significant amount of *Photo-Photo* is devoted to the description and analysis of this drawing. The narrator explains that her teacher had asked the class to draw 'le plus beau bonhomme possible' ('the finest-looking character possible'; p. 129).[15] While the rest of the class had interpreted this as meaning that they must draw a man, the narrator alone drew a girl. This exposed her to the ridicule of her classmates, although eliciting the approval and sympathy of the (female) teacher. The child's outrage is directed at her imprisonment, their imprisonment, within gender; within a (symbolic) order that insists on the male norm, and that inclines people to see everything through the lens of gender. The child takes pride in her discovery that faces are not contained by a black line, as they are in children's drawings. But all her classmates perceive is that she has had the ridiculousness to draw a girl when a 'bonhomme' had been required. And so:

> Homme ou femme, peu importe, cette intuition qui me touche, profondément, encore en en parlant aujourd'hui elle me touche, ce qui est important, c'est qu'un visage ne se termine pas par un trait. Et ne se termine pas tout court. [...] J'ai honte d'être la seule, je ne suis pas encore à l'âge où l'on tire une certaine fierté à être original ou simplement différent.
>
> (Man or woman, what's the difference, the intuition that touches me, deeply, that touches me even today when I speak of it, and that matters here, is that a face does not end in a line. And it simply does not 'end'. [...] [At the age of 8] I am ashamed to be the only one [to notice this], I have not yet reached the age where one takes a certain pride in being original or simply different.) (pp. 131–2)

The narrator's younger self is doubly different: different because she noticed that faces are not bound by lines, and different because she does not spontaneously 'think' through gender. And she is still different in both respects now; as an adult, she constantly finds that others see her as culpably transgressing gender boundaries, as she presumes to exercise the same profession as her father. Among her many observations on how society creates images of writers (sitting or, if they are 'écrivains voyageurs', standing; with or without legs/a cigarette and so on), she cites anonymous voices objecting to the creation of the word 'écrivaine' ('female writer') on the grounds that in the word in question, 'on entend le mot "vaine"' ('one hears the word "vain[e]"'); but, she asks pointedly of the (masculine) word 'écrivain' ('writer'), 'on n'entendrait pas le mot "vain"?' ('one apparently does not hear the word "vain" there?'; p. 46). She is still fighting the battle of her 8-year-old self, when all the other children (she states in her adult voice) endowed their 'bonshommes' with substitutes for the all-important penis: 'Tous les personnages ont une pipe ou un chapeau, une moustache, un marteau, une cravate pour évoquer cette chose un peu mystérieuse qui pend entre leurs jambes et que l'on ne voit pas' ('All the [drawn] characters have a pipe or a hat, a moustache, a hammer or a tie to imply that slightly mysterious thing that hangs between their legs, out of sight'; p. 131). However, Frederika (as if by chance) is practised in the analysis of children's drawings, for this is the main part of her therapeutic work with the children with whom she works. And when she is shown the drawing, she immediately understands: 'Tu ne t'es jamais vraiment remise de ce dessin...' ('you have never really recovered from this drawing...'; p. 184). From this moment on, the narrator feels relief.

Frederika is the instrument that Karl Lagerfeld has used to 'heal' the narrator. Her key role is stressed by Stephen in one of the novel's self-reflexive passages. By way of encouraging the narrator out of her writer's block, he suggests: 'Quand tu mets en scène tous ces éléments qui marchent par deux (paire de chaussures, paire de lunettes, Otto et Toto [...]) j'ai l'impression de voir se dessiner le portrait de cette femme, cette Allemande qui anime un atelier de dessin pour les enfants, celle qui te ressemble tant' ('When you bring in all those elements that go in pairs (a pair of shoes, a pair of glasses, Otto and Toto [...]), I have the impression that I'm watching you draw the portrait of that woman, that German woman who runs a drawing studio for children, the one who resembles you so closely'; p. 124).

But of course, it is Karl that has drawn the two 'sosies' together. When the narrator is surprised that Frederika has guessed that she is hoping to meet her in Baden-Baden, Frederika explains that Karl had told her of the narrator's existence (p. 169). In the closing pages, Karl's all-pervasive influence is emphasized as follows:

> Inutile de me débattre, d'essayer de m'échapper, tout me ramenait à Lagerfeld, à cette première photo dans son studio de la rue de Lille. Sans lui, je n'aurais pas rencontré Huguette Malo. [...] Pas rencontré Frederika surtout [...]. Si j'enlevais le personnage qu'il m'avait inspiré, il y aurait un gros trou au milieu du livre.

> (It was pointless to struggle, to try to escape, everything led me back to Lagerfeld, to that first photograph in his studio in the rue de Lille. Without him, I wouldn't have met Huguette Malo [...] or, above all, Frederika [...]. If I took out the character whom he inspired, there would be a great hole in the middle of the book.) (p. 192)

The 'godfather' has played his role discreetly, but effectively. And 'discreetly', too, Nimier has used him as a divergent double for the absent father.

Concluding Remarks

We saw that Nimier mentions her father directly only once, but the rest of the text invites us to see the father's absence/presence as all-pervasive and his figure as all-important.[16] In Lacanian theory, the 'non du père' insists on the necessity, for health, of leaving behind the 'imaginary', dyadic relation to the other, inaugurated in the mirror stage, to enter into the Symbolic, with its triangular relations.[17] However, Lacan also insists that we do not leave the Imaginary behind; a work such as the *Séminaire sur la lettre volée* (*Seminar on the Purloined Letter*), to name one of the most famous that explores this question, suggests, rather, that we may remain between the Imaginary and the Symbolic, in ways that may blind or hamper us.[18] In *Photo-Photo*, Nimier puts a similar idea into play. Yet in her version, the entry into the Symbolic marked by gender is reversed by the imaginary relation with Frederika. At the same time, not the father but the father's substitute, the 'godfather' Karl Lagerfeld, has permitted this 'regression' to the Imaginary. The apparently perfect, dyadic relationship may indeed be a mirage, for Karl continues to supply the third term. At least, the narrator suspects as much. After all, as the moment at which she meets her double approaches, she asks herself: 'Pourquoi suis-je ici? Est-ce vraiment pour voir à quoi je ressemble?' ('Why am I here? Is it really to see what I am like [or what I look like]?'; p. 152). Her answer takes the form of a further question: 'N'est-ce pas plutôt ça qui m'anime, même si je ne veux pas me l'avouer, en savoir un peu plus sur le roi de la Mode?' ('Isn't it, rather, even if I don't want to admit it to myself, to know a bit more about the King of Fashion?'; p. 153).

The narrator has 'chosen' a father who chooses, for her, an object on the basis of resemblance rather than difference. And the narrator works hard to suggest that there is nothing pathological in this; rather, it is a form of recovery or healing. It is also a kind of liberation; in the process, she realizes that this is a release from the trap of gender. She can finally effect a split from her former self, who was 'stuck', to take flight, like one of the angels made of 'stuc' ('stucco') which she observes in the ophthalmologist's waiting room.[19] Margaret-Anne Hutton has noted: '[in Nimier's works] paternal figures precipitate a splitting process in protagonists and narrators, [so that,] divided between silence and voice, the latter can achieve unity only when and if they overcome the imposed silence and find a new voice in the form of authorship; when they become creators in their own right and name'.[20] This remark holds true for *Photo-Photo*.

It seems appropriate to finish this chapter, the last in this collection, by referring to Alison Finch's masterful survey of the concept of influence. Effecting a broad historical sweep, Finch shows the vicissitudes of the word/concept 'influence'. She charts its relative decline through the twentieth century, but shows that, in spite of all, influence will not allow itself to fall into oblivion or disuse, or be theorized away.[21] The pieces in this volume show something of the resilience of influence as a concept and as a phenomenon, and as a vital concern for critical theory and practice alike.

Notes

1. Series of interviews for 'Interlignes' hosted by Dominique Antoine, available at http://education.francetv.fr/videos/marie-nimier-son-dernier-roman-photo-photo-v109567.
2. Often in her work, Nimier blurs the boundary between narrator and author. In *Photo-Photo*, there is no definitive indication that the narrator is *not* 'supposed to be' the author in the process of writing her latest book, a process during which she is portrayed as weaving facts and fantasy together.
3. See Marie Nimier, *Photo-Photo* (Paris: Gallimard, 2010), pp. 126–7. All subsequent references are to this edition and all translations are my own.
4. In French, 'endroit' can mean 'place' or, as the opposite of 'envers', it can mean the upper side (for instance of a coin); so in the French original cited here, there is a wordplay.
5. *Mise-en-abyme* of various kinds is a recurring device in Nimier's writing, notably in *Les Inséparables* (Paris: Gallimard, 2008).
6. See note 1 above.
7. Margaret-Ann Hutton observes: 'In the case of the Nimier corpus we find an important variation on the general theme of paternal dysfunction in the form of the recurring motif of the absent father'. Margaret-Anne Hutton, 'Authority and Authorship in the Works of Marie Nimier: "*Points de re-père*"', *Cincinnati Romance Review*, 25 (2006), 232–46 (p. 234).
8. See Sigmund Freud, 'The Uncanny' in *The Standard Edition of the Complete Psychological Works of Sigmund Freud*. trans. and ed. by James Strachey, 24 vols (London: Hogarth Press, 1953–74), XVII, pp. 217–56.
9. Though this point is not central to our argument, it is interesting to note that the photograph itself is twinned with an imaginary double, and the two together become an allegory of a story (the story, no doubt, that we are reading). For as the narrator, as though exhausted by the makeup session, begins to fall asleep, she grasps hold of a memory that is only half-conscious: 'Il pourrait s'agir d'un cliché, au moins retenir cette idée-là, de la lente disparition d'un cliché. Une histoire inscrite entre deux angles, deux points de vue. Deux photographies, en somme, l'une qui se voit, et l'autre, qui ne se voit pas' ('It could be a photograph, at least I should hold on to that idea, the idea of the slow disappearance of a photograph. A story inscribed between two angles, two points of view. Two photographs, in short, one that is seen and the other that is not'; p. 32).

10. In his contribution to this volume, Fabien Arribert-Narce cites Barthes's assertion in *Camera Lucida* that 'toute photo est un certificat de présence' ('every photograph is a certificate of presence'); see Chapter 10, note 12. Of course, Barthes wrote this before the advent of digital photography, which has allowed the convincing manipulation of photographic images to become routine.
11. The reader will remember also that photographs have played a key role in Nimier's autobiographical narratives in the past, as it is in part through photos of her father's car crash published in *Paris Match* that she reconstitutes her image of the absent father. See for instance *La Reine du silence* (Paris: Gallimard, 2004).
12. 'Un déclic, et clac! dans la boîte, comme les autres écrivains qui m'avaient précédée. Une mort sans cadavre, pensai-je, sans pleurs ni couronnes, sans compassion, sans rien' ('A click, and all done! Into the box, like the other authors who had gone before me. A death without a body, I thought, without tears or crowns, without compassion, without anything'; p. 28).
13. The narrator describes two occasions on which she and Édouard Levé (1965–2007) had supposedly collaborated: once when he wanted to be told about her dreams as he was doing a work based on the dreams of various people, and another when he took a series of photographs of unknown people with famous names: 'Ces hommes s'appelaient bien Klein, Breton, Léger, aucun doute sur la question. Mangeaient, dormaient, rêvaient et faisaient l'amour. N'étaient pas moins vrais que les autres' ('Those men were really called Klein, Breton, Léger, that was beyond doubt. They ate, slept, dreamed and made love. They were no less real than the others'; p. 51). This may be connected with Nimier's sense of bearing her father's name, especially as she is painfully aware of following in his footsteps.
14. While waiting to meet Frederika, the narrator asks herself whether she is truly in Baden-Baden 'pour voir à quoi je ressemble?' (p. 152). This passage will be discussed below.
15. It is impossible to translate 'bonhomme' precisely here, as English is not a gendered language. Dictionary definitions include 'chap' and 'fellow', but Nimier's point is that while all nouns in French are gendered, some can be seen as conceptually masculine or feminine (for instance, 'un chat' might be male or female).
16. In one passage, the narrator's absent boyfriend remembers how Levé taught him to play *osselets* (a game of dexterity) in their schooldays. The fact that one piece is the 'father' allows him to suggest that he and Levé shared an obsession with paternal figures: 'Édouard l'avait-il deviné? Tous ces efforts pour protéger le père de la chute me touchaient plus que de raison, et c'est comme ça, autour de ça me semble-t-il, que notre amitié se constitua' ('Had

Edouard guessed? All these efforts to protect the father from falling touched me more than they should have, and I think it is in this way, around this [feeling], that our friendship was formed'; p. 52).

17. For a masterful exposé of Lacan's theory, see Malcolm Bowie, *Lacan* (Cambridge, MA: Harvard University Press, 1991). See Chapters 2 and 4 respectively for the mirror stage and for the Imaginary, the Symbolic and the Real.

18. Bowie argues that '[Lacan's use of the term "Imaginary"] has a strong pejorative force, and suggests that the subject is seeking, in a wilful and blameworthy fashion, to remove himself from the flux of becoming. The Symbolic order, on the other hand, is often spoken of admiringly'. Nevertheless, he also observes that 'To some extent, the Symbolic and the Imaginary are a contrasting and interdependent pair' (*Lacan*, pp. 92, 93).

19. Nimier's narrator puns on 'stuck' and 'stuc' as follows: 'Stick, stock, stuc, ou Stephen, tu es bien aimable de me le rappeler [...]: stuc, sans "k"' ('Stick, stock, stucco; yes, Stephen, it's kind of you to remind me [...] stucco, without a 'k'; p. 127).

20. Hutton, 'Authority and Authorship in the Works of Marie Nimier', p. 238.

21. See Alison Finch, 'The French Concept of Influence', in *'When Familiar Meanings Dissolve...': Essays in French Studies in Memory of Malcom Bowie*, ed. by Naomi Segal and Gill Rye (Oxford and Bern: Peter Lang, 2011), pp. 235–48.

Bibliography

Abraham, Nicolas and Maria Török, *L'Écorce et le noyau*, 2nd edn (Paris: Flammarion, 1987).
Abraham, Nicolas and Maria Török, *The Shell and the Kernel: Renewals of Psychoanalysis*, trans. by Nicholas T. Rand (Chicago: Chicago University Press, 1994).
Alpers, Svetlana, *The Vexations of Art: Velázquez and Others* (New Haven, CT: Yale University Press, 2005).
Aragon, Louis, *Henri Matisse, roman* (Paris: Gallimard, 1998).
Aragon, Louis, *Sur Henri Matisse: entretiens avec Jean Ristat* (Paris: Stock, 1999).
Aragon, Louis, *Œuvres poétiques complètes*, ed. by Olivier Barbarant (Paris: Gallimard, 2007).
Arendt, Hannah, *Eichmann in Jerusalem: A Report on the Banality of Evil* (London: Penguin, 2006).
Ariès, Philippe, *Essais sur l'histoire de la mort en Occident du Moyen Age à nos jours* (Paris: Seuil, 1977).
Ariès, Philippe, *Images de l'homme devant la mort* (Paris: Seuil, 1983).
Ariès, Philippe, *Images of Man and Death*, trans. by Janet Lloyd (Cambridge: Harvard University Press, 1985).
Bachelard, Gaston, *L'Eau et les rêves, essai sur l'imagination de la matière* (Paris: Corti, 1942).
Bair, Deirdre, *Samuel Beckett: A Biography* (London: Simon, 1990).
Baldick, Chris, *Oxford Concise Dictionary of Literary Terms* (Oxford: Oxford University Press, 2004).
Balibar, Étienne, *Nous, citoyens d'Europe? Les frontières, l'État, le peuple* (Paris: La Découverte, 2001).
Baretti, Giuseppe, *Dissertation upon the Italian Poetry* (London, 1753).
Barthes, Roland, *The Pleasure of the Text*, trans. by Richard Miller (New York: Farrar, Straus and Giroux, 1975).
Barthes, Roland, *Image, Music, Text*, ed. and trans. by Stephen Heath (London: Fontana Press, 1977).
Barthes, Roland, *Sade, Fourier, Loyola*, trans. by Richard Miller (London: Jonathan Cape, 1977).
Barthes, Roland, *Empire of Signs*, trans. by Richard Howard (New York: Hill and Wang, 1982).
Barthes, Roland, *Camera Lucida*, trans. by Richard Howard (London: Vintage Books, 2000).
Barthes, Roland, *Œuvres complètes*, ed. by Éric Marty, 5 vols (Paris: Seuil, 2002).
Barthes, Roland, *L'Empire des signes* (Paris: Seuil, 2005).
Barthes, Roland, 'Texte (théorie du)', *Encyclopaedia universalis*, http://asl.univ-montp3.fr/e41slym/Barthes_THEORIE_DU_TEXTE.pdf.
Bashō, Matsuo, *The Narrow Road to the Deep North and Other Travel Sketches*, trans. by Nobuyuki Yuasa (Harmondsworth: Penguin, 1966).

Bataille, Georges *et al.*, *L'Affaire Sade, compte rendu exact du procès intenté par le Ministère public* (Paris: Pauvert, 1957).
Baxandall, Michael, *Patterns of Intention: On the Historical Explanation of Pictures* (New Haven, CT and London: Yale University Press, 1985).
Bayard, Pierre, *Le Plagiat par anticipation* (Paris: Minuit, 2009).
Beauvoir, Simone de, *Faut-il brûler Sade?* (Paris: Gallimard, 1972).
Beckett, Samuel, *Comment c'est* (Paris: Minuit, 1961).
Beckett, Samuel, *The Grove Centenary Editions of Samuel Beckett*, ed. by Paul Auster, 4 vols (New York: Grove Press, 2006).
Blanchot, Maurice, *L'Arrêt de mort* (Paris: Gallimard, 1948).
Blanchot, Maurice, *Le Livre à venir* (Paris: Gallimard, 1959).
Blanchot, Maurice, 'Le Grand Renfermement', *Nouvelle Revue Française*, 106 (October 1961), 676–86.
Blanchot, Maurice, *L'Entretien infini* (Paris: Gallimard, 1969).
Blanchot, Maurice, 'La Folie par excellence', in Karl Jaspers and Maurice Blanchot, *Strindberg et Van Gogh, Swedenborg et Hölderlin* (Paris: Minuit, 1970).
Blanchot, Maurice, *Lettres à Vadim Kozovoï suivi de La Parole ascendante*, ed. by Denis Aucouturier (Houilles: Manucius, 2009).
Bloom, Harold, *Poetry and Repression: Revisionism from Blake to Stevens* (New Haven, CT and London: Yale University Press, 1976).
Bloom, Harold, *The Anxiety of Influence: A Theory of Poetry*, 2nd edn (New York and Oxford: Oxford University Press, 1997).
Bloom, Harold, *A Map of Misreading*, 2nd edn (New York and Oxford: Oxford University Press, 2003).
Bonald, Louis Gabriel Ambroise de, *Œuvres complètes*, ed. by J. P. Migne, 3 vols (Paris: Migne, 1859).
Borges, Jorge Luis, *Collected Fictions*, trans. by Andrew Hurley (New York: Penguin, 1998).
Borges, Jorge Luis, *The Total Library: Non-Fiction, 1922–1986*, ed. by Eliot Weinberger, trans. by Esther Allen *et al.* (Harmondsworth: Penguin, 1999).
Bourdieu, Pierre, 'Les Conditions sociales de la circulation internationale des idées', *Romanistische Zeitschrift für Literatur*, 1–2 (1990), 3–8.
Bourdieu, Pierre, 'The Social Conditions of the International Circulation of Ideas' in *Bourdieu: A Critical Reader*, ed. by Richard Shusterman (Oxford: Wiley-Blackwell, 1999), pp. 220–28.
Bowie, Malcolm, *Lacan* (Cambridge, MA: Harvard University Press, 1991).
Buci-Glucksmann, Christine, *L'Esthétique du temps au Japon: du Zen au virtuel* (Paris: Galilée, 2005).
Burgin, Victor (ed.), *Thinking Photography* (London: Macmillan, 1982).
Canault, Nina, *Comment paye-t-on les fautes de ses ancêtres: l'inconscient transgénérationnel* (Paris: Desclée de Brouwer, 1998).
Certeau, Michel de, *The Writing of History*, trans. by Tom Conley (New York: Columbia University Press, 1975).
Chalais, François, *Lettre ouverte aux pornographes* (Paris: Albin Michel, 1975).
Challemel-Lacour, P., 'Un bouddhiste contemporain en Allemagne. Arthur Schopenhauer', *Revue des Deux Mondes*, 86 (1870), 296–332.
Chateaubriand, François-René de, *Génie du christianisme*, ed. by M. Regard (Paris: Gallimard, 1978).

Clayton, Jay and Eric Rothstein (eds), *Influence and Intertextuality in Literary History* (Madison: University of Wisconsin Press, 1991).

Comment, Bernard, *Roland Barthes, vers le neutre* (Paris: Bourgois, 2002).

Compagnon, Antoine, *Les Antimodernes: de Joseph de Maistre à Roland Barthes* (Paris: Gallimard, 2005).

Compagnon, Antoine, 'Écrire la vie: Montaigne, Stendhal, Proust', in *Cours et travaux du Collège de France: résumés 2008–2009, annuaire 109ème année* (Paris: Collège de France, 2010), pp. 863–85.

Concannon, Amy and Kerry Sweeney, interview with Darrieussecq (2004), http://darrieussecq.arizona.edu/eng/eninterview.html.

Condorcet, Nicolas de, *Œuvres*, ed. by A. Condorcet *et al.*, 12 vols (Paris: Firmin Didot Frères, 1847).

Dante Alighieri, *Commedia del divina poeta Danthe Alighieri, con la dotta e leggiadra spositione di Christophoro Londino* (Venice: G. G. da Trino, 1536), in *Bibliothèque de Voltaire: catalogue des livres*, ed. by M. P. Alekseev and T. N. Kopreeva (Moscow: Éditions de l'Académie des Sciences de l'URSS, 1961), n° 940.

Dante Alighieri, *Inferno*, ed. and trans. by Robin Kirkpatrick (London: Penguin, 2006).

Dante Alighieri, *Purgatorio*, ed. and trans. by Robin Kirkpatrick (London: Penguin, 2007).

Danto, Arthur, *The Abuse of Beauty: Aesthetics and the Concept of Art* (Chicago: Open Court, 2004).

Darrieussecq, Marie, 'Dans la maison de Louise' in *Louise Bourgeois – œuvres récentes* (Paris: Seuil, 1997).

Darrieussecq, Marie, 'Sorguina – la réponse de l'auteur de *Truismes* et de *Naissance des fantômes* à Marie Ndiaye', *Libération*, 10 March 1998.

Darrieussecq, Marie, *Il était une fois... la plage* (Paris: Roger-Viollet/Plume, 2000).

Darrieussecq, Marie, 'Interview by Becky Miller and Martha Holmes' (2001), http://darrieussecq.arizona.edu/eng/eninterview2001.html.

Darrieussecq, Marie, *Bref séjour chez les vivants* (Paris: Gallimard, 2002).

Darrieussecq, Marie, Untitled text in Annette Messager (ed.), *Hors-jeu* (Arles: Actes Sud Nantes, Musée des beaux-arts, 2002), pp. 69–71.

Darrieussecq, Marie, 'L'Arrière-saison', in Dolorès Marat (ed.), *Illusion* (Trézélan: Filigranes Éditions, 2003), pp. 5–14.

Darrieussecq, Marie, *White* (Paris: P.O.L., 2003).

Darrieussecq, Marie *et al.* (eds), *Ghostscape* (Paris: Monum, 2004).

Darrieussecq, Marie, Untitled text in Bernard Faucon *et al.* (eds), *Bernard Faucon* (Arles: Actes Sud, 2005), pp. 21–3.

Darrieussecq, Marie, 'Je suis devenue psychanalyste', *Lire* (01 November 2006), http://www.lexpress.fr/culture/livre/je-suis-devenue-psychanalyste-par-marie-darrieussecq_811700.html?xtmc=Darrieussecq_&xtcr=19.

Darrieussecq, Marie, *Zoo* (Paris: P.O.L., 2006).

Darrieussecq, Marie *et al.* (eds), *Jeanne Susplugas – Expiry Works – Date 1999/2007* (Paris: Archibooks, 2007).

Darrieussecq, Marie, 'Je est unE autre', in Annie Olivier (ed.), *Écrire l'histoire d'une vie* (Rome: Edizioni Spartaco, 2007), http://darrieussecq.arizona.edu/fr/collautofiction.doc.

Darrieussecq, Marie *et al.* (eds), *B2B2SP: Édouard François* (Paris: Éditions Archibooks, 2008).

Darrieussecq, Marie, 'Écrire, qu'est-ce que c'est?', transcript of a seminar held at the Institut des Hautes Etudes en Psychanalyse/ENS (2008).
Darrieussecq, Marie, 'Être libéré de soi', *Le Magazine littéraire*, 473 (March 2008), p. 58.
Darrieussecq, Marie et al. (eds), *Louise Bourgeois au Centre Pompidou* (Paris: Beaux Arts Éditions, 2008).
Darrieussecq, Marie, *Rapport de police – accusations de plagiat et autres modes de surveillance de la fiction* (Paris: P.O.L., 2010).
Deforges, Régine, *O m'a dit. Entretiens avec Pauline Réage* (Paris: Pauvert, 1995).
Deimier, Pierre de, *L'Académie de l'art poétique* (Paris: J. de Bordeaulx, 1610).
Deleuze, Gilles, *Deux régimes de fous: textes et entretiens 1975–1995*, ed. by David Lapoujade (Paris: Minuit, 2003).
Delon, Michel, *Les Vies de Sade* (Paris: Éditions Textuel, 2007).
Derrida, Jacques, *De la grammatologie* (Paris: Minuit, 1967).
Derrida, Jacques, *L'Écriture et la différence* (Paris: Seuil, 1967).
Derrida, Jacques, *Marges – de la philosophie* (Paris: Minuit, 1972).
Derrida, Jacques, *Writing and Difference*, trans. by Alan Bass (London: Routledge, 1978).
Derrida, Jacques, *La Carte postale: de Socrate à Freud et au-delà* (Paris: Flammarion, 1980).
Derrida, Jacques, 'Les Morts de Roland Barthes', *Poétique*, 47 (1981), 269–92.
Derrida, Jacques, *Margins of Philosophy*, trans. by Alan Bass (Chicago: University of Chicago Press, 1982).
Derrida, Jacques, *The Post Card: From Socrates to Freud and Beyond*, trans. by Alan Bass (Chicago: University of Chicago Press, 1987).
Derrida, Jacques, *Mal d'archive: une impression freudienne* (Paris: Galilée, 1995).
Derrida, Jacques, *Résistances: de la psychanalyse* (Paris: Galilée, 1996).
Derrida, Jacques, *Archive Fever: A Freudian Impression*, trans. by Eric Prenowitz (Chicago: University of Chicago Press, 1998).
Derrida, Jacques, *Parages* (Paris: Galilée, 2003).
Derrida, Jacques, 'The Deaths of Roland Barthes', trans. by Catherine Porter, in *Psyche: Inventions of the Other*, ed. by Peggy Kamuf and Elizabeth G. Rottenberg (Stanford, CA: Stanford University Press, 2007), pp. 264–98.
Derrida, Jacques, *Copy, Archive, Signature*, ed. by Gerhard Richter and trans. by Jeff Fort (Stanford, CA: Stanford University Press, 2010).
Derrida, Jacques and Elisabeth Roudinesco, *De quoi demain... Dialogue* (Paris: Flammarion, 2001).
Derrida, Jacques and Elisabeth Roudinesco, *For What Tomorrow...: A Dialogue*, trans. by Jeff Fort (Stanford, CA: Stanford University Press, 2004).
Descombes, Vincent, *Le Même et l'autre: quarante-cinq ans de philosophie française (1933–1978)* (Paris: Minuit, 1979).
Destais, Alexandra, 'L'Émergence de la littérature érographique féminine en France: 1954–1975' (unpublished doctoral thesis, Université de Caen, 2006).
Diderot, Denis and Jean Le Rond d'Alembert (eds), *Encyclopédie, ou Dictionnaire raisonné des sciences, des arts et des métiers*, 17 vols (Paris: Briasson, David, Le Breton, Durand, 1751–65).
Didi-Huberman, Georges, *L'Image survivante. Histoire de l'art et temps des fantômes selon Aby Warburg* (Paris: Minuit, 2002).
Didi-Huberman, Georges, *Images malgré tout* (Paris: Minuit, 2003).

Disson, Agnès et al., 'Projet Jet Stream', *Inventaire-Invention*, June 2011, http://www.a360.org/article.php3?id_article=99 (texts no longer accessible online).
Dosse, François, *Histoire du structuralisme*, 2 vols (Paris: La Découverte, 1991–92).
Dumas, Didier, *L'Ange et le fantôme. Introduction à la clinique de l'impensé généalogique* (Paris: Minuit, 1985).
Duras, Marguerite, *L'Amant* (Paris: Minuit, 1984).
Elderfield, John, *The Drawings of Henri Matisse* (London: Arts Council of Great Britain and Thames & Hudson, 1984).
Emanuel, Michelle, *From Surrealism to Less-Exquisite Cadavers: Léo Malet and the Evolution of the French Roman Noir* (Amsterdam and New York: Rodopi, 2006).
Espagne, Michel and Michael Werner (eds), *Transferts: les relations interculturelles dans l'espace franco-allemand (XVIIIe-XIXe siècles)* (Paris: Éditions Recherche sur les civilisations, 1988).
Farinelli, Arturo, 'Voltaire et Dante', *Studien zur vergleichenden Literaturgeschichte*, 6 (1906), 86–128.
Fein, David, *Charles d'Orléans* (Boston: Twayne, 1983).
Finch, Alison, 'The French Concept of Influence', in *'When Familiar Meanings Dissolve...': Essays in French Studies in Memory of Malcolm Bowie*, ed. by Naomi Segal and Gill Rye (Oxford and Bern: Peter Lang, 2011), pp. 235–48.
Finer, Emily, *Turning into Sterne: Viktor Shklovskii and Literary Reception* (Oxford: Legenda, 2010).
Flower, John (ed.), *Patrick Modiano* (Amsterdam and New York: Rodopi, 2007).
Fraser, David, 'Polarcauste: Law, Justice and the Shoah in French Detective Fiction', *International Journal of Law in Context*, 1.3 (2005), 237–60.
Freud, Sigmund, *The Standard Edition of the Complete Psychological Works of Sigmund Freud*. trans. and ed. by James Strachey, 24 vols (London: Hogarth Press, 1953–74).
Frey, Pascale, 'Darrieussecq: l'écriture pour toujours', *Lire* (October 2001), http://www.lire.fr/portrait.asp/idC=37851/idTC=5/idR=201/idG=3.
Fry, Paul H., 'How to Live with the Infinite Regress of Strong Misreading', *Modern Language Quarterly*, 69.4 (December 2008), 437–59.
Garcin, Jérôme, 'Comment on a lancé les livres cultes: 1954, "Histoire d'O"', *Le Nouvel Observateur*, 8 August 2002, pp. 58–61.
Gaudemar, Antoine de, 'Marie NDiaye polemique avec Darrieussecq', *Libération*, 3 March 1998, http://www.liberation.fr/culture/0101241197-marie-ndiaye-polemique-avec-marie-darrieussecq.
Gaudet, Jeanette, '"Des livres sur la liberté": conversation avec Darrieussecq', *Dalhousie French Studies*, 59 (2002), 108–18.
Gorrara, Claire, 'Cultural Intersections: The American Hard-Boiled Detective Novel and Early French *roman noir*', *Modern Language Review*, 98.3 (2003), 590–601.
Gorrara, Claire, 'Forgotten Crimes? Representing Jewish Experience of the Second World War in French Crime Fiction', *South Central Review*, 27.1-2 (2010), 3–20.
Goulbourne, Russell, '"Bizarre, mais brillant de beautés naturelles": Voltaire and Dante's *Commedia*', *La parola del testo*, 17 (2013), 31–44.
Grammont, Claudine, 'Recreations', in *Matisse: A Second Life*, ed. by Hanne Finsen (Paris: Hazan, 2005), pp. 55–65.

Guibert, Hervé, *L'Image fantôme* (Paris: Minuit, 1981).
Guibert, Hervé, *Ghost Image*, trans. by Robert Bononno (Los Angeles, CA: Sun and Moon Press, 1996).
Hagglünd, Martin, *Radical Atheism: Derrida and the Time of Life* (Stanford, CA: Stanford University Press, 2008).
Halbreich, Harry, 'From Semiramis... to Blues', article in booklet accompanying 1992 Timpani recording of Arthur Honegger, *Sémiramis et autres inédits d'orchestre*, Orchestre symphonique de RTL, cond. by Leopold Hager, November 1992 (France: Timpani, 1993 [Audio CD]), pp. 10–13.
Hannoosh, Michele, *Parody and Decadence: Laforgue's 'Moralités légendaires'* (Colombus: Ohio State University Press, 1989).
Hartmann, Eduard von, *Philosophie de l'insconscient*, trans. by D. Nolen, 2 vols (Paris: Germer Baillière, 1877).
Hassan, Ihab H., 'The Problem of Influence in Literary History: Notes towards a Definition', *Journal of Aesthetics and Art Criticism*, 14.1 (September 1955), 66–76.
Hesiod, *'Theogony' and 'Works and Days'*, ed. and trans. by Martin L. West (Oxford: Oxford University Press, 2008).
Hokenson, Jan Walsh, *Japan, France, and East-West Aesthetics: French Literature, 1867–2000* (Madison, NJ: Fairleigh Dickinson University Press).
Holland, Michael, 'The Time of His Life', *Paragraph*, 30.3 (November 2007), 46–66.
Hutton, Margaret-Anne, 'Authority and Authorship in the Works of Marie Nimier: "*Points de re-père*"', *Cincinnati Romance Review*, 25 (2006), 232–46.
Jackson, Julian, *France: The Dark Years 1940–1944* (Oxford: Oxford University Press, 2001).
Jordan, Shirley, 'Saying the Unsayable: Identities in Crisis in the Early Novels of Darrieussecq', in *Women's Writing in Contemporary France: New Writers, New Literatures in the 1990s*, ed. by Gill Rye and Michael Worton (Manchester: Manchester University Press, 2002), pp. 142–53.
Kaprièlan, Nelly, 'Voyages en terres inconnues', special issue of *Nouvelles littératures françaises* (2010), 54–6.
Karatani, Kojin and Sabu Kohso (trans.), 'Uses of Aesthetics: After Orientalism', *boundary 2*, 25.2 (1998), 145–60.
Kawakami, Akane, *Travellers' Visions: French Literary Encounters with Japan, 1881–2004* (Liverpool: Liverpool University Press, 2005).
Kawakami, Akane, '"Un coup de foudre photographique": Autobiography and Photography in Hervé Guibert', *Romance Studies*, 25.3 (2007), 211–25.
Kimyongür, Angela, 'Patrick Pécherot, Eugenics and the Occupation of France', in *Violence and War in Culture and the Media: Five Disciplinary Lenses*, ed. by A. Karatzogianni (London: Routledge, 2012).
Klossowski, Pierre, *'Sade mon prochain' précédé de 'Le Philosophe scélérat'* (Paris: Seuil, 1947).
Knowlson, James, 'Beckett the Tourist: Bamberg and Würzburg', in *Beckett at 100: Revolving It All*, ed. by Linda Ben-Zvi and Angela Moorjani (Oxford: Oxford University Press, 2008), pp. 21–31.
Krieger, Murray, *Ekphrasis: The Illusion of the Natural Sign* (Baltimore, MD and London: Johns Hopkins University Press, 1992).
Kristeva, Julia, *La Révolution du langage poétique: l'avant-garde à la fin du XIXe siècle, Lautréamont et Mallarmé* (Paris: Seuil, 1974).

Kristeva, Julia, *Desire in Language: A Semiotic Approach to Literature and Art* (New York: Columbia University Press, 1980).
Lafayette, Marie-Madeleine Pioche de la Vergne, comtesse de, *La Princesse de Clèves* (Paris: Flammarion, 2009).
Laforgue, Jules, *Moral Tales*, trans. by William J. Smith (New York: New Directions, 1985).
Laforgue, Jules, *Œuvres complètes*, 3 vols (Lausanne: L'Age d'homme, 1986).
Laforgue, Jules, *Moralités légendaires*, ed. by Daniel Grojnowski and Henri Scepi (Paris: GF Flammarion, 2000).
Lambeth, John, 'Entretien avec Darrieussecq', *The French Review*, 79.4 (March 2006), 806–18.
Lamennais, *Œuvres complètes*, ed. by L. Le Guillou, 11 vols (Geneva: Slatkine, 1980).
Lane, Philippe and Michael Worton (eds), *French Studies in and for the Twenty-First Century* (Liverpool: Liverpool University Press, 2011).
Laufer, Laurie, 'Quand le traumatisme de la perte a plastiqué la mémoire', in *La Chose traumatique*, ed. by Franck Chaumon and Véronique Meneghini (Paris: L'Harmattan, 2005), pp. 97–118.
Laurens, Camille, 'Darrieussecq ou le syndrome de coucou', *La Revue littéraire*, 32 (Autumn 2007), 1–14.
Lehut, Bernard, and Thierry Grandillot, interview with Darrieussecq on RTL, radio broadcast entitled *Les Livres ont la parole* (September 2007).
Le Naire, Olivier, 'Singeries', *L'Express*, 19 March 1998, http://www.lexpress.fr/informations/singeries_628270.html.
Lévesque, Claude and Christie McDonald (eds), *L'Oreille de l'autre: otobiographies, transferts, traductions. Textes et débats avec Jacques Derrida* (Montréal: VLB, 1982).
Levi, Primo, *Les Naufragés et les rescapés: quarante ans après Auschwitz* (Paris: Gallimard, 1989).
Libération, online chat, 'Darrieussecq: "La littérature s'est toujours faite de lectures et d'influences"', *Libération*, 12 January 2010, http://www.liberation.fr/livres/1201233-dialoguez-avec-marie-darrieussecq.
Maistre, Joseph de, *Du Pape*, ed. by J. Lovie and J. Chetail (Geneva: Droz, 1966).
Maistre, Joseph de, *Œuvres*, ed. by P. Glaudes (Paris: Robert Laffont/Bouquins, 2007).
Malcolm, Janet, *In the Freud Archives* (London: Macmillan, 1997).
Malet, Léo, *Nestor Burma. Les Nouveaux Mystères de Paris*, ed. by Nadia Dhoukar, 2 vols (Paris: Robert Laffont, 2006).
Malet, Léo, *Nestor Burma. Premières enquêtes*, ed. by Nadia Dhoukar (Paris: Robert Laffont, 2006).
Marty, Éric, *Pourquoi le XXe siècle a-t-il pris Sade au sérieux?* (Paris: Seuil, 2011).
Masson, J. M., *The Assault on Truth: Freud's Suppression of the Seduction Theory* (Harmondsworth: Penguin, 1985).
Matisse, Henri, *Marianna Alcoforado, Lettres portugaises* (Paris: Tériade, 1946).
Matisse, Henri, *Charles Baudelaire, Les Fleurs du mal* (Paris: La Bibliothèque française, 1947).
Matisse, Henri, *Florilège des amours de Ronsard* (Paris: Skira, 1948).
Matisse, Henri, *Poèmes de Charles d'Orléans* (Paris: Tériade, 1950).
Matisse, Henri, *Correspondance Matisse-Rouveyre*, ed. by Hanne Finsen (Paris: Flammarion, 2001).

Matisse, Henri, *Écrits et propos sur l'art*, ed. by Dominique Fourcade (Paris: Hermann, 2005).

McDonald, Ronan, *The Cambridge Introduction to Samuel Beckett* (Cambridge: Cambridge University Press, 2006).

McLeod, Enid, *Charles of Orleans: Prince and Poet* (London: Chatto & Windus, 1969).

Menand, Louis, *The Marketplace of Ideas: Reform and Resistance in the American University* (New York: W.W. Norton, 2010).

Mœglin-Delcroix, Anne, *Sur le livre d'artiste: articles et écrits de circonstance (1981–2005)* (Marseille: Le Mot et le reste, 2005).

Mora, Gilles and Claude Nori, *L'Été dernier: manifeste photobiographique* (Paris: Éditions de l'étoile, 1983).

Mortier, Roland, 'L'Idée de décadence littéraire au XVIIIe siècle', *Studies on Voltaire and the Eighteenth Century*, 57 (1967), 1013–29.

Mortier, Roland, *L'Originalité: une nouvelle catégorie esthétique au siècle des Lumières* (Geneva: Droz, 1982).

Mourier-Casile, Pascaline and Dominique Moncond'Huy, 'Entretien avec Jacques Roubaud', *Revue La Licorne*, 40 (2006), http://edel.univ-poitiers.fr/licorne/document3347.php.

Nancy, Jean-Luc, *L'Adoration (Déconstruction du christianisme, 2)* (Paris: Galilée, 2010).

Narjoux, Cécile, 'Darrieussecq et "l'entre-deux-mondes" ou le fantastique à l'œuvre', *IRIS*, 24 (Winter 2002–3), 233–7.

Nimier, Marie, *La Reine du silence* (Paris: Gallimard, 2004).

Nimier, Marie, *Les Inséparables* (Paris: Gallimard, 2008).

Nimier, Marie, *Photo-Photo* (Paris: Gallimard, 2010).

Nussbaum, Martha C., *Not for Profit: Why Democracy Needs the Humanities* (Princeton, NJ: Princeton University Press, 2010).

Orr, Mary, *Intertextuality: Debates and Contexts* (Cambridge: Polity Press, 2003).

Parrochia, Daniel, *Ontologie fantôme: essai sur l'œuvre de Patrick Modiano* (Fougère La Versanne: Encre Marine, 1996).

Pascal, Blaise, *Œuvres complètes*, ed. by L. Lafuma (Paris: Seuil, 1963).

Pauvert, Jean-Jacques, *La Traversée du livre, mémoires* (Paris: Viviane Hamy, 2004).

Pécherot, Patrick, *Les Brouillards de la Butte* (Paris: Gallimard, 2001).

Queneau, Raymond, *Introduction à une lecture de Hegel* (Paris: Gallimard, 1947).

Rajewsky, Irina O., *Intermedialität* (Tübingen: A. Francke, 2002).

Rajewsky, Irina O., 'Intermediality, Intertextuality and Remediation: A Literacy Perspective on Intermediality', *Intermedialités*, 6 (Spring 2006), 43–64, cri.histart.umontreal.ca/cri/fr/intermedialities/interface/numeros.html/.../p6_rajewsky_text.pdf.

Rancière, Jacques, *Le Destin des images* (Paris: La Fabrique, 2003).

Rancière, Jacques, *The Future of the Image*, trans. by Gregory Elliott (London: Verso, 2007).

Reyns-Chikuma, Chris, *Images du Japon en France et ailleurs* (Paris: L'Harmattan, 2005).

Ribot, Théodule, *La Philosophie de Schopenhauer* (Paris: Germer Baillière, 1874).

Rilke, Rainer Maria, *Sämtliche Werke*, ed. by the Rilke Archive, Ruth Sieber-Rilke and Ernst Zinn, 6 vols (Frankfurt a.M.: Insel, 1966).

Roche, Denis, 'Un discours affectif sur l'image', *Le Magazine littéraire*, 314 (1993), 65–7.
Rodgers, Catherine, 'Lectures de la sorcière, ensorcellement de l'écriture', in *Marguerite Duras: lectures plurielles*, ed. by Catherine Rodgers and Raynalle Udris (Amsterdam and Atlanta, GA: Rodopi, 1998), pp. 17–34.
Rodgers, Catherine, '"Entrevoir l'absence des bords du monde" dans les romans de Darrieussecq', in *Nouvelles écrivaines: nouvelles voix?*, ed. by Nathalie Morello and Catherine Rodgers (Amsterdam and New York; Rodopi, 2002), pp. 83–103.
Roubaud, Jacques, *Mono no aware ou le sentiment des choses: cent-quatre poèmes empruntés au japonais* (Paris: Gallimard, 1970).
Roubaud, Jacques, *Poèmes de métro* (Paris: P.O.L., 2000).
Roubaud, Jacques, *La Bibliothèque de Warburg: version mixte* (Paris: Seuil, 2002).
Roubaud, Jacques, *Tokyo infra-ordinaire* (Paris: Inventaire-Invention, 2005).
Roudinesco, Élisabeth, *Mais pourquoi tant de haine?* (Paris: Seuil, 2010).
Rousso, Henry, *Le Syndrôme de Vichy* (Paris: Seuil, 1987).
Ruffel, Lionel, 'Le Temps des spectres', in *Le Roman français aujourd'hui: transformations, perceptions, mythologies*, ed. by Bruno Blanckeman and Jean-Christophe Millois (Paris: Prétexte Éditeur, 2004), pp. 95–117.
Sagan, Françoise, *Bonjour Tristesse* (Paris: Julliard, 1954).
Saint-Amand, Pierre, 'Mort à blanc: Guibert et la photographie', in *Le Corps textuel d'Hervé Guibert*, ed. by Ralph Sarkonak (Paris: La Revue des lettres modernes, 1997), pp. 81–95.
Samoyault, Tiphaine, *L'Intertextualité: mémoire de la littérature* (Paris: Nathan, 2001).
Sarrey-Strack, Colette, *Fictions contemporaines au féminin – Darrieussecq, Marie Ndiaye, Marie Nimier, Marie Redonnet* (Paris: L'Harmattan, 2002).
Sauvage, Jérémi, '"Ce qui m'a toujours déçue dans les films ou dans la littérature fantastique, c'est quand on voit le monstre" – Entretien avec Marie Darrieussecq', *Ténèbres*, 8 (October/December 1999), 61–6.
Schopenhauer, Arthur, *Pensées et fragments*, trans. by J. Bourdeau (Paris: Germer Baillière, 1881).
Shakespeare, William, *Hamlet*, bilingual edition, with French translations by François Maguin (Paris: GF-Flammarion, 1995).
Shirane, Haruo (ed.), *Early Modern Japanese Literature: An Anthology* (New York: Columbia University Press, 2008).
Shirane, Haruo, *Traces of Dreams: Landscape, Cultural Memory and the Poetry of Bashō* (Stanford, CA: Stanford University Press, 1998).
Shusterman, Richard (ed.), *Bourdieu: A Critical Reader* (Oxford: Wiley-Blackwell, 1999).
Spurling, Hilary, *Matisse: The Life* (London: Penguin, 2009).
Steiner, George, *After Babel: Aspects of Language and Translation* (Oxford: Oxford University Press, 1975).
Szlovak, Charlotte, interview with Darrieussecq for *Ulysse à Dublin* (documentary), Zeugma Films/Art France, 2004.
Todorov, Tzvetan, *Introduction à la littérature fantastique* (Paris: Seuil, 1970).
Todorov, Tzvetan, *The Fantastic: A Structural Approach to a Literary Genre*, trans. by Richard Howard (Cleveland, OH: Case Western Reserve University Press, 1973).
Trollope, Anthony, *He Knew He Was Right*, ed. by John Sutherland (Oxford: Oxford University Press, 2008).

Valéry, Paul, *Œuvres*, ed. by Jean Hytier, 2 vols (Paris: Gallimard, 1957–60).
Voltaire, *Œuvres complètes*, ed. by Louis Moland, 52 vols (Paris: Garnier, 1877–85).
Voltaire, *Mélanges*, ed. by J. Van Den Heuvel (Paris: Gallimard, 1961).
Voltaire, *Essai sur les mœurs*, ed. by René Pomeau, 2 vols (Paris: Garnier, 1963).
Voltaire, *Lettres philosophiques*, ed. by Gustave Lanson and André-Michel Rousseau, 2 vols (Paris: Didier, 1964).
Voltaire, *Œuvres complètes*, ed. by Theodore Besterman *et al.* (Oxford: Voltaire Foundation, 1968–).
Voltaire, *Corpus des notes marginales*, ed. by O. Golubiéva *et al.* (Berlin: Akademie Verlag, 1979–).
Vovelle, Michel, *La Mort et l'occident de 1300 à nos jours* (Paris: Gallimard, 1983).
Wagner, Richard, *Quatre poèmes d'opéra traduits en prose française, précédés d'une lettre sur la musique* (Paris: A. Bourdilliat, 1861).
Wolin, Richard, *Heidegger's Children: Hannah Arendt, Karl Löwith, Hans Jonas and Herbert Marcuse* (Princeton, NJ: Princeton University Press, 2001).
Wright, Alastair, *Matisse and the Subject of Modernism* (Princeton, NJ and Oxford: Princeton University Press, 2004).
Yerushalmi, Yosef Hayim, *Freud's Moses: Judaism Terminable and Interminable* (New Haven, CT: Yale University Press, 1991).
Žižek, Slavoj, *Looking Awry* (Cambridge, MA: MIT Press, 2000).

Index

Note: 'n.' after a page reference denotes a note number on that page.

Abraham, Nicolas, xx, 190 n. 11
Adam, Philippe, 179 n. 14
Adorno, Theodor, 53
Alcoforado, Marianna, 93
Alembert, Jean Le Rond d', 22, 29 n. 4
Alighieri, Dante, xvii, 18–31
Alpers, Svetlana, 88
Althusser, Louis, 6, 7
Amila, John, 164 n. 2
Annunzio, Gabriele D', *see* D'Annunzio
Antoine, Dominique, 205 n. 1
Anzieu, Didier, 6
Aragon, Louis, 87, 89–90, 92
Arcouët, Serge, *see* Stewart, Terry
Arendt, Hannah, 57 n. 21
Ariès, Philippe, 104, 108 n. 6
Artaud, Antonin, 112, 113–15, 119

Bachelard, Gaston, 137, n. 2
Bair, Deirdre, 110 n. 62
Bakhtin, Mikhail, xiv, 4
Bakst, Léon, 75, 76
Baldick, Chris, 138 n. 10
Balibar, Étienne, 7
Baretti, Giuseppe, 31 n. 22
Barthes, Roland, xv–xvi, xiii, 4, 55, 140–53, 168, 170–1, 172
Bashō, Matsuo, 166–7, 168, 175, 178
Bass, Alan, 123 n. 5, 137 n. 3, 138 n. 8
Bataille, Georges, xvi–xviii, 48, 51, 53, 56 n. 2, 112
Baudelaire, Charles, xviii, 51, 52, 89, 93–4
Baxandall, Michael, xvi–xvii
Bayard, Pierre, 31 n. 20
Beauvoir, Simone de, xviii, 54–5
Beckett, Samuel, xix, 99–110, 120–1
Benois, Alexandre, 75, 76
Bernabé, Jean, 9

Blanchot, Maurice, xviii, xix, 53, 54, 111–25
Bloom, Harold, xiii–xv, xvii, xxi n. 4, 21, 71, 128, 137 n. 2
Boisdeffre, Pierre de, 50
Boltanski, Christian, 146, 148
Bonald, Louis Gabriel Ambroise de, 34, 36–8, 40, 41
Bonnefoy Yves, 115
Borges, Jorge Luis, xviii, 12, 85, 94–5, 30–1 n. 20
Bossuet, Jacques-Bénigne, 32, 35
Bourdieu, Pierre, 11–12
Bourgeois, Louise, xx, 188
Bowie, Malcolm, xxi n. 8, 207 n. 17, 207 n. 18
Breton, André, 51, 140
Brody, Elaine, 76, 82 n. 16
Browning, Robert, 30–1 n. 20
Buci-Glucksmann, Christine, 171, 172
Burgin, Victor, 142
Butor, Michel, 168

Calle, Sophie, 146, 148
Camus, Albert, 49
Canault, Nina, 191 n. 11
Casanova de Seingalt, Giacomo, 50
Certeau, Michel de, 14–15
Cervantes, Miguel de, xviii
Césaire, Aimé, 9
Cézanne, Paul, xvi–xvii
Chalais, François, 50
Challemel-Lacour, P., 68 n. 1
Chamoiseau, Patrick, 9
Chateaubriand, François-René, vicomte de, xvii, 34–6, 41
Claudel, Paul, 168
Clayton, Jay, 138 n. 9
Cocteau, Jean, 51, 96
Comment, Bernard, 151 nn. 17 & 18
Compagnon, Antoine, 3, 140, 147

219

Concannon, Amy, 190 n. 1, 191 n. 18
Condillac, Étienne Bonnet, abbé de, xxi n. 8, 137 n. 2
Condorcet, Nicolas de, 33, 36
Confiant, Raphaël, 9
Conley, Tom, 17 n. 14
Constant, Benjamin, xiii

Daeninckx, Didier, 163
D'Annunzio, Gabriele, 76
Dante, see Alighieri, Dante
Danto, Arthur, 97 n. 21
Darrieussecq, Marie, xx, 180–93
Darwin, Charles, 60, 61
Debussy, Claude, 76
Deforges, Régine, see Réage, Pauline
Declercq, Alain, 193 n. 40
Desclos, Anne, see Réage, Pauline
Deimier, Pierre de, 31 n. 22
Deleuze, Gilles, xxi n. 18, 6, 55
Delon, Michel, 46
Derrida, Jacques, xiii, xiv–xv, xix, xx, xxi n. 8, 6, 10, 111–15, 126–39, 142, 147, 149, 152 n. 28, 152 n. 29
Descartes, René, 5, 32, 37, 60, 61
Descombes, Vincent, 6
Destais, Alexandra, 47–8
Diaghilev, Sergei, xviii, 71, 75
Diderot, Denis, 29 n. 4
Didi-Huberman, Georges, 47, 52, 55, 56 n. 4
Disson, Agnès, 179 n. 14
Donne, John, 29
Dosse, François, 4
Duhamel, Marcel, 154
Dumas, Didier, xx, 191 n. 11
Duras, Marguerite, 152 n. 26, 187

Elderfield, John, 88–9
Eleanor of Aquitaine, 108 n. 6
Eliot, T. S., xiv
Emanuel, Michelle, 164 n. 3, 164 n. 10
Engels, Friedrich, 131
Espagne, Michel, 10, 11

Fanon, Franz, 9
Farinelli, Arturo, 30 n. 14
Faucon, Bernard, xx, 188, 189
Fein, David, 86

Fénelon, François de Salignac de la Mothe, 35
Finch, Alison, xiv, xxi n. 8, xxii n. 23, 204
Finer, Emily, 124 n. 12
Flaubert, Gustave, xiii, 52
Fokine, Isabelle, 81 n. 7
Fokine, Michel, 72, 76
Foucault, Michel, xiii, 4, 6, 55, 111, 112, 115–16
François, Édouard, 188
Fraser, David, 161
Freud, Sigmund, xix, xxi n. 12, 6–7, 16 n. 6, 51, 111, 126–39
Frey, Pascale, 191 n. 13
Fry, Paul H., xiv

Gadamer, Hans-Georg, xiv
Garcin, Jérôme, 56 n. 13
Garçon, Maurice, 51
Gaudemar, Antoine de, 190 n. 2
Gaudet, Jeanette, 191 n. 16
Genette, Gérard, 3
Geoffroy-Schneiter, Bérénice, 193 n. 40
Gide, André, xiii, 76, 78
Goldbert, Itzhak, 193 n. 40
Gorrara, Claire, 164 n. 1, 165 n. 22
Goulbourne, Russell, 29 n. 2
Grammont, Claudine, 92, 93
Grandillot, Thierry, 191 n. 17
Grigorian, Natasha, 81 n. 12
Gross, Béatrice, 193 n. 40
Guibert, Hervé, xx, 140, 144–5, 146, 148, 189

Hagglünd, Martin, 138 n. 15
Halbreich, Harry, 73
Hannoosh, Michele, 65
Harding, Frank, see Malet, Léo
Hartmann, Eduard von, xviii, 58–70
Hartog, François, 12
Hassan, Ihab H., 138 n. 10
Hegel, Georg Wilhelm Friedrich, 6, 47, 54, 56 n. 2
Heidegger, Martin, xxi n. 12, 6, 111
Helvétius, Claude Adrien, xiii
Hergé, 163
Hesiod, 30 n. 11

Hobbes, Thomas, 33
Hokenson, Jan Walsh, 179 n. 9
Hokusai, 174
Hölderlin, Friedrich, 112, 113–15, 117, 119
Holland, Michael, 24 n. 13
Holmes, Martha, 192 n. 27
Homer, 19, 95
Honneger, Arthur, 72, 76, 78, 80
Hume, David, xvi
Huot, Sylviane, 81 n. 13
Husserl, Edmund, 6
Hutton, Margaret-Anne, 204, 205 n. 7

Irigaray, Luce, 6
Iser, Wolfgang, 10

Jackson, Julian, 165 n. 28, 165 n. 30
Jaeckin, Just, 50, 55
Jaucourt, Louis, chevalier de, 22
Jauss, Hans Robert, xiv, 10
Jensen, Wilhelm, 135–7
Jordan, Shirley, 192 n. 32
Jouet, Jacques, 167
Joyce, James, xx

Kafka, Franz, 53, 112, 30–1 n. 20
Kamo no Chomei, 177
Kant, Immanuel, 53, 60, 61, 57 n. 21
Kaprièlen, Nelly, 191 n. 19
Karatani, Kojin, 168, 177
Kawakami, Akane, 152 n. 25, 179 n. 9
Kimyongür, Angela, 165 n. 31
Klossowski, Pierre, xviii, 6, 48, 50
Knowlson, James, 99
Kojève, Alexandre, 6, 56 n. 2
Kopreeva, T. N., 29 n. 2
Krieger, Murray, xvii
Kristeva, Julia, 4

Lacan, Jacques, 6, 203–4
Lacoue-Labarthe, Philippe, 6
Lafayette, Marie-Madeleine Pioche de La Vergne, comtesse de, 192 n. 28
Laforgue, Jules, xviii, 58–70
Laing, R. D., 128
Lamartine, 51
Lambeth, John, 191 n. 12

Lamennais, Félicité Robert de, xvii, 34, 38–43
Lane, Philippe, 16 n.1
Laufer, Laurie, 184
Laurens, Camille, 190 n. 2
Laurenti, Huguette, 82 n. 18
Lautréamont, comte de, 112
Le Corbusier, 188
Lehut, Bernard, 191 n. 17
Leiris, Michel, 53
Le Naire, Olivier, 190 n. 2
Leonardo da Vinci, 71
Lequeux, Emmanuelle, 193 n. 40
Lévesque, Claude, 114
Levinas, Emmanuel, 6, 115
Levi, Primo, 57 n. 24
Lévi-Strauss, Claude, xv
Lyotard, Jean-François, 6

Macé, Gérard, 168
Maistre, Joseph de, xvii, 34, 41–3
Malcolm, Janet, 139 n. 20
Malet, Léo, xix, 154–65
Mallarmé, Stéphane, 18, 28, 72, 75, 76, 77, 89, 112
Mandiargues, André-Pieyre de, 48
Marat, Dolorès, 188
Marinetti, Filippo Tomaso, 12
Marty, Éric, 53
Marx, Karl, 7, 113, 131
Masson, J. M., 139 n. 20
Matignon, Renaud, xv, 148
Matisse, Henri, xviii, 84–98
McLeod, Enid, 97 n. 6
Meckert, Jean, *see* Amila, Jean
Menand, Louis, 9–10
Menard, Pierre, xviii, 95
Merleau-Ponty, Maurice, 6
Messager, Annette, 188
Meudal, Gérard, 165 n. 33
Miller, Becky, 192 n. 27
Milton, John, xiv, 19
Modiano, Patrick, xx, 188
Mœglin-Delcroix, Anne, 90
Moncond'Huy, Dominique, 179 n. 8
Montaigne, Michel de, 3, 32, 38
Mora, Gilles, 140
Moreau, Gustave, 75, 76, 78
Mortier, Roland, 30 n. 6

Mourier-Casile, Pascaline, 179 n. 8
Muther, Richard, 82 n. 14

Nancy, Jean-Luc, 6, 111, 112
Narjoux, Cécile, 184
Nietzsche, Friedrich, xxi n. 12, 51, 115, 126
Nimier, Marie, xx, 194–207
Nimier, Roger, xx
Nori, Claude, 140
Nussbaum, Martha, 14–16

Onfray, Michel, 16 n. 6
Orléans, Charles d', xviii, 84–98
Orr, Mary, 29 n. 3

Parrain, Brice, 56 n. 2
Parrochia, Daniel, 192 n. 35
Pascal, Blaise, xvii–xviii, 32–45
Pasolini, Pier Paolo, 55
Paulhan, Jean, xviii, 47, 48, 51
Pauvert, Jean-Jacques, 47, 50–2, 55
Pécherot, Patrick, xix, 154–65
Perec, Georges, 168
Picasso, Pablo, xvi–xvii, 96
Plato, 137 n. 2
Porquet, Jean-Louis, 165 n. 33
Proust, Marcel, 147
Pyman, Avril, 82 n. 14

Queneau, Raymond, xviii, 53, 56 n. 2

Rahm, Philippe, 193 n. 40
Rajewsky, Irina, 83 n. 31
Rancière, Jacques, 141–2
Ravel, Maurice, 76
Réage, Pauline, xviii, 47–9, 55
Rémi, Georges, *see* Hergé
Reyns-Chikuma, Chris, 168–9, 177
Ribot, Théodule, 59
Richter, Gerhard, 152 n. 28
Rilke, Rainer Maria, xviii, 85, 93–4, 95
Rimsky-Korsakov, Nikolai, 73, 78
Roche, Denis, 141, 144, 146–7, 148
Roger-Viollet, 188
Ronsard, Pierre de, 89
Rothstein, Eric, 138 n. 9
Roubaud, Jacques, xiii, xx, 166–79
Roudinesco, Élisabeth, 6, 139 n. 43

Rousseau, André-Michel, 30 n. 19
Rousseau, Jean-Jacques, xiii, 32, 34, 35, 49 n. 11, 137 n. 2
Rousso, Henry, 14
Rouveyre, André, 85–8, 90–1, 95, 96
Rubinstein, Ida, 72–3, 75–8, 82 n. 30
Ruffel, Lionel, 189
Rye, Gill, xxi, n. 8, 207 n. 21

Sade, Donatien-Alphonse-François, marquis de, xviii, 46–57
Sagan, Françoise, 56 n. 5
Said, Edward, 168
Saint-Amand, Pierre, 151 n. 19
Samoyault, Tiphaine, 69 n. 7
Sarraute, Nathalie, 187–8
Sarrey-Strack, Colette, 190 n. 2
Sartre, Jean-Paul, xiii, 6, 54
Sauvage, Jérémi, 191 n. 15
Scepi, Henri, 68 n. 4
Schopenhauer, Arthur, xviii, 58–70
Segal, Naomi, xxi, n. 8, 207 n. 21
Shakespeare, William, xiii, 60, 61–2, 78
Shirane, Haruo, 178
Shklovsky, Viktor, 115
Sollers, Philippe, 55
Spurling, Hilary, 97 n. 8
Steiner, George, 29
Stewart, Terry, 164 n. 2
Stravinsky, Igor, 76
Sue, Eugène, 155
Sutherland, John, 128–9
Sweeney, Kerry, 190 n. 1, 191 n. 18
Szlovak, Charlotte, 192 n. 36

Teika, Fujiwara, 172
Teller, Juergen, 188
Tocqueville, Alexis de, xiii
Todorov, Tzvetan, 184
Török, Maria, xx, 190 n. 11
Toussaint, Jean-Philippe, 179 n. 14
Tran Ba Vang, Nicole, 188
Trollope, Anthony, 128

Valéry, Paul, xiii, xviii, xix, 18, 28–9, 71–83, 126–39
Verlaine, Paul, 60
Vilmouth, Jean-Luc, 193 n. 40

Virgil, 95
Voltaire, xiii, xvii, 18–31, 33, 34, 36, 42
Vovelle, Michel, 105

Wagner, Richard, 66–8, 71–2, 78
Warburg, Aby, 47, 54, 55
Weil, Simone, 115
Werner, Michael, 10, 11
Wilde, Oscar, 75
Wittgenstein, Ludwig, xx

Wolfskehl, Otto von (Bishop), 99
'Wolfskehlmeister', 99–110
Wolin, Richard, 123 n. 2
Woodman, Francesca, xx, 188–9
Wright, Alastair, 88, 92

Yerushalmi, Yosef Hayim, 132–3
Yourcenar, Marguerite, 168

Žižek, Slavoj, 13